Fairness in Criminal Appeal

Helena Morão • Ricardo Tavares da Silva
Editors

Fairness in Criminal Appeal

A Critical and Interdisciplinary Analysis of the ECtHR Case-Law

Springer

Editors
Helena Morão
Research Centre for Criminal Law and Criminal Sciences (CIDPCC)
University of Lisbon School of Law
Lisbon, Portugal

Ricardo Tavares da Silva
Research Centre for Criminal Law and Criminal Sciences (CIDPCC)
University of Lisbon School of Law
Lisbon, Portugal

ISBN 978-3-031-13000-7 ISBN 978-3-031-13001-4 (eBook)
https://doi.org/10.1007/978-3-031-13001-4

This Springer imprint is published by the registered company Springer Nature Switzerland AG
The registered company address is: Gewerbestrasse 11, 6330 Cham, Switzerland

Acknowledgments

This book is the result of a research seminar held between July 2021 and June 2022 at CIDPCC (Research Centre for Criminal Law and Criminal Sciences), the Portuguese research centre specifically focused on Criminal Law, supported by FCT (Fundação para a Ciência e Tecnologia).

The editors are very grateful to all the authors. Special mention must be made of Professors Massimo Ceresa-Gastaldo and Antonio Mª Lara López who accepted to join our project.

This work is dedicated to Criminal Law Professor Maria Fernanda Palma on the 30th anniversary of her PhD, the first PhD in Criminal Law awarded in Portugal to a woman.

Helena Morão
Ricardo Tavares da Silva

About This Book

This book addresses the European Court of Human Rights' fairness standards in criminal appeal, filling a gap in this less researched area of studies. Based on a fair trial immediacy requirement, the Court has found several violations of Article 6 of the European Convention on Human Rights at the appellate level by at least eighteen States of the Council of Europe in a vast array of cases, particularly in contexts of first instance acquittals overturning and of sentences increasing on appeal.

On the one hand, the book critically engages this case-law with the law revisions it has recently inspired in European countries, as well as with the critiques and difficulties that it continues to raise. On the other hand, it interweaves insight from criminal procedure theory with new discoveries in the field of cognitive sciences (neuroscience of memory, philosophy of knowledge, AI), shedding an interdisciplinary light on the (in)adequacy and limits of the Strasbourg Court's jurisprudence.

About This Book

Contents

About the Editors

Helena Morão is a Criminal Law Professor at the University of Lisbon School of Law where she was awarded her PhD. She is the Deputy Director of the Research Centre for Criminal Law and Criminal Sciences (CIDPCC), the Portuguese research centre specifically focused on criminal law, as well as the Deputy Director of the journal Anatomy of Crime, Journal of Law and Crime Sciences. Her main field of research is criminal law from both normative and interdisciplinary perspectives. She is the author of several works on criminal law, including criminal appeal law, and has participated as an expert in various criminal law reforms.

Ricardo Tavares da Silva is an Invited Assistant in Criminal Law at the University of Lisbon School of Law, where he was awarded his bachelor's degree. He also has a Master's degree and a PhD degree in Philosophy from the School of Arts and Humanities of the University of Lisbon. He is especially interested in Normative Theory and in the foundations of Law, but also in related issues in Philosophy of Action and Philosophy of Mind, Metaphysics and Epistemology, Cognitive Science and Neuroscience. He is a member and executive coordinator of the Research Centre for Criminal Law and Criminal Sciences (CIDPCC).

About the Editors

Abbreviations

CCA	Coimbra Court of Appeal
CEPEJ	European Commission for the Efficiency of Justice
ECA	Évora Court of Appeal
ECHR	European Convention on Human Rights
ECtHR	European Court of Human Rights
FCCouncil	French Constitutional Council
GCA	Guimarães Court of Appeal
ICCass	Italian Court of Cassation
ICConst	Italian Constitutional Court
ICCPR	International Covenant on Civil and Political Rights
ICPP	Italian *Codice di Procedura Penale* (Italian Criminal Procedure Code)
LCA	Lisbon Court of Appeal
LECrim	*Ley de Enjuiciamiento Criminal* (Spanish Criminal Procedure Act)
LOPJ	*Ley Orgánica del Poder Judicial* (Spanish Judicial Power Organic Act)
PCA	Porto Court of Appeal
PCC	Portuguese Constitutional Court
PCPP	Portuguese *Código de Processo Penal* (Portuguese Criminal Procedure Code)
SC	Spanish Constitution
SCC	Spanish Constitutional Court
SCJ	Supreme Court of Justice (Portugal)
SSC	Spanish Supreme Court
SStPO	*Schweizerische Strafprozessordnung* (Swiss Criminal Procedure Code)
StPO	*Strafprozeßordnung* (German Criminal Procedure Code)

Part I
Introduction

Chapter 1
The ECtHR Case-Law on Immediacy in Criminal Appeal

Helena Morão

> It appears that European appellate courts are, in a sense, allergic to immediacy. Thaman (2019), p. 946

1.1 The ECtHR Case-Law on Immediacy in Criminal Appeal

The European Court of Human Rights (ECtHR)—in line with its early jurisprudence that upheld the right of the accused to be present, participate, and be heard in person in the appeal proceedings involving questions of fact, which dates back to the case Ekbatani v. Sweden[1]—has continued to hold in more recent judgments that the principles of fair trial contained in Article 6 § 1 of the European Convention on Human Rights (ECHR) require, as a rule, that the court of appeal requested to globally appraise both facts and law relating to the guilt or innocence of the

[1] Ekbatani v. Sweden, no. 10563/83, 26 May 1988, § 32, *hudoc.echr.coe.int*: '(. . .) the Court of Appeal was called upon to examine the case as to the facts and the law. In particular, it had to make a full assessment of the question of the applicant's guilt or innocence (. . .). In the circumstances of the present case that question could not, as a matter of fair trial, have been properly determined without a direct assessment of the evidence given in person by the applicant – who claimed that he had not committed the act alleged to constitute the criminal offence (. . .) – and by the complainant. Accordingly, the Court of Appeal's re-examination of Mr. Ekbatani's conviction at first instance ought to have comprised a full rehearing of the applicant and the complainant.'

H. Morão (✉)
University of Lisbon School of Law, Research Centre for Criminal Law and Criminal Sciences (CIDPCC), Lisbon, Portugal
e-mail: helenamorao@fd.ulisboa.pt

H. Morão, R. Tavares da Silva (eds.), *Fairness in Criminal Appeal*,
https://doi.org/10.1007/978-3-031-13001-4_1

defendant directly evaluates the oral evidence, by rehearing the witnesses and the accused at an appeal hearing.[2]

The ECtHR puts it this way:

> Where an appellate court is called upon to examine a case as to the facts and the law and to make a full assessment of the question of the applicant's guilt or innocence, it cannot, as a matter of fair trial, properly determine those issues without a direct assessment of the evidence.[3]

This immediacy case-law covers, namely, the overturning of first instance acquittals on appeal, as, among others, in the case Dan v. Moldova,[4] as well as the increasing of sentences on appeal as, for example, in the case of Zahirović v. Croatia.[5]

On account of the breach of this immediacy requirement in criminal appeal, the Strasbourg Court has found a violation of Article 6 § 1 (and sometimes also § 3 c) of the Convention in vast array of cases, by a significant number of Contracting States such as Albania, Austria, Croatia, France, Finland, Iceland, Italy, Moldova, the Netherlands, Norway, Poland, Portugal, Romania, Russia, San Marino, Spain, Sweden, or Ukraine.[6] Actually, the ECtHR considers that, although Article 6 § 1 does not compel the States of the Council of Europe to establish appellate courts,

---

[2]See Trechsel (2005), pp. 257 et seq.; Summers (2007), pp. 114 et seq.; Fanego (2012), p. 172; Morão (2020), pp. 179 et seq.; Spano and Bårdsen (2020), pp. 583 et. seq.; European Court of Human Rights (2022), §§ 294–303.

[3]Dan v. Moldova, no. 8999/07, 5 July 2011, § 30, *hudoc.echr.coe.int*. By contrast, this demand does not apply to appeals implicating simply legal aspects—a different legal interpretation or its application to settled facts—(Bazo González v. Spain, no. 30643/04, 16 December 2008, § 36, *hudoc.echr.coe.int*), though 'the facts and the legal interpretation can be intertwined to an extent that it is difficult to separate the two from each other.' (Suuripää v. Finland, no. 43151/02, 12 January 2010, § 44, *hudoc.echr.coe.int*).

[4]Dan v. Moldova, §§ 31–33.

[5]Zahirović v. Croatia, no. 58590/11, 25 April 2013, § 57, *hudoc.echr.coe.int*: '(. . .) where the appellate court is called upon to examine whether the applicant's sentence should be increased and when the appeal proceedings are capable of raising issues including such matters as the applicant's personality and character, which makes such proceedings of crucial importance for the applicant since their outcome could be of major detriment to him, the Court considers that the appellate court cannot examine the case properly without having heard the applicant directly and gaining a personal impression of him.'

[6]See, for instance, Ekbatani v. Sweden, no. 10563/83, 26 May 1988, §§ 32–33; Botten v. Norway, no. 6206/90, 19 February 1996, §§ 48–53; Michael Edward Cooke v. Austria, no. 25878/94, 8 February 2000, §§ 40–44; Destrehem v. France, no. 56651/00, 18 May 2004, §§ 45–47; Dondarini v. San Marino, no. 50545/99, 6 July 2004, §§ 27–29; Dănilă v. Romania, no. 53897/00, 8 March 2007, §§ 35–43; Strzałkowski v. Poland, no. 31509/02, 9 June 2009, §§ 47–48; Suuripää v. Finland, no. 43151/02, 12 January 2010, § 44–48; Sinichkin v. Russia, no. 20508/03, 8 April 2010, § 38; Dan v. Moldova, no. 8999/07, 5 July 2011, §§ 30–35; Cani v. Albania, no. 11006/06, 6 March 2012, § 63; Zahirović v. Croatia, no. 58590/11, 25 April 2013, §§ 57 and 61–64; Sobko v. Ukraine, no. 15102/10, 17 December 2015, §§ 76–78; Gómez Olmeda v. Spain, no. 61112/12, 29 March 2016, §§ 33–40; Lorefice v. Italy, no. 63446/13, 29 June 2017, §§ 36–47; Júlíus Þór Sigurþórsson v. Iceland, no. 38797/17, 16 July 2019, §§ 39–44; Paixão Moreira Sá Fernandes v. Portugal, no. 78108/14, 25 February 2020, §§ 59–66; X v. the Netherlands, no. 72631/17, 27 July 2021, §§ 45 and 53–56; *hudoc.echr.coe.int*.

States which do institute such appeal courts must comply with the guarantees of Article 6 on appeal,[7] even if they are not bound by Protocol no. 7 to the Convention which enshrines the right of appeal in criminal matters in its Article 2.

As far as can be ascertained, most of these ECtHR's decisions concern appeal proceedings purely based on written records of the first instance trial,[8] and, according to the Strasbourg Court, the 'assessment of the trustworthiness of a witness is a complex task which usually cannot be achieved by a mere reading of his or her recorded words.'[9] However and somewhat surprisingly, in Gómez Olmeda v. Spain, the ECtHR identified an infringement of Article 6 § 1 as well, even though the reversal of the acquittal by the court of appeal was, in this case, grounded on the viewing of the first instance trial video-recording. Furthermore, the main argument given for this judgement did not rest on a theoretical approach to a possible insufficiency of this indirect immediacy in criminal procedure, but merely on the understanding of the Spanish Constitutional Court in similar rulings.[10]

Especially lately and not without important criticism,[11] the European Court has likewise recognized some exceptions to its immediacy in criminal appeal case-law, which allow the appeal court to take a new position on the relevant facts established

---

[7] See Delcourt v. Belgium, no. 2689/65, 17 January 1970, § 25; and, linking this affirmation to an effective right of access to the courts, Maresti vs Croatia, no. 55759/07, 25 June 2009, § 33.

[8] See, e. g., Dan v. Moldova, § 32: 'The first-instance court acquitted the applicant because it did not trust the witnesses after having heard them in person. In re-examining the case, the Court of Appeal disagreed with the first-instance court as to the trustworthiness of the accusation witnesses' statements and convicted the applicant. In so doing the Court of Appeal did not hear the witnesses anew but merely relied on their statements as recorded in the file.'

[9] Dan v. Moldova, § 33.

[10] Gómez Olmeda v. Spain, §§ 38–39: '(. . .) the Spanish Constitutional Court, in ruling on similar cases, has found that the viewing of a video-recording of the first-instance trial does not enable an appellate court to assess personal evidence (. . .). Consequently, it may not be considered that the viewing of the video-recording placed the *Audiencia Provincial* in the same position as the first-instance judge.' See also *Sentencia* no. 167/2002, §§ 9–11, *hj.tribunalconstitucional.es*, of the Spanish Constitutional Court.

The Spanish Government had '(. . .) argued that the viewing of the video-recording by the judges of the Audiencia Provincial equated to holding a hearing for the purposes of Article 6 § 1 of the Convention. They conceded that a public hearing was not exactly the same as a viewing of a video-recording but stressed that this viewing had provided the judges with full access to all the evidence produced to the criminal judge. In the Government's opinion, the viewing of the video-recording had placed the judges of the Audiencia Provincial in a better position to take a sound decision on the case than if a new hearing had been held, since the former had allowed them to have full and personal access to all the evidence produced to the criminal judge.' (Gómez Olmeda v. Spain, § 27).

[11] See the dissenting opinion of Judge Ranzoni, § 8, to Marilena-Carmen Popa v. Romania, no. 1814/11, 18 February 2020, *hudoc.echr.coe.int*: '(. . .) the Court establishes principles which, however, in subsequent cases it dilutes by accepting various kinds of exceptions. That makes the interpretation of such principles unpredictable and causes uncertainty for the national authorities in their application. Unfortunately, that is exactly what the majority did in the present case by artificially differentiating it from other cases instead of adhering to the clear principle established by the Court in its case-law.'

by the lower instance and reach a conviction for the first time on appellate level without directly hearing the witnesses, when:

(a) The charges brought against the accused involve solely minor crimes;[12]
(b) It turns out physically or legally impossible to examine a witness in person at the appeal trial;[13]
(c) The higher instance court decides based on the weight that can be attached to the evidentiary value of an expert report directly assessed, and not on the reliability of a witness,[14] or, more broadly, not based on the reassessment of the credibility of a testimony or on a reinterpretation of the testimonial evidence;[15]
(d) The appellate court's fundamental task is not to evaluate the trustworthiness of an essential witness, but rather to verify whether his or her statements are corroborated by other evidence which the court of appeal is able to assess directly, such as camera footage, phone transcripts, and documents;[16]
(e) The unheard witness on appeal is merely corroborative and not decisive to the conviction;[17] or
(f) The defence has not asked for the witnesses to be summoned at the appeal proceedings.[18]

Yet, our focus here will not be these exceptions, but instead the principle that the appeal court that has the responsibility for deciding the guilt or innocence of a defendant in reference to factual issues ought to—as a rule and in order not to

[12]Fejde v. Sweden, no. 12631/87, 29 October 1991, §§ 33–34; and Jan-Åke Andersson v. Sweden, no. 11274/84, 29 October 1991, §§ 29–30, *hudoc.echr.coe.int*, both with dissenting opinions of Judges Cremona, Walsh, Russo, Spielmann, De Meyer, Loizou and Bigi: 'I (. . .) find it difficult, in the context of a fair trial, to distinguish, as the majority do in this case, between the minor and major character of an offence. For the persons concerned, whom this provision of the Convention seeks to protect, all cases have their importance.' (Judge Cremona).

The ECtHR may be here drawing a parallel with the first part of Article 2 § 2 of Protocol no. 7 ('This right [of appeal in criminal matters] may be subject to exceptions in regard to offences of a minor character (. . .).'

[13]Dan v. Moldova, § 33, in *obiter dictum*: '(. . .) because, for example, he or she has died, or in order to protect the right of the witness not to incriminate him- or herself'. See also Chiper v. Romania, no. 22036/10, 27 June 2017, §§ 63–69, *hudoc.echr.coe.int*.

[14]Marilena-Carmen Popa v. Romania, no. 1814/11, 18 February 2020, §§ 41–46, *hudoc.echr.coe.int*, with the above-mentioned dissenting opinion of Judge Ranzoni.

[15]Zirnīte v. Latvia, no. 69019/11, 11 June 2020, §§ 53–56, *hudoc.echr.coe.int*.

[16]Lamatic v. Romania, no. 55859/15, 1 December 2020, §§ 56 and 59–60; Ignat v. Romania, no. 17325/16, 9 November 2021, §§ 51 and 53–59; *hudoc.echr.coe.int*.

[17]Di Martino and Molinari v. Italy, no. 15931/15 and 16459/15, 25 March 2021, §§ 41–45, *hudoc.echr.coe.int*; and, partly, Zirnīte v. Latvia, §§ 53 and 56.

[18]Kashlev v. Estonia, no. 22574/08, 26 April 2016, § 51, *hudoc.echr.coe.int*. This rationale is clearly more controversial (see the dissenting opinion of Judge Karakaş, §§ 7–14). As an illustration, the following Lazu v. the Republic of Moldova, no. 46182/08, 5 July 2016, § 42, *hudoc.echr.coe.int*, states the exact opposite: '(. . .) the Court notes that the requirements of a fair trial necessitated the rehearing of witnesses and that the Court of Appeal was under an obligation to take positive measures to such an end, even if the applicant did not request it'.

undermine the overall fairness of the criminal appeal—rehear itself the evidence given orally by the witnesses and the accused, and, most importantly, the inference drawn from it in Gómez Olmeda v. Spain that for this purpose it is usually not enough to examine the audio-visual recording of the first instance trial, when available.

In fact, addressing this concern, the Spanish *Ley de Enjuiciamiento Criminal* (LECrim) was altered in 2015 to prohibit *de novo* convictions and penalties increasing on appeal in the event of an error in the evidence assessment, which can only lead to the quashing of the appealed decision and a retrial of the case (Article 792 § 2 LECrim),[19] though, since 2009, the first trial recorded evidence can be reproduced at appeal hearings (Article 791 LECrim). On the contrary, in the solution of the Italian *Legge Orlando* of 2017, in situations of *appello* by the *Pubblico Ministero* of acquittals for reasons relating to the assessment of declarative evidence, a 'renewal of evidence' (*rinnovazione dell'istruzione dibattimentale*) takes place in the court of appeal (new § 3-bis of Article 603 of the Italian *Codice di Procedura Penale).* Still, these ECtHR case-law inspired law revisions raised critiques as well as difficulties, and new legislative reforms are underway in both Spain and Italy.[20]

I would not question the right of the defendant to appear personally at the appeal hearing to argue his or her case and guarantee adversarial and defence rights, as a matter of fair appeal, in cases of global evaluation of the accused's guilt or innocence as regards to points of fact, particularly in contexts of overturning acquittals. Not even that, the appellate court is under the duty to take positive measures to secure his or her presence to that effect when deemed necessary,[21] even if the defence has not requested a hearing to be held. Quite the opposite: within the frame of reference of an expressive theory of punishment, this obligation appears indisputable with respect to cases of acquittal reversal or sentence aggravation, taking into account the expressive function and the nature of the communicative vehicle of the conviction itself.[22] It is, indeed, in the moment of the conviction that the communication of criminal censure by the State reaches its exponent, addressing the accused as a rational agent, declaring his or her guilt and expressing the public disapproval deserved by the crime committed.

But should we agree with the European Court when it advocates a right of the defendant to give evidence in person before the court of appeal in all these situations, although he or she has already made statements at the first instance trial that have

---

[19]The Spanish legislator thus followed the alternative to the rehearing of personal evidence in appeal suggested in Július Þór Sigurþórsson v. Iceland, §§ 38 and 42: 'In the alternative, the appeal court must limit itself to quashing the lower court's acquittal and referring the case back for a retrial.' (§ 38).

[20]On all these legislative reforms see Chaps. 2 and 3.

[21]Botten v. Norway, § 53, for example.

[22]See Duff (2003), pp. 80 and 132 et seq.; Duff (2018), no. 5; Simester and von Hirsch (2011), p. 5; and, for a communicative theory of the trial itself and on the participatory role of the defendant within this framework, Duff et al. (2007), pp. 97 et seq. and 199 et seq.

been video recorded and which the appeal court can directly assess? And should we also accept that, in general, so one may weigh differently the same witness evidence and rebut the lower instance version of facts, all the crucial testimonies must be repeated at the appellate stage, even if video recorded as well and the high instance court sees no need to further question the witnesses?

An affirmative answer seems, at first glance, technologically outdated, considering, on the one hand, the historical role of technological advancements that made records of trials possible in the recognition of the right to appeal,[23] and, on the other hand, our postmodern technological society which considerably strengthened a remote audio-visual component in the late pandemic context.

Moreover, the ECtHR appears to conceive the appeal on factual elements more as a second trial or a retrial in a higher instance, in the image of the German *Berufung*,[24] than as a review of the first instance proceedings. The disadvantages of double trials are, nevertheless, well known: a second trial leads, to a greater or lesser extent, to the practical uselessness of the first trial and, therefore, to evident procedural efficiency losses; it may jeopardize the discovery of the truth, for participants know what has been previously said; and it weakens the *ne bis in idem* principle, due to the burden that a second trial for the same facts represents for the accused.

Finally, the ECtHR's jurisprudence on immediacy in criminal appeal does not look consistent with its own case-law on immediacy in case of a change in the composition of the trial court, as, in Chernika v. Ukraine, where the case was remitted for retrial before a different judge, the Court appears to concede that the viewing of video recorded statements of the key witnesses by the new judge could have compensated for the lack of a personal examination of those same witnesses.[25]

1.2 Key Question and Structure

This book aims, in short, to carry out a critical and interdisciplinary analysis of the fair criminal appeal immediacy criteria adopted in the ECtHR's case-law in the light of Article 6 of the ECHR, considering its relevance for the Contracting States and their future legislative amendments as well as for criminal process theory in general.

To this effect, Part I (Criminal appeal immediacy models and the ECtHR case-law) covers the advantages and disadvantages of models of appeal on factual points that lay out an alternative to the classic second trial at second instance, focusing, on

[23] Marshall (2011), pp. 36–37.

[24] See §§ 323 et seq. StPO; and Roxin and Schünemann (2017), p. 465; Bohlander (2021), pp. 226 et seq.

[25] Chernika v. Ukraine, no. 53791/11, 12 March 2020, § 73, *hudoc.echr.coe.int.*: '(. . .) the trial judge who eventually convicted the applicant had no opportunity personally to examine any of the three key witnesses for the prosecution. Neither did he have at his disposal a video recording of their statements even though domestic law envisaged a possibility of such video recording (. . .) and the latter may have provided an important additional safeguard'.

the one hand, on systems recently adapted to respond to the ECtHR's immediacy requirements, and, on the other hand, on the first instance trial's recorded evidence system deemed unfair by the Strasbourg Court. Chapter 2 (The evidence renewal model in Italy) begins with the partially inspired by the ECtHR's jurisprudence 'declarative evidence renewal', which can be used in the Italian *appelo* by the *Pubblico Ministero* to challenge an acquittal, but not by the defence to challenge a conviction. Chapter 3 (The retrial model in Spain) discusses the Spanish dialogue with the ECtHR's case-law, from the previous appeal system attached to the video-recordings viewing of the first instance hearing, to its replacement by a retrial system in cases of prosecution appeals directed to first-time convictions and sentences increasing, along with the expected novelties of the ongoing reform. Chapters 4 and 5 (The recordings model in Portugal) reflect on the insufficiencies of the Portuguese appeal system—rooted on the audio-recording of the first instance hearing and which the defendant and the prosecution can equally access—, both from the appellate court perspective (Chapter 4) as well as from the accused and the victim perspectives (Chapter 5).

Part II (Immediacy in criminal procedure theory and cognitive sciences) turns to the fundamentals of immediacy in the theory of criminal process and to its compatibility with new discoveries in the field of cognitive sciences, seeking to measure the scientific adequacy of the ECtHR's appeal immediacy requisite from an interdisciplinary point of view. Chapter 6 (Immediacy at the first instance trial) explores the foundations of the criminal procedure immediacy principle and its exemptions, in particular the technological exceptions, at the first instance trial. Chapter 7 (Audio-visual recordings as evidence in criminal procedure) tackles the validity of trials mainly or exclusively based on recorded evidence from the standpoint of immediacy. Chapter 8 (Neuroscience of memory and philosophy of knowledge challenges to immediacy) deals with current research in the neuroscience of memory and the philosophy of knowledge and its implications in the choice between trial repetition or recorded evidence reproduction in appeal. Chapter 9 (AI assistance in the courtroom and immediacy) explains how the employment of AI assistants in the courtroom, during testimonies, might shape the immediacy requirement, including at the appellate level.

Chapter 10 (Concluding thoughts) integrates the findings of the previous chapters, drawing overall conclusions on the legitimacy of the ECtHR's immediacy standard of fairness at the appellate stage with some remarks on its limits.

Cited Case-Law

ECtHR

hudoc.echr.coe.int

Delcourt v. Belgium, no. 2689/65, 17 January 1970
Ekbatani v. Sweden, no. 10563/83, 26 May 1988

Fejde v. Sweden, no. 12631/87, 29 October 1991
Jan-Åke Andersson v. Sweden, no. 11274/84, 29 October 1991
Botten v. Norway, no. 6206/90, 19 February 1996
Michael Edward Cooke v. Austria, no. 25878/94, 8 February 2000
Destrehem v. France, no. 56651/00, 18 May 2004
Dondarini v. San Marino, no. 50545/99, 6 July 2004
Dănilă v. Romania, no. 53897/00, 8 March 2007
Bazo González v. Spain, no. 30643/04, 16 December 2008
Strzałkowski v. Poland, no. 31509/02, 9 June 2009
Maresti vs Croatia, no. 55759/07, 25 June 2009
Suuripää v. Finland, no. 43151/02, 12 January 2010
Sinichkin v. Russia, no. 20508/03, 8 April 2010
Dan v. Moldova, no. 8999/07, 5 July 2011
Cani v. Albania, no. 11006/06, 6 March 2012
Zahirović v. Croatia, no. 58590/11, 25 April 2013
Sobko v. Ukraine, no. 15102/10, 17 December 2015
Gómez Olmeda v. Spain, no. 61112/12, 29 March 2016
Kashlev v. Estonia, no. 22574/08, 26 April 2016
Lazu v. the Republic of Moldova, no. 46182/08, 5 July 2016
Chiper v. Romania, no. 22036/10, 27 June 2017
Lorefice v. Italy, no. 63446/13, 29 June 2017
Júlíus Þór Sigurþórsson v. Iceland, no. 38797/17, 16 July 2019
Marilena-Carmen Popa v. Romania, no. 1814/11, 18 February 2020
Paixão Moreira Sá Fernandes v. Portugal, no. 78108/14, 25 February 2020
Chernika v. Ukraine, no. 53791/11, 12 March 2020
Zirnīte v. Latvia, no. 69019/11, 11 June 2020
Lamatic v. Romania, no. 55859/15, 1 December 2020
Di Martino and Molinari v. Italy, no. 15931/15 and 16459/15, 25 March 2021
X v. the Netherlands, no. 72631/17, 27 July 2021
Ignat v. Romania, no. 17325/16, 9 November 2021

Spanish Constitutional Court

hj.tribunalconstitucional.es

Sentencia no. 167/2002

References

Bohlander M (2021) Principles of German criminal procedure, 2nd edn. Hart Publishing, Oxford
Duff A (2003) Punishment, communication and community. Oxford University Press, New York
Duff A (2018) Theories of criminal law. In: Zalta EN (ed) The Stanford encyclopedia of philosophy, Summer 2018 Edition. https://plato.stanford.edu/archives/sum2018/entries/criminal-law/
Duff A, Farmer L, Marshall S, Tadros V (2007) The trial on trial, vol 3: Towards a normative theory of the criminal trial. Hart Publishing, Oxford/Portland

European Court of Human Rights (2022, 30th April) Guide on Article 6 of the European Convention of Human Rights – Right to a fair trial (criminal limb). http://www.echr.coe.int

Fanego CA (2012) The right to a double degree of jurisdiction in criminal offences (Art. 2 P7). In: Roca JG, Santolaya P (eds) Europe of rights: A Compendium on the European Convention of Human Rights. Martinus Nijhoff Publishers, Leiden/Boston, pp 167–176

Marshall PD (2011) A comparative analysis of the right to appeal. Duke J Comp Int Law 22:1–45

Morão H (2020) Pela Renovação da Renovação da Prova. Anatomia do Crime 12:171–195

Roxin C, Schünemann B (2017) Strafverfahrensrecht – Ein Studienbuch, 29th edn. C. H. Beck, München

Simester AP, von Hirsch A (2011) Crimes, harms and wrongs – On the principles of criminalisation. Hart Publishing, Oxford/Portland

Spano R, Bårdsen A (2020) On the right to a fair hearing in criminal appeal proceedings. In: Spano R et al (eds) Fair trial: regional and international perspectives/Procès Équitable: Perspectives Regionales et Internationales – Liber Amicorum Linos-Alexandre Sicilianos. Anthemis, Limal, pp 583–594

Summers SJ (2007) Fair trials – The European criminal procedural tradition and the European Court of Human Rights. Hart Publishing, Oxford/Portland

Thaman SC (2019) Appeal and cassation in continental European criminal justice systems: guarantees of factual accuracy, or vehicles for administrative control? In: Brown DK, Turner JI, Weisser B (eds) The Oxford handbook of criminal process. Oxford University Press, Oxford, pp 937–959

Trechsel S, with the assistance of Summers SJ (2005) Human rights in criminal proceedings. Oxford University Press, Oxford

Part II
Criminal Appeal Immediacy Models and the ECtHR Case-Law

Chapter 2
The Evidence Renewal Model in Italy

Massimo Ceresa-Gastaldo

2.1 The Physiognomy of Appeal in the Criminal Justice Review System

Conceived as a broad-spectrum remedy, aiming to establish the unfairness of a judgment (albeit lawfully) delivered at the outcome of a trial, as well as to quash (for reasons strictly provided by the law) a first-instance judgment, criminal appeal is structured by the Italian criminal procedure legislator on the basis of a unique framework, which borrows features from the other appeal models and doesn't allow to include it within one of the traditional dogmatic categories thereof.

The devolutionary effect arising from the appellant's appeal—based on the provisions of Article 597 § 1 ICPP, according to which "the appeal assigns to the second-instance judge the duty to hear and determine the case strictly with reference to the issues of the lower court's judgment that were raised on appeal"—means that criminal appeal does not qualify as a second trial or retrial of the case, but rather as a review of the firs-instance proceedings.

This characteristic translates differently than the typical motion to quash: the latter remedy allows a party to request the quashing of a judgment on the basis of a specified list of grounds, so that the court may (except in the case of vacation of judgment on the court's own motion) either grant or dismiss the motion on the grounds put forward; conversely, in criminal appeal, the parties dispose of a "free scrutiny" tool, where the scope of review is not defined by the grounds for appeal but by the points in the appealed judgment to which the grounds relate back to. This means that the judge, within the subject-matter of examination, is free to redefine any question abstractly possible, regardless of any appellant's specific request, having

M. Ceresa-Gastaldo (✉)
Department of Law, Bocconi University, Milan, Italy
e-mail: massimo.ceresa@unibocconi.it

H. Morão, R. Tavares da Silva (eds.), *Fairness in Criminal Appeal*,
https://doi.org/10.1007/978-3-031-13001-4_2

the power to review all case file documents. This results in the fact that, when all the points of the decision are under appeal, the scope of review extends to the entire case.

What is meant by "point" of the decision has been clear for some time now: every finding of fact or of law that may be considered and examined independently[1] and that has a direct impact not so much on the reasons for the ruling, but on the disposition of the judgment; every "conclusion" in judgments relating to joinder of offenses or defendants (i.e. each individual decision referring to each offender, or, in case of multiple charges, to each count), is made up of different "points", relating to conduct, circumstances, defences, malicious intent or negligence, legal qualification of the offence, sentencing, benefits and so on. While every individual conclusion is abstractly capable of becoming irrevocable (when none of the points that compose it have been subject to appeal), with reference to the points of a judgment, partial *res iudicata* cannot be applied, as challenging any part of a conclusion prevents even the parts of that conclusion that were not challenged from becoming final, the only bar in their respect being related to the devolutionary effect;[2] this bar, moreover, that does not apply to the parts of the judgment that are bound by an essential connection to the issues raised on appeal, since even criminal appeal is subject to the rule and general principle set forth in Article 624 § 1 ICPP on reviews before the Court of Cassation.[3]

This legislative approach clearly aims to create a suitable balance between the needs at play: having ruled out the solution of a second trial—which would have entailed too great a sacrifice in terms of procedural economy,[4] not necessarily counterbalanced by an increasingly reliable result[5]—the choice was made for a means of review guided by the complaints of the interested party. This allows to make a targeted selection of the subject-matter submitted to the court's examination and, at the same time, to put to good use, in light of the arguments put forward by the

[1] As held in the "historic" judgment ICCass, joint sections, 26 February 1955, Zoccola, which has become a crucial precedent regularly referred to by subsequent case-law.

[2] Lozzi (2020), p. 703.

[3] Bargis (2020), p. 807.

[4] Peroni (2001), p. 728. Consistent with the opinion that "any approach departing from the traditional one would have necessarily entailed a reform of the 1941 judicial system" is: 'Relazione al progetto preliminare del codice di procedura penale', *Gazzetta ufficiale della Repubblica italiana*, 24 October 1988, no. 250, suppl. ord. no. 2, p. 124.

[5] The second-instance court, by examining the facts from scratch, faces the same probability of error as the first-instance court; as a matter of fact, since it is often called to rule on facts long after they took place, it faces an even greater difficulty in reconstructing the events compared to that of the first judge. This observation in scholarship is rather dated: see Cesarini (1878), p. 115.

appellant,[6] the experience of the first examination, thereby securing, overall, a smaller risk of error compared to other models.[7]

Furthermore, the court of appeal's scope of review, in addition to extending beyond the boundaries of the issues raised on appeal, by reason of application of the above-mentioned rule set forth Article 597 § 1 ICPP, also includes a number of assessments on the court's own motion.

A significant number of exceptions to the rule of partial devolution is set forth by the code provisions that impose, also in the second instance, and even in the absence of a party request, the statements of lack of jurisdiction (Article 20 § 1 ICPP), of the lower court's lack of subject-matter jurisdiction, not arising from joinder (Articles 21, §§ 1 and 3, and 23 § 2 ICPP), of absolute grounds for nullity (Article 179 ICPP), of the relative grounds for nullity that may still be invoked (Article 180 ICPP), and of the double jeopardy bar (Article 649 ICPP). Furthermore, appeal proceedings are also subject to the rule set forth in Article 129 ICPP, which require immediate declaratory judgments in relation to affirmative defences; likewise, the declaration of excluded evidence under Article 191 ICPP is also included within the powers that the second-instance judge may exercise on its own motion.

It should also be noted that, by express provision of Article 597 § 5 ICPP, "by judgment, the court may, also on its own motion, order the suspension of sentence, no conviction to be recorded and the application of one or more mitigating circumstances; when necessary, the court may also proceed with the weighing and balancing of any mitigating and aggravating circumstances under Article 69 of the Criminal Code". Falling within the scope of application of this provision, according to influential scholarship, are two other similar cases, namely the exclusion of one or more aggravating circumstances, erroneously considered by the trial court, and the recalculation of the sentence according to the criteria set forth in Article 133 ICPP.[8] An unexpressed ground for devolution by law is the violation of the lawfulness principle, in cases where the first-instance court determined a wrongful sentence either in type or amount.

[6]Siracusano (2016), p. 18, acutely notes that "it is the very "argumentative" coefficient of evidence that is neglected in solutions that do not give proper value to the "re-examination" of previously adduced evidence"; "these theories do not take into account the "refuting" implication of evidence, and refutation as an ideal strategy to clot alternative theories to those supported in the first instance", "nor do they consider the "persuasive" resources of evidence, and evidence as a tool capable of providing an account of the facts that is convincing and, perhaps, different from the one outlined in the reasoning of the court's or appellate court's judgment"; "the "persuasive" and "refuting" moments are intrinsically tied... to the evidence as an argument, and may allow, in the transition from the first to the second stage of the proceedings, and through new parameters of persuasion, an adequate documentary re-examination of the facts".

[7]Liebman (1980), p. 404, referring to Carnelutti (1956), p. 551, observes that the review judge is favoured "by the very fact of being called to rule no longer on a blank case, as presented to the trial judge, but rather on a previously solved case, and thus the review court has something the first judge did not have, that is the experience of the first instance proceedings, on which it is called to apply its critical thinking, encouraged by the parties' observations and cross-observations".

[8]Cordero (2012), p. 1148.

2.1.1 The Proceedings. Hearing of the Appeal

The 1988 legislator designed two appeal procedures: one ordinary, held in open court, according to the general rules governing first instance proceedings, generally referred to in Article 598 ICPP, and to those specified in Title II Volume IX of the ICPP; and one simplified, in chambers, according to the rules set forth in Article 127 ICPP.

The ordinary procedure envisages that the hearing, following the fulfilment of preliminary requirements under Article 601 ICPP, begins with a "report of the case" by the presiding judge or by a delegated judge (Article 603 § 1 ICPP).

This requirement serves the purpose to inform the bench of judges of the facts, the events of the trial and the issues raised by the appellant that shall form the subject-matter of the decision. Upon drafting the above provision, evaluations were made as to whether or not maintaining this requirement, borrowed from previous code provisions, by virtue of the undeniable conditioning effect of the information selection process by the reporting judge on the hearing and examination of the case by the bench, and the risk of discouraging the involvement and study of the case by the judges not called to report on it; the decision was, however, made to maintain it, on the ground that "assigning to each of the judges the examination of the case files of individual trials entails a more in-depth study and better assessment, which, if the report is made with appropriate care and information, the other members of the bench may equally, if not better, be a part of".[9]

In the appeal hearings, the court may order the "reading, also on its own motion, of the case file documents and, within the limits set forth in Articles 511 ff., of the documents pertaining to the preliminary stages" (Article 602 § 3 ICPP). The wording, which is very straightforward with regards to the "case file documents" (clearly referring to the transcripts of the trial),[10] deserves to be clarified with reference to the "documents pertaining to the preliminary stages": only the documents already adduced in the first instance, and thereby contained in the case file, may be taken into consideration on appeal, while any other documents, that may be examined under Articles 511 ff. ICPP but were not examined at the time, may be examined on the basis of the evidence renewal tool regulated by Article 603 ICPP (a tool that would, on the contrary, be eluded with an extensive interpretation of Article 602 § 3 ICPP).[11]

---

[9] 'Relazione al progetto preliminare del codice di procedura penale', p. 130.

[10] Bargis (2020), p. 820; Fiorio (1998), p. 336.

[11] Bargis (2020), p. 820; Peroni (1995), p. 183; Zappalà (1991), p. 198; of a contrary opinion Nobili (1989), p. 71, according to whom the reference made to the "limits set forth in Articles 511 ff." should be interpreted in such a way that in appeal "the rule of documents that may be subject to examination but were not examined at the trial must in any case be re-applied".

Precisely because the appeal is structured as a review of the lower court's decision, and not as a retrial of the case,[12] it is essentially dedicated to a critical reassessment of the evidence submitted in the first instance and made available in full to the appellate court.[13]

After an appeal has been filed, the court of appeal receives, from the trial court clerk's office, the appealed judgment, the notice of appeal and the case file (Article 590 ICPP); in other words all the documents that were available to the trial court that handed down the appealed judgment. Among these, all trial recorded evidence, including any phonographic or audio-visual recordings and transcripts, (which, by express provision of Article 139 § 6 ICPP, are included in the case file).[14]

2.1.1.1 Renewal of Evidentiary Hearings

Only exceptionally,[15] therefore, by way of departure from the general rule of completeness of the evidence taken at first instance,[16] a fresh examination of

[12]Unlike the provisions laid out in the 1978 preliminary draft project whereby (by way of implementation of Directive No. 74 of the Enabling Act of 1974) this remedy—as noted by Zappalà (1991), p. 201—was described as a "re-do" of the first-instance proceedings" precisely by virtue of the provision imposing a mandatory renewal of hearings upon motion (not manifestly groundless) of the parties.

[13]Tranchina and Di Chiara (1999), p. 214.

[14]Article 134 ICPP provides that proceedings be recorded in minutes, to be "drawn up in full or summarized by means of stenotype or other mechanical means or, in case of impossibility, by hand" (§ 1); the provision adds that "when the minutes are drawn up in summary form, a phonographic recording is also made" (§ 2) and that when "the recording means specified in paragraphs 2 and 3 are deemed to be insufficient, an audio-visual recording may be added where considered absolutely necessary. The audio-visual representation of statements made by the victim of the offence who is in a particularly vulnerable position is in any case allowed even outside the cases of absolute necessity." (§ 4). A critical legislative choice that to subject the court's decision to order, in addition to an audio-recording, the video-recording of statements, to a "rather elusive" requirement such as absolute necessity, which is "on the one hand, the result of a subjective assessment and, on the other, rather undefined", Signorato (2020), p. 483.

[15]Highlighting the exceptional nature of the rule is 'Relazione al progetto preliminare', pp. 125 and 129; in scholarship, among others, Bargis (2020), p. 821; Ceresa-Gastaldo (2010), p. 30; Lozzi (2020), p. 689; Peroni (1995), p. 258; Tranchina and Di Chiara (1999), p. 214.

[16]Zappalà (1991), p. 201; in case-law the principle was established by ICCass, joint sections, 24 January 1996, Panigoni and others, and confirmed, among others, by ICCass, joint sections, 17 December 2015, Ricci: "the renewal of evidence in appeal represents an exceptional remedy that may be resorted to, by way of departure from the presumption of trial evidence completeness, when the court considers it necessary, in that it would not be able to rule on the sole basis of the evidence already available. Essentially, following a request for evidence renewal, on the ground of pre-existing evidence not yet adduced (*noviter producta*), the court, under Article 603 §1 ICPP, has the power to grant or reject the motion, in accordance with the standard of "inability to decide based on the current state of the case file", simply by specifying, without incurring in manifest illogicality defects, the reasons for its choice".

evidence may be admitted "at a hearing between the parties by order of the court" (Article 603 § 5, ICPP).

This approach carries a specific meaning: in order to ensure consistency with the adversarial principle and the oral and immediacy requirements applied in the first instance proceedings, the appeal is not aimed at repeating the entire evidence-taking procedure (albeit without structuring it as a second trial *tout court*), but at reviewing the appealed decision, also with regards to the strict fulfilment of the rules provided for the purpose of establishing the facts of the case.

Therefore, the possibility that, for the reasons put forward by the appellant or autonomously identified by the court, the examination of the recorded evidence and transcripts (or of the audio and visual files from the trial evidentiary hearings)[17] may not be not sufficient, such as to require a direct hearing of previously adduced evidence or of "fresh" evidence, is only residual.

This may occur, precisely, either upon the appellant's request, in the notice of appeal or in the supplementary grounds for appeal, to "rehear evidence previously adduced at the trial or to introduce fresh evidence", either upon the court's own motion; the court may order a renewal of evidence, in the first case, when "fresh or after-discovered evidence" has emerged (Article 603 § 2 ICPP), or, in any case, if "it holds that it is unable to rule based on the current state of the case file" (Article 603 §

[17] It should also be noted that the examination of audio and visual files of the trial evidence is a practice entirely unknown to Italian appellate courts. The only sources on which the courts generally base their assessments are the minutes and phonographic transcripts of the hearings: there is no record of decisions where, even in light of doubts on the interpretation of an answer given by a witness or the defendant, the court resorted to the audio or visual recordings of the hearing, albeit the files being available to the court. As a matter of fact, the Court of Cassation diminished the value of such means, holding that "as to the recording of proceedings, the loss, for any reasons, of the audiotapes relating to the testimonies duly transcribed does not constitute ground for nullity of the relevant witness statements, considering it is not expressly provided and that the events of the hearing are in any case documented by the transcripts, which are an integral part of the minutes of the hearing" (ICCass, joint sections, 27 February 2020, no. 12778; similarly already ICCass, section III, 26 July 1993, no. 1698, Petrone). In this case, the applicant had explained that, in the appeal, the defence sought leave to extract a copy or otherwise proceed to the listening of the phonographic recordings of the hearings held at the first-instance trial. The request had been only partially satisfied since the recording of the hearing held on 13 April 2012 was missing, while in the defence's opinion that hearing had been decisive for the case, as a statement had been given, among others, by the judicial police offer who had conducted the investigation. Thus a general nullity defence had been invoked for violation of the defence's right to listen to the phonographic recordings of the first-instance trial hearings in order to verify the correctness of the related transcript. The Court of Appeal had dismissed the argument, on the one hand, holding that the case file contained the transcripts of all the hearings—including the one held on 13 April—and, on the other, by referring to the principle of law (affirmed in the Petrone judgment of 1993) according to which Article 139 § 6 ICPP sets forth that the phonographic recordings be included in the case file but no penalty is envisaged, particularly in terms of exclusion of the transcript, in case of non-compliance with the rule.

1, part II ICPP);[18] and, in the second case, any time it considers supplementary evidence "absolutely necessary" (Article 603 § 3 ICPP).[19]

This is the epistemological structure of criminal appeal defined by the 1988 Italian criminal procedure code, which, despite the criticism raised in scholarship from several quarters,[20] remained unchanged for nearly thirty years, preserved by courts that were rather reluctant to flexible interpretations of the legal framework, that is up until the amendment of Article 111 Italian Constitution,[21] the reform of fair trial requirements,[22] and, in particular, a number of decisions of the ECtHR on convictions of defendants on appeal after acquittal at trial,[23] from which point on the case-law on the matter radically shifted direction.

[18] The "fresh evidence" that may be introduced on appeal under Article 603 § 1 ICPP, other than any "evidence arising or discovered after the trial", is evidence that already existed or was already known to the parties but not introduced in the trial, either because it was not admitted or because it was not requested by the parties. This rule shows a doubtful compatibility with the adversarial principle since it allows the parties, by way of departure from discovery obligations and the penalties of inadmissibility and disqualification, to introduce on appeal "surprise" evidence never mentioned at the trial: Fassone (1991), p. 634; Nappi (1990), p. 975.

[19] In addition to these cases, Article 604 § 6 ICPP allows the judge to order, if necessary, the renewal of evidence in case of an erroneous declaration at first instance of the crime being no longer punishable or of a bar to prosecution.

Article 603 § 4 ICPP, in its original version, provided another ground for the renewal of evidence, relating to the violation of the right to be heard during the trial due to the defendant's absence for valid reasons. The provision, repealed by Article 11 § 2 of Act No 67 of 28 April 2014, had raised many doubts, not only because it placed on the defendant the burden to prove the lack of knowledge of the first-instance proceedings (where Article 175 § 2 ICPP, as transposed from Law Decree No 17 of 21 February 2005, converted into Act No. 60 of 22 April 2005, places on the judicial authority the burden to conduct "all necessary checks" on the fulfilment of the requirements to grant the applicant a new deadline to challenge the judgment in absentia or the summary conviction order); but also because, by admitting in the case at hand only a renewal of the evidentiary hearing and not a retrial of the case before the trial court due to absence of the accused, it actually deprived the defendant of a first-instance trial: on this matter see, for all, Bargis (2020), p. 822.

[20] See Amodio (1999), p. 3620; Gaito (2015), p. 5; Lozzi (2004), p. 641.

[21] Constitutional Act No. 2 of 23 November 1999.

[22] Implemented, after the amendment of Article 111 Constitution, by Act No. 63 of 1° March 2001.

[23] As known, after a first ruling holding that fair trial guarantees do not necessarily require to be replicated in all instances of the proceedings (Ekbatani v. Sweden, no. 10563/83, 26 May 1988, *hudoc.echr.coe.int*), the case Destrehem v. France, no. 56651/00, 18 May 2004, *hudoc.echr.coe.int*, which found a violation of Article 6 § 3 ECHR in cases where the appellate court overturns an acquittal and convicts the defendant after having denied the latter's motion to rehear the witnesses for the defence, seemed bound to consolidate the Court's line of interpretation supporting the principle that a new direct examination of the witness before the appellate court is necessary in order to reassess, to the detriment of the defendant, the related statement that had grounded the acquittal: Dan v. Moldavia, no. 8999/07, 5 July 2011; Manolachi v. Romania, no. 36605/04, 5 March 2013; Hanu v. Romania, no. 10890/04, 4 June 2013; Luzu v. Moldavia, no. 46182/08, 5 July 2016; *hudoc.echr.coe.int*. In reality, the Court itself ruled on other occasions that the standard of guarantee of direct examination of the witnesses on appeal is not mandatory as it may be compensated for by other guarantees provided by the criminal justice system which protect the overall fairness of the

With two judgments by the full bench, the Court of Cassation, between 2016 and 2017, paved the way for the necessary implementation of the evidence renewal model in the event of appeals against acquittals, with a view to overturning them into convictions.

With the first judgment, in the *Dasgupta* case,[24] the Court of Cassation firstly stated that, in principle, an acquittal at first instance may not be overturned solely on the basis of a different documentary assessment of the evidence on appeal: a second-instance judgment convicting the defendant without having ordered a fresh hearing of the evidence is null on the ground of lack of reasoning, since the conviction conflicts with the "reasonable doubt" standard.[25] According to the Court, on the basis of a traditional interpretation of Article 603 ICPP,[26] in these cases the appellate court is under an obligation to proceed, even on its own motion (Article 603 § 3 ICPP), with a new hearing of those[27] who in the first instance gave statements on

trial: in this direction, Kashlev v. Estonia, no. 22574/08, 26 April 2016, *hudoc.echr.coe.int*, according to which there is no violation of Article 6 when a renewal of evidence was not ordered but the system still ensures "the existence of ... safeguards against arbitrary or unreasonable assessments of the evidence or establishment of the facts" (§ 50), such as the obligation for the appellate court, when overturning an acquittal, to provide particularly thorough reasoning for departing from the assessment given by the trial court, with indication of the mistakes made by the lower court, and the provision of a duty to verify whether such obligation has been fulfilled ("the fair trial guarantees enshrined in Article 6 §§ 1 and 3 (d) has not been put into question, that the applicant, who was assisted by a lawyer, did not request the examination of witnesses at the appellate court's hearing, that the Court of Appeal followed the requirement of domestic law to provide particularly thorough reasoning for departing from the assessment given to the evidence by the first-instance court, including the indication of mistakes made by it, and that an appeal against the Court of Appeal judgment to the country's highest court allowed the latter to verify whether the requirements of domestic law, including those of a fair trial, had been met": § 51). In the same direction, Chiper v. Romania, no. 22036/10, 27 June 2017, *hudoc.echr.coe.int*. On the matter see, for all, Caneschi (2021), p. 214.

[24] ICCass, joint sections, 28 April 2016, Dasgupta, with comment by Aiuti (2016), p. 3214. For a comment on the decision see also Capone (2016), p. 52 ff.; Lorenzetto (2016), p. 1; Tesoriero (2017a), p. 79 ff.

[25] Called to rule on the question of whether "the issue regarding the violation of Article 6 ECHR when the appellate court overturns a judgment of acquittal and determines the defendant's guilt, solely on the basis of a different assessment of the credibility of the witness statements without personally rehearing the witnesses, may be examined on the supreme court's own motion", the Joint Chambers of the Court of Cassation have affirmed that "outside the cases of inadmissibility of the appeal, when the appellant has appealed the second-instance judgment on the grounds of insufficient, contradictory or manifestly illogical reasoning for the reassessment of declarative evidence considered decisive, albeit without specifically referring to the principle set forth in Article 6 § 3 (d) ECHR, the Court of Cassation shall quash the appealed judgment and remand the case".

[26] According to the court, "the principles contained in the European Convention for the protection of human rights and fundamental freedoms, as defined in the ECtHR's consolidated case-law, albeit not translating into rules that are directly applicable in the domestic legal systems, constitute interpretation criteria – inspired by the Convention – which the national courts must draw on when enforcing domestic provisions".

[27] Regardless of the capacity of the person giving the statement: witness, defendant called as a witness, co-defendant in connected proceedings, co-defendant in the same proceedings,

facts considered decisive for the acquittal by the trial court.[28] Even if it were impossible to proceed with a direct hearing of the declarative evidence—e.g. if the person is deceased, incapacitated or cannot be traced—according to the Court, an acquittal may not be overturned simply based on an examination of previously recorded evidence, "without prejudice to the court's duty to establish the actual impossibility to conduct a direct examination, and that the unavailability does not depend on the intention to favour the defendant or on the unlawful conduct of third parties, in which cases the judgment may be grounded on previously recorded statements".

Likewise, according to the *Patalano* judgment,[29] the appeal judgment is vitiated for lack of reasoning, by way of violation of the reasonable doubt standard, when, upon appeal filed by the prosecution against an acquittal delivered within an unconditional accelerated trial procedure,[30] the judgment finds the defendant guilty on the basis of a different assessment of declarative evidence considered decisive, without the court having directly reheard the witnesses that gave such statements.[31]

In parallel, while on the one hand, the case-law confirming and stretching the extensive interpretation of the provision began to multiply,[32] on the other, the

"vulnerable" party, defendant. Even the examination of expert witnesses is to be repeated on appeal when their statements were decisive for the acquittal at first-instance: this was established—already with reference to the new Article 603 § 3 *bis* ICPP—in ICCass, joint sections, 28 January 2019, Pavan, with comment by Galluccio Mezio (2019), p. 3859.

[28] According to the Court of Cassation, "evidence considered decisive for the purpose of deciding whether to order a new hearing of witness statements in cases where the appellate court intends to overturn an acquittal based on a different assessment of the oral evidence, is evidence that, on the basis of the first-instance judgment, determined, or even only contributed to determine, the acquittal and that, albeit in the presence of other types of evidence, if expunged from the case file, is potentially capable of affecting the outcome of the proceedings, as well as those which, albeit regarded as having little to no value by the lower court, are, in the appellant's perspective, in fact relevant – alone or jointly with other evidence – for the conviction".

[29] ICCass, joint sections, 19 January 2017, Patalano, with comment by Aprati (2017), p. 2672; Tesoriero (2017b), p. 3668.

[30] It may be of use to recall that the accelerated trial procedure, regulated by Articles 438–443 ICPP, is ordered upon motion of the defendant and conducted in a "simplified" form in the chambers of the preliminary hearing judge, who rules based on the current state of the case file, consisting of the preliminary investigation file (unless the judge decides to take, on his own motion, other evidence necessary for reaching a judgment when he holds to be unable to rule on the current state of the case file: Article 441 § 5 ICPP). The defendant may condition his motion to a supplementary taking of evidence (so-called "conditional" accelerated trial procedure); the judge grants the request if he considers supplementary evidence necessary for the purpose of judgment and consistent with the underlying procedural economy needs; if the motion is granted, the prosecution may file a motion to introduce counterevidence (Article 438 ICPP).

[31] Conversely, if the appellate court intends to overturn a lower court's judgment of acquittal delivered at an ordinary or accelerated trial it is not under an obligation to order a new hearing of the oral evidence if it finds that the evidence assessed by the lower court was misread due to omission, invention or falsification (ICCass, joint sections, 19 January 2017, Patalano).

[32] For example, ICCass, section II, 17 May 2017, Salute and others, with comment by Caneschi (2017), p. 1, has established that the appellate court overturning a lower court's judgment to the

legislation took steps towards adjusting the wording of Article 603 ICPP to the new sensitivity: the Orlando Reform (Act No. 103 of 2017) added a new paragraph 3 *bis*, which sets forth that "in case of appeal by the prosecution against an acquittal for reasons relating to the assessment of declarative evidence, the court shall order a renewal of the evidence".[33]

2.1.1.2 Procedure for Introducing Evidence

As to the procedure for the taking of evidence, the reference in Article 598 ICPP to the first-instance procedural rules, the absence of express exceptions, and, in any case, the general scope of application of the adversarial principle as an epistemological criterion operating at every stage of the proceedings, lead to consider the rules on cross-examination certainly applicable.[34]

This applies not only in the case of fresh evidence, but also when the renewal aims to repeat the evidence already adduced at first instance; although in this case it wouldn't be completely out of place to have some reservations about the effectiveness of the cross-examination, considering its "psychological effects, partly based on the element of surprise, tend to wear out in the original contribution".[35]

After the evidence has been directly examined, where necessary, the parties make their closing submissions and, once the hearing is closed, the court delivers its judgment.

2.1.2 Proceedings in Chambers

The second procedural model, regulated by Article 599 ICPP, was introduced by the legislator in order to allow a more rapid procedure for appeals regarding limited issues but that still have a significant impact in number: appeals strictly regarding sentencing, the weighing of circumstances or the granting of benefits, or (this option was abolished and then reinstated) selected grounds for appeal pursuant to an "agreement" between the parties.[36] Subject to the same procedural rules are also

detriment of the defendant, including by reason of a more serious legal qualification of the offence than the one made by the trial court, must in any case order a new hearing of the witness statements if the overturning is grounded on a different interpretation of said oral evidence.

[33] The provision was included in Article 1 § 58 of Act No. 103 of 23 June 2017; on the issue see Sect. 2.2 below.

[34] On the matter see, also for further bibliography and case-law, Fiorio (2008), p. 190.

[35] Peroni (1995), p. 218; in similar terms Fassone (1991), p. 633; Renon (1994), p. 3019.

[36] Paragraphs 4 and 5 of the original Article 599 ICPP provided for a so-called "agreement" on the grounds for appeal (an agreement between the parties—not binding on the court—on the acceptance of all or part of the grounds for appeal, with waiver—bound to become ineffective in case of rejection of the "agreement"—of any other grounds, and with indication of the new sentence

appeals against judgments issued in accelerated trial procedures (Article 443 § 4 ICPP), and those regarding the enforceability of civil judgments.

Compared to the standard procedure outlined in Article 127 ICPP, the code envisages a number of specific rules in relation to a number of aspects, such as the summons of the defendant, which is issued by decree under Article 601 § 1 ICPP, the deadline to file an appearance (Article 601 § 3 ICPP), the defendant's participation in the hearing, in case of absence with good cause, when the defendant has requested to attend (since Article 599 § 2 ICPP provides for the power to request an adjournment of the hearing), the necessary presence of the parties in case of evidentiary hearings (Article 599 § 3 ICPP), and the decision, which in this case is delivered in the form of a judgment (Article 605 § 1 ICPP).

On the one hand, there is no doubt that the chamber proceedings can include supplementary evidence-taking, considering the express reference contained in Article 599 § 3 ICPP ("in case of renewal of evidence, the court shall proceed with the taking of evidence in the judge's chambers, under Article 603, with the required participation of the prosecution and defence counsels").

More problematic, on the other hand, is establishing whether the scope of the above-mentioned provision extends to all chamber proceedings and, particularly, to accelerated appeal procedures. The affirmative response[37] does not seem to encounter any exceptions other than that of an appeal filed after an accelerated trial procedure upon a so-called "simplified" petition, where the defendant's waiver to the right to introduce evidence is projected onto the appeal, thereby preventing the possibility to request a renewal of evidence,[38] except upon the court's own motion in accordance with the requirements set forth in Article 603 § 3 ICPP.[39]

2.1.3 The Decision

The appellate court, in cases that do not require a judgment of inadmissibility, (power reserved to the appellate court under Article 591 ICPP), delivers a judgment

---

sought); the provisions were declared inconsistent with the Constitution, due to conflict with the delegated law (Article 2 of Act No. 93) and, therefore, with Article 96 of the Italian Constitution, in the judgment ICConst 10 October 1990, no. 435 "in the part where they allow the determination of the case according to the procedures provided therein even outside the cases specified in the first paragraph of the same Article 599 ICPP", since the Court held that the delegating legislator had not intended to "indiscriminately depart, in appeal proceedings, from the general principle of discussion on the merits of criminal proceedings, which is crucial in that it allows any citizen to verify the reasons and procedures of the criminal justice administration". The rule had then been reinstated, in essentially identical terms, by Article 11 of Act No. 14 of 19 January 1999, and then repealed by Article 2 § 1 (i) of Law Decree No. 92 of 23 May 2008, (converted into Act No. 125 of 24 July 2008).

[37] Fiorio (2008), p. 226.

[38] Bargis (2020), p. 820.

[39] Fiorio (2008), p. 186.

by which it either makes a finding on the merits of the case, by upholding or overturning the appealed judgment, or it quashes the judgment and remands the case to the lower court for retrial.

The judgment is upheld if the court has determined that the findings of the lower court are correct and thus the assignments of error raised by the appellant are groundless. In respect of these issues, the court, in its reasoning—which must meet the requirements set forth in Article 546 ICPP—must provide brief but accurate arguments:[40] "coessential to the principle of devolution is the power-duty of the appellate court to hear and decide on the appellant's requests; thus, given the correlation between the grounds for appeal and the court's scope of hearing and determination, it is not acceptable that the court should be exempt from such a duty", with the result that, any such omission would be "ground for appeal to the highest court for failure to address an argument on appeal".[41]

When the court—upholding one of the grounds for appeal put forward by the appellant, or for other reasons, within the limits set forth by Article 597 ICPP[42]—finds that the lower court's decision was incorrect, it amends the judgment; the same outcome shall apply to a number of other cases governed by Article 604 ICPP (despite the inaccuracy of Article 605 § 1 ICPP which seems to point to quashing):[43] namely, when the appeal court decides on the merits, keeping the case file, despite having found one or more of the case file documents to be void (Article 604 § 5 ICPP), or when it finds error in the previous ruling declaring a bar to prosecution (Article 604 § 6 ICPP), or in the judgment rejecting an application for a tender of payment in satisfaction of a fine, which, in the court's opinion, should on the contrary have been granted (Article 604c§ 7 ICPP).

The court's decision-making powers—just as in the granting of benefits and assessment of the circumstances surrounding the crime (Article 597 § 5 ICPP)—have no limitations when it comes to the legal qualification of the offence, which can also be changed (within the limits of Article 597 § 1 ICPP) to the detriment of the defendant, provided that the jurisdiction of the trial judge is not exceeded (Article 597 § 3, second part, ICPP).

The law thus does not impose any "qualitative" limitations on the review, but it does provide for a significant bar to the power to amend judgments to the detriment of the defendant, with reference to the treatment of the latter (convicted or acquitted): "when the appellant is only the defendant, the judge cannot increase the sentence, in type or amount, issue a new or more severe security measure, acquit the defendant on less favourable grounds than the ones stated in the judgment or revoke any benefits granted" (Article 597 § 3, first part, ICPP).

---

[40] As pointed out by Zappalà (1991), p. 221.

[41] ICCass, joint sections, 19 January 2000, Tuzzolino.

[42] See Sect. 2.1 above.

[43] The introduction to the provision—"outside the cases set forth by Article 604, the court of appeal delivers a judgment. . .overturning"—seems, indeed, to hint to the fact that in the cases specified by the mentioned provision only quashing is admitted.

Without analysing the provision in too much detail, it should however be noted that the principle aiming to protect the defendant against a worst outcome when the adverse party has accepted the judgment, does not have a counterweight in the cross-appeal filed by the prosecution, which allows the public-party appellee to react to the defendant's motion for appeal precisely in order to avoid triggering the above-mentioned guarantee.[44]

The appeal, by virtue of its dual "essence" as a remedy against un unfair judgment or against the invalidity of measures ordered at the trial, may also function as a purely rescinding judgment, after which the rescinding stage is remitted to the referring judge.

In accordance with the severability doctrine and procedural economy needs, the rules laid out in this regard by Article 604 ICPP especially serve the purpose to restrict the scope of application of remand for retrial, thereby limiting the quashing of judgments to specific and exceptional cases.

2.2 Immediacy in Criminal Appeal Under the New Article 603 § 3 *bis* ICPP

Having outlined, in broad terms, the physiognomy of criminal appeal, we may now focus on the meaning and scope of the latest developments undergone by Article 603 ICPP which, as seen, regulates the cases subject to evidence renewal.

It should firstly be noted that the direct hearing of evidence in appeal, which represents an exception to the rule of trial evidence completeness, does not however entail a departure from the procedural model: criminal appeal, even when the court orders a renewal of evidence previously adduced at the trial or the taking of fresh evidence, continues to be a review of the trial court's decision, a "judgment on the judgment",[45] in the context of which supplementary evidence-taking aims to overcome the decision-making *impasse* faced by the judge in upholding or dismissing the issues raised by the appellant against the appealed judgment.[46]

In other words, the conduct of new evidentiary hearings does not, in itself, from a conceptual standpoint, transform the nature of the procedure and turn it into a second trial on the charges: it is simply a legal tool that allows the court to confirm or reject an assignment of error in the judgment submitted for review.

So much so that the appellate court, even in the event of a new hearing of evidence, continues to rest its decision on previously recorded evidence (in addition, naturally, to the evidence directly taken before it) and its scope of examination is confined within the perimeter traced by the devolutionary mechanism

[44]The cross-appeal, after the amendment brought to Article 595 ICPP by Legislative Decree No. 11 of 6 February 2018, is now provided for the defendant only.

[45]Critical judgment defined as such by Carnelutti (1949), p. 89.

[46]Massa (1969), p. 250.

guided by the grounds for appeal; and even its decision-making powers, as seen,[47] are those typical of review.

Hence, second-instance proceedings in the Italian criminal procedure system continue to serve a function that is complementary to, rather than competing with, the previous procedural stage,[48] even when the examination takes place other than "on paper" and immediacy is restored by the judge's direct contact with the evidence.

This also applies to the renewal of evidence in case of appeal filed by the prosecution against an acquittal, as introduced by the legislator in Article 603 § 3 *bis* ICPP in the aim to adjust the Italian judicial system to the indications provided by the ECtHR.[49]

Even in the latter case, the court does not proceed with a full new reconstruction of the facts underlying the criminal charges by repeating the evidence-taking procedure in its entirety: the rather vague statutory wording ("in case of appeal by the prosecution. . . .the judge orders a renewal of evidence"), led to believe that an obligation of full reiteration had been imposed,[50] but subsequent case-law immediately took a stand in the opposite direction:[51] only the evidence whose assessment the appellant deems to have been conducted incorrectly by the judge who handed down the judgment of acquittal must be directly re-examined in appeal. After the evidence has been given before the appellate court, the latter may decide to assess it differently than the trial court, and thereby grant the prosecution's motion to overturn the judgment.

Immediacy in appeal, even with a view to overturning an acquittal, thus remains a partial immediacy limited to the scope of review of the grounds for appeal.

The new provision, from this standpoint, adds very little to the previous rule, whose scope of application, in truth, seemed—according to the interpretation provided by the Joint Chambers of the Court of Cassation in the *Dasgupta* case—even broader and more functional, allowing the judge to order a renewal of all the evidence (for the prosecution and for the defence) subject to reassessment to the

[47] See Sect. 2.1.3 above.

[48] See, if ever, Ceresa-Gastaldo (2017), p. 164.

[49] See Sect. 2.1.1.1 above.

[50] This indeed seemed to be the interpretation of the provision contained in the bill, and then approved and incorporated in the Orlando Act—Ceresa-Gastaldo (2017), p. 166—, also in consideration of the fact that the appeal, for the purpose of verdict, opens up to the possibility of a reassessment to the detriment of the accused of any evidence introduced and examined at first instance, and not just of the evidence grounding the acquittal (or in other words, the evidence held decisive by the judge who delivered the appealed judgment), but also and especially the counterevidence, which had been held unreliable in the first instance.

[51] See, among the many decisions in this direction, ICCass, section I, 27 February 2020, no. 12412; ICCass, section III, 4 February 2020, no. 16444; ICCass, section I, 27 March 2019, no. 35696.

detriment of the defendant, and not just of the evidence selected by the appealing prosecution.[52]

Perhaps the only advantage of the new provision is that it has made the decision-making criteria for renewal more objective, in that it is subject to the grounds for appeal put forward by the appellant, thereby securing the judge's impartial position.[53]

Having said that, it is doubtful whether the new provision, as set forth, truly does represent a guarantee for the defendant rather than a chance unilaterally offered to the prosecution—losing party at the trial—to have the first-instance outcome overturned.[54] If the reinstatement of immediacy, fastening the appeal to a more reliable heuristic approach, is meant to reduce the degree of error in judgments, it is difficult to understand why this tool should be made available to the prosecution only, in order to challenge and correct an allegedly wrongful acquittal, and not also to the defendant, in order to have a wrongful conviction overturned.[55]

It should also be added that the solution adopted by means of the Orlando Reform seems to have been rounded down, but also up.

No indication is provided by the legislator to ensure that the renewal take place only with regards to evidence examined before the first-instance judge, and not with regards to previously recorded evidence assessed by the trial court: consider

[52]See Sect. 1.1.1 above. It is not without reason that, precisely by referring to this influential precedent and to the interpretation of the rules on evidence renewal in force before the 2017 reform, a number of more recent decisions of the Court of Cassation try to stretch the scope of application of Article 603 § 3 *bis* ICPP, admitting that "any oral evidence which determined, or contributed to determine, the acquittal and which, if expunged from the case file, could potentially affect the outcome of the trial, is to be considered decisive for the acquittal and therefore subject to renewal in case of appeal by the prosecution. To these one must add the evidence that the appellant has considered relevant, whether alone or jointly with other evidence": ICCass, section V, 18 February 2021, no. 29864.

[53]Capone (2018), p. 64, who notes that the decision of the judge to order a fresh hearing of the evidence risks to result in an anticipation of the conviction.

[54]See Macchia (2017), p. 8; and, if ever, Ceresa-Gastaldo (2017), p. 168. The restriction of the right of defence seems particularly evident in the case of appeal by the prosecution against an acquittal delivered within an accelerated trial procedure (see below, in the text and following footnote), if we consider that the examination and cross-examination of evidence on appeal takes place—as acutely observed by Tesoriero (2017b), p. 3683—to the detriment of the defendant, who had possibly chosen the simplified trial procedure, where he was acquitted, precisely because he was aware of the weaknesses of the investigation file.

[55]While it is true that on appeal an acquittal can be overturned into a conviction simply by reassessing previously recorded evidence against the defendant—as stressed by ICCass, joint sections, 21 December 2017, Troise, with comment by Capone (2019), p. 288—it is also true that ordering a fresh hearing of a prosecution witness before the new judge could have a greater chance of success in proving the errors in the conviction delivered at first instance. While Article 603 § 3 *bis* ICPP grants the public prosecutor a vested right to the renewal of evidence—Capone (2018), p. 68—, the defendant who appeals a conviction for reasons relating to declarative evidence has access only to the milder remedy provided by Article 603 §1 ICPP, with an evident unequal treatment: Aiuti (2017), p. 257; Caneschi (2018), p. 842; Ceresa-Gastaldo (2017), p. 168.

unconditional accelerated trial procedures,[56] or the case of evidence taken at a pre-trial hearing,[57] or preliminary investigation records introduced as evidence upon agreement of the parties.[58]

As will be examined further below,[59] in order to remedy this inconvenience and to attempt to narrow the provision's scope of application, the legislator is putting in place a new amendment of Article 603 ICPP.

2.3 Convictions Against Italy for Violation of Article 6 § 1 ECHR

In 2017, 2020 and 2021, Italy received three convictions by the European Court of Human Rights for violation of Article 6 § 1 ECHR: namely in Lorefice v. Italy,[60] Tondo v. Italy,[61] and Maestri and others v. Italy.[62]

Despite these judgments being handed down subsequently to the approval of the Orland Act, all three cases examined took place under the regulatory framework previously in force (the appeals were filed, respectively, in 2013, 2014 and 2015), as implemented before the interpretation of Article 603 ICPP shifted in another direction following the *Dasgupta* judgment handed down by the Joint Chambers of the Court of Cassation.[63]

---

[56] On this matter the Constitutional Court has dismissed as groundless the questions of unconstitutionality of Article 603 § 3 *bis* ICPP "as to the part where such provision, as interpreted by case-law, in the case of appeal by the prosecution against an acquittal for reasons relating to the assessment of declarative evidence, imposes on the court a duty to order a fresh hearing of the evidence even in the event of a first-instance trial conducted in simplified form and thus on the basis of the "state of the case file" at that stage under Articles 438 ff.": ICConst 23 May 2019, no. 124, which found that "the rules on the renewal of evidence do not introduce any unbalance between the parties' procedural powers, considering they place a requirement on the court, and not a free choice on the parties, to be implemented even in the absence of a request from the latter".

[57] According to ICCass, section III, 3 July 2020, no. 24597, "the appellate court is under an obligation to conduct a fresh hearing of evidence pursuant to Article 603 § 3 *bis* ICPP also when the different assessment of declarative evidence considered decisive concerns evidence taken during the preliminary investigation and not heard again before the trial court". The case at hand regarded the direct examination on appeal of the victim of the crime, already conducted at the preliminary hearing and recorded on camera, whereby the recordings were deemed to be irrelevant for the purpose of excluding the direct hearing of the evidence by the judge who had overturned the first-instance acquittal to the detriment of the defendant.

[58] Capone (2018), p. 70.

[59] See Sect. 2.5 below.

[60] Lorefice v. Italy, no. 63446/13, 29 June 2017, *hudoc.echr.coe.int*.

[61] Tondo v. Italy, no. 75037/14, 22 October 2020, *hudoc.echr.coe.int*.

[62] Maestri and others v. Italy, no. 20903/15, 8 July 2021, *hudoc.echr.coe.int*.

[63] See Sect. 2.1.1.1 above.

All three convictions involve cases of first-instance acquittals overturned on appeal, following a reassessment of recorded evidence.

It is interesting to note that, according to the ECtHR, the criminal procedure code actually included a provision that would have prevented the violation of the Convention, but the judges had failed to enforce it. Specifically, the Court held that Article 603 ICPP was in itself compliant with the Convention rules, but its concrete application—bear in mind this is before the interpretation shift by the Joint Chambers—was inadequate.

From this viewpoint, the Strasbourg Court's position would seem to confirm the impression that the legislator's amendment in 2017 was not at all necessary, if the interpretation of Article 603 ICPP had complied, in practice, with the indications provided in the *Dasgupta* judgment.[64]

2.3.1 *Lorefice v. Italy*

In the Lorefice v. Italy case, the applicant had been convicted by the Court of Appeal of Palermo, which had granted the appeal filed by the prosecution and the civil party against the acquittal delivered by the Court of Sciacca.

The trial court had heard a number of witness statements alleging the applicant's guilt for the offences charged (extortion, possession of explosive devices, third-party property damage, collusion and attempted robbery), and had found that the statements made, also in light of the evidence introduced at the trial, not only were unreliable and not corroborated by further evidence, but were also so imprecise, illogical and incoherent to be deemed false. Subsequently the Court of Appeal, after having reassessed the evidence included in the case file, had held that these statements were, on the contrary, credible, having found that overall the statements made were precise and corroborated by several other factors, which the lower court had failed to consider. Mr Lorefice thus filed an appeal to the Supreme Court of Cassation, for violation of Article 6 ECHR, which the Court had however dismissed, finding that there was no general rule that required the appellate court to rehear evidence in order to reverse a first-instance judgment to the detriment of the appellant, and that the only obligation the court was bound to was to provide a clear and thorough reasoning for its decision to depart from the lower court's verdict.[65]

---

[64] In these terms Caneschi (2021), p. 217; Pressacco (2017), p. 1554.

[65] The Court of Cassation in this case adhered to the dated and well-established case-law—in some respects not far from the stand the ECtHR took in the Kashlev v. Estonia judgment—according to which "the appellate court overturning a lower court's judgment is under an obligation to outline the pillars of its own, alternative reasoning on the evidence, and to specifically refute the most relevant arguments put forward in the first judgment's reasoning, accounting for the related incompleteness and such as to justify the overturning of the appealed judgment" (ICCass, joint sections, 12 July

The European Court's ruling revolved precisely around this line of interpretation, stating that the mere thorough examination of the reasons for the first-instance judgment, even when this allows to highlight the shortcomings of the appealed judgment in light of all the evidence included in the case file, "does not release the appellate court from the obligation to personally hear the witnesses whose statements, which the Court was ready to assess in a completely opposite direction than that of the trial court and to the detriment of the defendant, constituted the main evidence on which the conviction was based".[66] Furthermore, the Court of Appeal—which had the power to deliver a fresh judgment on the merits, either to uphold or overturn the appellant's acquittal—"could have ordered, on its own motion, the reopening of the investigation, in accordance with Article 603 § 3 ICPP, and a new hearing of the witnesses".[67]

As seen, the Court's judgment does not point to any discrepancies in the Italian statutory framework before the Orland Reform: quite the opposite, the European judges have acknowledged that the ICPP already envisaged the proper legal device, which, however, the court of appeal failed to enforce, thereby violating Article 6 § 1 ECHR.

2.3.2 *Tondo v. Italy*

Italy's second conviction came in a rather singular case, where the Italian judges acknowledged the right to a renewal of evidence on appeal only for one of the two defendants on trial, while denying this guarantee to the other, since the evidence reassessed in order to overturn the acquittal for both co-defendants had been considered decisive only for one of the two convictions.

The appellant had been charged, together with his brother, of murder and attempted murder; the Trial Court of Lecce had acquitted both co-defendants, finding that one had acted in self-defence and that the other had committed no crime. The version of facts presented at the trial by the defence, claiming the absence of any intent to kill, had been considered reliable; in particular, the Court had found, on the one hand, that the credibility of the only eye witness had been impeached, by reason of a personal interest, and, on the other, that none of the other witnesses heard had provided any useful information to the case.

Both the prosecution and the civil parties appealed the judgment, filing a motion with the Court of Appeal to rehear the co-defendant, since his statements at the trial hearing differed from the ones previously made during the preliminary investigation. After hearing the co-defendant—but not the witnesses previously examined in the

2005, Mannino). Pointing out to the differences between the Kashlev case and the Lorefice case, Aiuti (2018), p. 682.

[66] Lorefice v. Italy, § 44.

[67] Lorefice v. Italy, § 39.

first instance—the Court of Appeal had overturned the acquittal and convicted both co-defendants, based on a negative reassessment of their statements, having found the eye witness' statement to be, on the contrary, credible and that the other statements adduced during the trial demonstrated that the defendants had intentionally caused the victim's death and could not, therefore, invoke a self-defence justification.

The two brothers subsequently brought an appeal to the Court of Cassation against the conviction, arguing, among other things, a violation of Article 6 ECHR on the ground that the Court of Appeal had reassessed the prosecution witness' statement as credible without ordering a new hearing of said witness. The Court of Cassation did, indeed, find a violation of Article 6 ECHR, as interpreted by the ECtHR in the judgment Dan v. Moldavia, since it had reassessed the credibility of a decisive witness statement without directly hearing the witness. However, the Court held that this conclusion applied to the accomplice only, and not to the principal offender, who was deemed indisputably guilty of having fired the deadly shot, and it had thus upheld his conviction, which had therefore become final. The reason for this decision, as briefly mentioned, was that according to the Court, the witness statement at hand was not in fact decisive for the verdict on the applicant, but only on the co-defendant, since with reference to the former, it merely confirmed what other evidence had already allowed to demonstrate.

The ECtHR, moved by the convicted applicant, did not share the differentiated outcomes. Clearly not because it does not agree with the distinction between decisive and non-decisive evidence, but because it believed that in the case at hand that specific piece of evidence was, in fact, also decisive for the verdict on the applicant, and that thus even the latter's conviction by the Court of Appeal had been delivered in violation of Article 6 ECHR, just as the Court of Cassation had found to be true for the co-defendant. The Strasbourg judges openly expressed their astonishment for the unjustified differential treatment of the co-defendants by the Italian judges, who correctly applied in one case and not the other the relevant domestic rules in light of the Convention's principle: "this Court does not understand...why the Court of Cassation found that this principle should apply only with regards to F.T., who was charged with participation in murder, and not with regards to the applicant. While there were no doubts as to the fact that the victim's death had been caused by the shots fired by the applicant, the judges had, however, based the conviction on a different version of the facts that took place in the final stage of the dispute, especially with regards to the position of the victim at the time the gun had been fired, and to the threat posed by the victim to the applicant. These elements should have required a direct examination of the relevant witnesses";[68] in addition to a hearing of the defendant, present at the trial.[69]

[68]Tondo v. Italy, § 44.

[69]Thus "denying him the possibility to express his arguments on factual questions that are decisive in assessing his guilt": Tondo v. Italy, § 46.

Unlike the Lorefice v. Italy case, where the interpretation of Article 603 ICPP was found to be inconsistent with Article 6 §1 ECHR, by loyalty to the theory of a "reinforced" reasoning as the sole requirement to be met in order to overturn an acquittal on appeal, in the Tondo v. Italy case, the Court of Cassation shows to have taken a step forward and set aside such theory, since it reversed the Court of Appeal's judgment precisely on the ground that it had not directly heard the witnesses whose statements it had reassessed to the detriment of the defendant.

This once more confirms that the legal system at the time (this is 2015, right before the Dasgupta ruling) already provided the appellate court with the remedy that would have secured the parties' right to a fair trial.[70]

2.3.3 Maestri and Others v. Italy

The judgment Maestri and others v. Italy undoubtedly has a wider reach than the previously mentioned judgments.

In the case at hand, out of the seven applicants, six had been convicted in the first instance by the Court of Saluzzo for aggravated fraud, while all had been acquitted on the charges of conspiracy. In granting the prosecution's appeal, the Court of Appeal of Torino had found all defendants guilty of both offences. The defendants had then brought an appeal to the Court of Cassation, arguing that the Court of Appeal had overturned the lower's court judgment to their detriment without ordering a fresh hearing of the prosecution witnesses and of the defendants themselves before convicting them. The Court of Cassation had dismissed the appeals, stating that the appellate court would have had an obligation to directly hear the witnesses if it had considered necessary a reassessment of their credibility and a new examination of the facts; this had not been the case as the appellate court had not given a different interpretation to the statements made by the witnesses, whose version of the facts had never been questioned. As to the obligation to hear the defendants in person, the Court of Cassation had ruled that the possibility for the defendants to make statements of their own free will at any stage of the proceedings (Article 494 ICPP) and their right to address the court last (Article 523 ICPP) was sufficient to guarantee their defence rights.

The European Court granted the appeals, finding that there had been a violation of Article 6 § 1 for failure to order a fresh examination of the witnesses (in this case, solely in relation to the conviction of one of the applicants)[71] and a hearing of the defendants.

[70] Cassibba (2021), p. 315.

[71] For the other six applicants, the Court held that the appellate court had relied on findings of fact undisputed by the parties and had reached a conclusion of law that differed as to the constituent elements of the conspiracy offence, thereby excluding a violation of Article 6 § 1 ECHR for failure to conduct a new hearing of the evidence (Maestri and others v. Italy, §§ 48–49). Pointing out to the contradictory reasoning of the Court as to the subject of the appellate court's assessments, here

As to the first issue, the Court confirmed the same conclusions laid out in the judgments Lorefice v. Italy and Tondo v. Italy,[72] namely that the Italian code of criminal procedure (Article 603) imposes on the second-instance judge a fresh examination of the witnesses before being in a position to reassess their statements to the detriment of the defendant who had been acquitted of all charges at first instance precisely on the basis of such statements. The Court of Appeal of Torino had, on the contrary, reached a different assessment of the evidence without conducting a direct examination of the sources.[73]

With regards to the second issue, the Court granted the appeals, having held that all applicants had been denied their right to be heard in person, in contrast with Article 6 ECHR. The appellate court, "by amending the lower court's verdict and determining the issue of the applicants' guilt as regards the offence of criminal conspiracy. . .had also considered the applicants' intentions and had ruled for the first time on subjective circumstances concerning them. . . In the Court's view, such an assessment, by virtue of its characteristics, implied taking a position on facts which were decisive for the determination of the applicants' guilt": and "where an inference drawn by the lower court related to subjective elements, it was not possible to perform a legal assessment of the accused's conduct without having first sought to prove that the conduct had actually occurred, which necessarily entailed ascertaining the element of intent on the accused's part in relation to the alleged acts".[74]

The applicants' waiver of the right to be present at the trial does not entail, in the Court's opinion, a waiver of their right to be heard by the appellate court;[75] "In those circumstances, the judicial authorities had to take all positive measures needed to guarantee the examination of the defendant, even if the defendant had neither

regarded as concerning only the legal qualification of the offence, but later (§ 52) clearly referred to the finding of fact that was decisive for the determination of the defendants' guilt: Caianiello and Tesoriero (2021), p. 4089.

[72]Even in this case, the Court acknowledged (albeit by improperly referring to the well-established case-law following the case examined: §§ 19 and 20) that the framework laid down in the ICPP (Article 603), as interpreted by the Court of Cassation, imposed on the appellate court the hearing of the witnesses before reassessing their statements to the detriment of the defendant (§ 60).

[73]Maestri and others v. Italy, § 64.

[74]Maestri and others v. Italy, § 52.

[75]As already affirmed by the ECtHR in Júlíus Þór Sigurþórsson v. Island, no. 38797/17, 16 July 2019, *hudoc.echr.coe.int*. This principle is acknowledged by the Court of Cassation: see ICCass, section VI, 16 February 2016, no. 12544, according to which "the absence of the defendant at the first appeal hearing, resulting in a formal declaration of trial in absentia, cannot be interpreted as a waiver to be heard upon the defence's request, it being understood that the intention to waive such a right, whether expressed or otherwise, is conceivable only when the examination of the defendant had been previously ordered and only at the hearing in which the statement was meant to be given". The appellate court may not therefore dismiss the defendant's motion to be heard, upon renewal of the evidence under Article 603 § 4 ICPP, solely on the basis of the defendant's absence at the first hearing.

attended the hearing, nor asked for leave to address the appellate court nor objected through his or her counsel to that court giving judgment on the merits".[76]

Nor can the possibility for the defendant to make statements of his own free will (Article 494 ICPP) "satisfy the requirement for the court to examine defendants in person regarding facts and questions that were decisive for the determination of their guilt"; on the contrary, in this regard the Court's opinion is that "it could not reasonably be maintained that in order to defend themselves, defendants should address the court on their own initiative and should choose to speak about facts in relation to which they had been acquitted at first instance".[77]

This decision, albeit without being a pilot-judgment under Article 61 of the Rules of the Court, or explicitly identifying a systemic and structural violation, seems, however, to have a general scope of application, since it ascertains "a violation of the Convention's rules on personal rights, likely to be repeated with similar adverse consequences against multiple parties other than the applicant who find themselves in the same situation".[78]

The Court of Cassation, underlying that the Italian procedural system does not set forth an obligation for the appellate court to order a hearing of the defendant in the cases specified in the Maestri v. Italy judgment, acknowledged the risk of a possible reiteration, in similar cases, of the procedural and substantive wrong identified by the Strasbourg judges, and thereby referred to the Joint Chambers the question of "general applicability of the *obiter dictum* of the judgment" Maestri v. Italia, "which reprimanded the Italian's justice system for not having envisaged, by way of protection of the defendant acquitted at first instance and then convicted on appeal, a specific requirement for the court to hear the defendant before delivering a conviction, while setting guiding criteria".[79]

By order of the deputy presiding judge of the Court, however, the Joint Chambers remitted the case file to the referring chamber for a new assessment,[80] having found that the case, in fact, fell under the scope of application of Article 603 ICPP, as interpreted by the Joint Chambers in the Dasgupta case, which does not allow distinctions based on the capacity of the person making the statement.[81]

[76] Maestri and others v. Italy, § 56.

[77] Maestri and others v. Italy, § 59.

[78] ICCass, joint sections, 24 October 2019, no. 8544, Genco.

[79] ICCass, section I, ord. 21 September 2021, no. 45179, Mannucci.

[80] ICCass, joint sections, ord. 17 January 2022, no. 11459, Mannucci.

[81] See Sect. 2.1.1.1 above (n 27). Doubts were raised about the fact that a similar provision, albeit certainly designed with the best intentions, might actually be counterproductive for the defendant, should the latter refuse to be examined: Caianiello and Tesoriero (2021), p. 4090.

2.4 Immediacy in Appeal and Accelerated Trial Procedure: The ECtHR Judgment in the Di Martino and Molinari v. Italy Case

As seen, domestic case law has recently shown to consider evidence renewal on appeal as mandatory even in cases of appeal against an acquittal delivered at the outcome of an accelerated trial procedure.[82]

In the case Di Martino and Molinari v. Italy—domestically resolved before the interpretation shift regarding Article 603 ICPP with the Dasgupta and Patalano judgments[83]—this rule was not applied. The two applicants, acquitted by the Italian judge at the preliminary hearing of the unconditional accelerated trial procedure had later been convicted by the court of appeal upon motion by the prosecution. In their appeal to the European Court the applicants complained about the appellate court's failure to hear the witnesses whose statements in the accelerated trial procedure had been examined solely "on paper", as well as the witness who had actually been personally heard by the trial court, which had ordered the hearing on its own motion under Article 441 § 5 ICPP. In both cases the applicants argued a violation of Article 6 §1 ECHR.

The European Court dismissed the appeals as it found the trial against the applicants, as a whole, fair.[84]

In abstract, the argument regarding the appellate court's failure to rehear the witness previously heard by the trial court, could have been upheld; nevertheless, according to the Court this evidence had not been decisive for the purpose of overturning the acquittal, since the witness statement merely confirmed the statements of other witnesses and corroborated the overall evidence against the applicants and had thus not been assigned decisive weight neither by the first-instance judge nor by the second-instance court.[85]

As to the second issue, that is the failure to order a renewal on appeal of the evidence merely assessed "on paper" by the trial court, the Strasbourg judges firstly stressed the compatibility with the Convention's rules of procedures that entail the voluntary waiver to fair trial guarantees;[86] and inferred that the applicant's request to be tried by means of a simplified procedure amounted to a waiver of oral evidence and a conduct of the trial based on the documentary evidence included in the case

[82] See Sect. 2.1.1.1 above.

[83] See nn 24 and 29 above.

[84] Di Martino and Molinari v. Italy, no.15931/5 and no. 16459/15, 25 March 2021, *hudoc.echr.coe.int.*

[85] Di Martino and Molinari v. Italy, § 44.

[86] Di Martino and Molinari v. Italy, § 33.

file.[87] Thus the appellate court had the power to re-examine the case on the basis of that same evidence.[88]

Furthermore, the European Court acknowledged that the Italian legal system (as interpreted by the Court of Cassation) offers a more advanced guarantee[89] than the one provided by the Convention.[90] And highlights—in line with its case-law—that "nothing in this Convention shall be construed as limiting or derogating from any of the human rights and fundamental freedoms which may be ensured under the laws of any High Contracting Party" (Article 53 ECHR).[91]

The decision of the ECtHR has thus paved the way for the next amendment to the rules on evidence renewal in appeal.

Before the Di Martino and Molinari v. Italy judgment it was difficult to imagine a shift in the courts' interpretation—albeit strongly criticized by scholarship[92]—or a legislative amendment, after even the Constitutional Court had endorsed the application, held compliant with the Convention, of Article 603 § 3 *bis* ICPP even to cases of appeal by the prosecution against acquittals delivered at the outcome of an accelerated trial procedure.[93]

To this day, the premise underlying the case-law theory that this interpretation of the procedural rule is guided by the Convention has been rejected. The European Court clearly states the contrary: evidence renewal in appeal is not, in these cases, imposed by the Convention.

---

[87] Di Martino and Molinari v. Italy, § 37.

[88] Di Martino and Molinari v. Italy, § 36.

[89] Regarding the doubts as to whether this is indeed a more advanced guarantee see Sect. 2.2 (n 54) above.

[90] In this regard, the Court observed (§ 39) that "the Italian Court of Cassation has recently given an extensive interpretation to Article 603 ICPP, providing an obligation for appellate courts to order, even on their own motion, the hearing of witnesses decisive for the conviction, in both ordinary and simplified criminal trial procedures (§ 16 above)".

[91] Di Martino and Molinari v. Italy, § 39.

[92] See, also for further bibliography, Caneschi (2018), p. 828.

[93] ICConst 23 May 2019, no. 124, which dismissed as groundless the questions of unconstitutionality of Article 603 § 3 *bis* ICPP "as to the part where such provision, as interpreted by case-law, in the case of appeal by the prosecution against an acquittal for reasons relating to the assessment of declarative evidence, imposes on the court a duty to order a fresh hearing of the evidence even in the event of first-instance proceedings conducted in simplified form. In particular, for the Constitutional Court, a direct contact between the judge and the witnesses—epistemologically considered the most reliable method for taking evidence—is required, even in the context of a trial procedure purely based on documentary evidence, by the need to lose the implied reasonable doubt resulting from the reaching of contrasting decisions.

2.5 Amendments on the Horizon: The "Cartabia Reform"

With Act No. 134 of 27 September 2021, the so-called Cartabia Act, the Parliament delegated to the Government the power to amend, inter alia, the Italian code of criminal procedure. The general objective is to achieve a greater efficiency in the criminal procedure system and, to this end, the legislator has prepared a number of amendments (some of which by statute, others, precisely, by delegated law in the frame of the directives issued by the Parliament) to the procedural and substantive criminal justice framework.

Among the amendments regarding appeals, set forth in Article 1 § 3 of the Cartabia Reform, there is also the one governing the renewal of evidence in appeal.

The guiding criterium laid down in Article 1 § 13(1), provides an obligation to "amend Article 603 § 3-*bis* of the criminal procedure code, in order to envisage that, in the case of appeal against an acquittal for reasons relating to the assessment of declarative evidence, the renewal of evidence be limited to statements heard at a hearing before the trial court".[94]

While the ministerial committee responsible for preparing the draft reform had directly proposed to repeal paragraph 3 *bis* of Article 603 ICPP, such as to revert to the state of affairs prior to the Orlando Act,[95] the text approved by the chambers of Parliament merely restricts the scope of application of the rule in order to exclude the obligation of renewal in all cases—e.g. in the event of accelerated trial procedures or of evidence taken during preliminary investigations[96]—in which the evidence subject to the appellate court's reassessment was not directly taken before the first-instance judge in accordance with the principle of immediacy.

The tormented history of evidence renewal in appeal, should, at this point, finally settle down.

Cited Case-Law

ECtHR

hudoc.echr.coe.int

[94] Highlighting how the amendment, consistent with the ECtHR's conclusions in the Di Martino and Molinari v. Italy judgment, pursues procedural economy objectives, in reaction to the case-law that "with little comprehension" extended the obligation to renew the hearing of evidence on appeal: Gialuz and Della Torre (2022), p. 321.

[95] See 'Riforma del processo penale, del sistema sanzionatorio e della prescrizione del reato: la relazione finale della Commissione Lattanzi', *Sistema penale* (25 May 2021).

[96] See Sect. 2.2 (n 57) above. Of the opinion that the delegating legislator thereby intended to "refute the statement of principle expressed in a number of recent rulings by the Court of Cassation according to which (on the contrary) declarative evidence must in any case be reheard": Bassi and Parodi (2021), p. 59.

Ekbatani v. Sweden, no. 10563/83, 26 May 1988
Destrehem v. France, no. 56651/00, 18 May 2004
Dan v. Moldavia, no. 8999/07, 5 July 2011
Manolachi v. Romania, no. 36605/04, 5 March 2013
Hanu v. Romania, no. 10890/04, 4 June 2013
Kashlev v. Estonia, no. 22574/08, 26 April 2016
Luzu v. Moldavia, no. 46182/08, 5 July 2016
Chiper v. Romania, no. 22036/10, 27 June 2017
Lorefice v. Italy, no. 63446/13, 29 June 2017
Júlíus Þór Sigurþórsson v. Island, no. 38797/17, 16 July 2019
Tondo v. Italy, no. 75037/14, 22 October 2020
Di Martino and Molinari v. Italy, no.15931/5 and no. 16459/15, 25 March 2021
Maestri and others v. Italy, no. 20903/15, 8 July 2021

ICCass

www.cortecostituzionale.it

Joint sections, 26 February 1955, Zoccola
Section III, 26 July 1993, no. 1698, Petrone
Joint sections, 19 January 2000, Tuzzolino
Joint sections, 12 July 2005, Mannino
Section VI, 16 February 2016, no. 12544
Joint sections, 28 April 2016, Dasgupta
Joint sections, 19 January 2017, Patalano
Section II, 17 May 2017, Salute and others
Joint sections, 28 January 2019, Pavan
Section I, 27 March 2019, no. 35696
Joint sections, 24 October 2019, no. 8544, Genco
Section III, 4 February 2020, no. 16444
Section I, 27 February 2020, no. 12412
Joint sections, 27 February 2020, no. 12778
Section III, 3 July 2020, no. 24597
Section V, 18 February 2021, no. 29864
Section I, ord. 21 September 2021, no. 45179, Mannucci
Joint sections, ord. 17 January 2022, no. 11459, Mannucci

References

Aiuti V (2016) Poteri d'ufficio della cassazione e diritto all'equo processo. Cassazione penale:3214–3235

Aiuti V (2017) Obbligo di rinnovazione e prova dichiarativa. In: Marandola A, Bene T (eds) La riforma della giustizia penale. Giuffré, Milan, pp 243–265

Aiuti V (2018) Corte europea e "motivazione rafforzata" nel caso Lorefice. Cassazione penale:682–691

Amodio E (1999) Riformare le impugnazioni dopo il ripristino di un primo grado deflazionato e garantito. Cassazione penale:3620–3624
Aprati R (2017) Overturning sfavorevole in appello e mancanza del riesame. Cassazione penale:2672–2682
Bargis M (2020) Impugnazioni. In: Bargis M (ed) Compendio di procedura penale, 10th edn. Cedam, Pasua, pp 754–903
Bassi A, Parodi C (2021) La riforma del sistema penale. L. n. 134/2021: la delega e le norme immediatamente applicabili. Giuffré, Milan
Caianiello M, Tesoriero S (2021) Diritto di difesa e appello penale: vecchie e nuove coordinate dalla giurisprudenza della Corte edu (a proposito di Maestri e altri contro Italia). Cassazione penale:4089–4103
Caneschi G (2017) Rinnovazione istruttoria anche in caso di reformatio in peius parziale: l'inarrestabile metamorfosi del giudizio di appello. Archivio penale 3:1–10
Caneschi G (2018) La rinnovazione istruttoria in appello dopo la riforma Orlando: una non soluzione ad un problema aparente. Rivista italiana di diritto e procedura penale:821–857
Caneschi G (2021) Il diritto a un doppio grado di giudizio e rinnovazione della prova in appello. In: Ceresa-Gastaldo M, Lonati S (eds) Profili di procedura penale europea. Giuffré, Milan, pp 210–221
Capone A (2016) Prova in appello: un difficile bilanciamento. Processo penale e giustizia:52–65
Capone A (2018) Appello del pubblico ministero e rinnovazione istruttoria. In: Bargis M, Belluta H (eds) La riforma delle impugnazioni tra carenze sistematiche e incertezze applicative. Giappichelli, Turin, pp 54–82
Capone A (2019) Appello dell'imputato contro la condanna. Le sezioni unite negano l'obbligo di rinnovazione istruttoria. Rivista italiana di diritto e procedura penale:288–301
Carnelutti F (1949) Lezioni sul processo penale, vol IV. Edizioni dell'Ateneo, Rome
Carnelutti F (1956) Istituzioni del processo civile italiano, vol III. Società Editrice del Foro Italiano, Rome
Cassibba F (2021) Prima condanna in appello e garanzie effettive. Rivista italiana di diritto e procedura penale:315–318
Ceresa-Gastaldo M (2010) Appello (dir. proc. pen.). In: Enciclopedia del diritto, vol III, Annali. Giuffré, Milan, pp 11–35
Ceresa-Gastaldo M (2017) La riforma dell'appello, tra malinteso garantismo e spinte deflative. Diritto penale contemporaneo Rivista trimestrale 3:163–172
Cesarini C (1878) Dell'appello in penale e dell'ordinamento della giustizia correzionale. Rivista penale 9:110–122
Cordero F (2012) Procedura penale, 9th edn. Giuffré, Milan
Fassone E (1991) L'appello. Un'ambiguità da scogliere. Questione Giustizia:632–635
Fiorio C (1998) L'appello. In: Gaito A (ed) Le impugnazioni penali, vol I. UTET, Torino, pp 299–366
Fiorio C (2008) La prova nuova nel processo penale. CEDAM, Padua
Gaito A (2015) Vecchio e nuovo a proposito della rinnovazione in appello. Archivio penale online:1–9
Galluccio Mezio G (2019) Riflessioni a margine delle Sezioni unite nel caso Pavan: la rinnovazione della 'prova tecnica' in appello tra luci ed ombre. Cassazione penale:3859–3893
Gialuz M, Della Torre J (2022) Giustizia per nessuno. L'inefficienza del sistema penale italiano tra crisi cronica e riforma Cartabia. Giappichelli, Turin
Liebman ET (1980) Il giudizio d'appello e la Costituzione. Rivista di diritto processuale:401–409
Lorenzetto E (2016) Reformatio in peius in appello e processo equo (art. 6 Cedu): fisiologia e patologia secondo le Sezioni unite. Diritto penale contemporâneo:1–7
Lozzi G (2004) Reformatio in peius del giudice di appello e cognitio ex actis della Corte di cassazione. Rivista italiana di diritto e procedura penale:631–641
Lozzi G (2020) Lezioni di procedura penale, 14th edn. Giappichelli, Turin

Macchia A (2017) Le novità dell'appello: la rinnovazione dell'appello, concordato sui motivi. Diritto penale contemporâneo:1–15
Massa M (1969) Contributo allo studio dell'appello nel processo penale. Giuffré, Milan
Nappi A (1990) Il nuovo processo penale: un'ipotesi di aggiornamento del giudizio di appello. Cassazione penale II:974–978
Nobili M (1989) La nuova procedura penale. Lezioni agli studenti. CLUEB, Bologna
Peroni F (1995) L'istruzione dibattimentale nel giudizio d'appello. CEDAM, Padua
Peroni F (2001) Giusto processo e doppio grado di giurisdizione nel mérito. Rivista di diritto processuale:710–732
Pressacco L (2017) Principio di immediatezza e reformatio in peius tra Strasburgo e Roma. Rivista italiana di diritto e procedura penale:1552–1557
Renon P (1994) Presupposti e limiti all'applicazione dell'esame incrociato nel giudizio di appello. Cassazione penale:3017–3020
Signorato S (2020) Articolo 135 c.p.p. In: Illuminati G, Giuliani L (eds) Commentario breve al codice di procedura penale, 3rd edn. Wolters Kluwer, Milano, pp 483–485
Siracusano D (2016) Ragionevole durata del processo e giudizi di impugnazione. Rivista italiana di diritto e procedura penale:16–28
Tesoriero S (2017a) Luci e ombre della rinnovazione istruttoria in appello per il presunto inocente. Giustizia penale III:79–108
Tesoriero S (2017b) Una falsa garanzia: l'obbligatoria attuazione del contradditorio nel giudizio abbreviato d'appello. Cassazione penale:3668–3687
Tranchina G, Di Chiara G (1999) Appello (diritto processuale penale). In: Enc. dir., III agg. Giuffré, Milan, pp 200–215
Zappalà E (1991) Articoli 601-605 c.p.p. In: Chiavario M (ed) Commento al nuovo codice di procedura penale, vol VI. UTET, Turin, pp 189–224

Chapter 3
The Retrial Model in Spain

Antonio Mª. Lara López

3.1 Introduction

The second instance in the criminal proceedings and, consequently, the appeal that opens this phase of the process, is a subject that after years of study and discussion continues to be highly topical in Spain.

This is marked by the fact that beyond the consideration of the second instance as a legal-technical instrument or as a new phase of the process of declaration, it reaches the category of a basic piece in criminal prosecution.

Moreover, and this is the central axis, today, our legal system, despite the 2015 reform of the Criminal Procedure Act of 1882[1] (hereinafter, LECrim) has not yet offered a complete legislative response to the fact that not every criminal sentence is going to have access to the full second instance. In fact, as a legacy of the original system of the LECrim, until very recently there was no appeal that opened the second instance in cases involving crimes with a sentence of more than 5 years. Although this circumstance has been resolved, the current appeal (nor the foreseeable future if the Draft Bill of a new Criminal Procedure Law of 2020—hereinafter, LECrim Preliminary Draft—which is not yet in the parliamentary process, is approved) does not fully satisfy the opening of a complete second instance with full review capacity of what happened in the first instance.

In line with the consideration of the second instance as a guarantee for the defendant, the right to appeal in criminal proceedings has been elevated to the category of fundamental right by the influence of the International Conventions

[1] Approved by Royal Decree of September 14, 1882 (Gaceta de Madrid, no. 260. of September 17, 1882.

A. M. Lara López (✉)
Department of Political Science, International Public Law and Procedure Law, Málaga University, Faculty of Law, Málaga, Spain
e-mail: antoniolara@uma.es

H. Morão, R. Tavares da Silva (eds.), *Fairness in Criminal Appeal*,
https://doi.org/10.1007/978-3-031-13001-4_3

signed by Spain which postulate, with few differences in content, that every convicted person has the right to have his case reviewed by a higher court.

But the right to appeal and the right to a second instance may not coincide from a technical-procedural point of view. From this perspective, the discussion on the subject has centered on the interpretation of the meaning and extent of such review. In other words, does the right to review the conviction constitute a right to a second instance, or is it fully satisfied with a remedy of whatever nature that allows a mere review of the legal basis of the decision? In essence, what constitutes the second instance in the criminal justice system and what characteristics must the appeal that opens this second instance have in order to effectively comply with this fundamental right is one of the main questions in this subject.

From this perspective, we will approach this study from the following aspects:

The fundamental right to an appeal and its configuration by the International Covenants and Conventions subscribed by Spain; the interpretation of the right to the second instance established by the UN Human Rights Committee; the nature of the appeal that has the quality of opening the second instance; what the second instance consists of and how it is configured; the appeal; the current situation of the second criminal instance and the immediacy in evidence and, finally, the recording of trials and their assessment in second instance.

3.2 The Right to Appeal in Criminal Proceedings

The right to appeal in our criminal justice system constitutes a fundamental right without legal conditions as in the rest of the jurisdictional fields. This is how the Spanish Constitutional Court (hereinafter, SCC) has considered it in a vacillating jurisprudence that sometimes includes it in the right to effective judicial protection of Article 24.1 and at other times in the right to a trial with all the guarantees of section 2 of the aforementioned article.

This express recognition does not arise from the Constitution itself, since it does not include the right to appeal in any passage. Therefore, in the criminal process, it must be sought in international law and its impact on the Spanish legal system granted by the Spanish Constitution (hereinafter SC) itself, either by integrating it as national law or as a hermeneutic criterion.

The legislative instruments referred are, specifically, the International Covenant on Civil and Political Rights (hereinafter ICCPR), approved by the General Assembly of the United Nations in 1966, ratified in 1977; and Protocol No. 7 to the European Convention on Human Rights of 1984 (hereinafter ECHR), ratified in 2009.

Thus, Article 14.5 of the ICCPR[2] and Article 2.1 of Protocol No. 7[3] provide that anyone convicted of a criminal offense [4] has the right to have his conviction and sentence reviewed by a higher court. Therefore, and by application of art. 10.2 in relation to art. 96.1 EC, our procedural system is obliged to establish an appeal, suitable for controlling the legal correctness of the conviction handed down at the trial level.

However, the link imposed by these instruments has not always been understood as a right to a second criminal instance; in fact, the SCC has not understood it in this way in numerous sentences. This was a response to the criticisms, which, in the form of a complaint to the UN Human Rights Committee, pointed out that in single instance trials with subsequent cassation (sentences of more than 5 years imprisonment) did not comply with the provisions of the Covenant, since the appeal in cassation did not allow for a full review of the conviction and sentence.

These complaints resulted in rulings against our country, the most significant of which is contained in the Opinion of July 20, 2000 in the "Gómez Vázquez v. Spain case", which we analyse, among other issues, in the following section.

---

[2]Art. 14.5 ICCPR: "Everyone convicted of a crime shall have the right to his conviction and sentence being reviewed by a higher tribunal according to law.".

[3]Art. 2 Protocol No. 7 to the Convention for the Protection of Human Rights and Fundamental Freedoms (Strasbourg, 22.XI.1984)

Right of appeal in criminal matters

1. Everyone convicted of a criminal offence by a tribunal shall have the right to have his conviction or sentence reviewed by a higher tribunal. The exercise of this right, including the grounds on which it may be exercised, shall be governed by law.
2. This right may be subject to exceptions in regard to offences of a minor character, as prescribed by law, or in cases in which the person concerned was tried in the first instance by the highest tribunal or was convicted following an appeal against acquittal.

[4]It should be borne in mind that the classification of a criminal offense, for the purposes of applying the requirement of the double degree of jurisdiction according to the ECHR, does not depend so much on what is established in the state system as on compliance with the Engel Criteria, which emanated from the doctrine of the ECtHR in the judgment of the Engel and others v. the Netherlands, of June 8, 1976. Recently, this court has extended the double degree requirement to administrative sanctioning processes in Spain by application of this doctrine in the judgment of the Saquetti Iglesias v. Spain Case, of June 30, 2020. This condemnation of the Spanish State will pose a problem since there is no legal provision for the double degree of jurisdiction in the contentious-administrative order for all administrative sanctioning proceedings that will have to be legally implemented, but, until then, the successive condemnations that will reach Spain from the Strasbourg Court will have a difficult legal solution for the appellants.

3.3 The Opinion of the United Nations Human Rights Committee and the Reaction of Spain

The complaint was based on the February 22, 1992, judgment of the Provincial Court of Toledo, which had convicted Mr. Gómez Vázquez to twelve years and one day of imprisonment for murder. The Spanish Supreme Court rejected the appeal in cassation against the sentence imposed and no appeal was filed before the Constitutional Court.

The basis of the complaint before the Committee was the structure of the Spanish procedural system, since, in relation to serious crimes (those punishable by more than six years imprisonment, the oral trial is held before the Provincial Court), after the investigation has been carried out by the investigating judge, while in relation less serious crimes, the oral trial is heard by the Juzgado de lo Penal (sic), in which case the appeal, if held, will first be made before the Provincial Court, with the possibility of filing a cassation appeal before the Supreme Court.

This claim, like many others, was based on Articles 14.5 of the ICCPR, which provide, as we have noted, that anyone convicted of a criminal offense has the right to have the conviction reviewed by a higher court. Thus, and by application of art. 10.2 in relation to art. 96.1 CE, Spanish procedural law is obliged to establish an appeal, capable of controlling the legal correctness of the conviction handed down at the trial level.

On July 20, 2000, the United Nations Human Rights Committee issued an opinion considering that the Spanish criminal cassation system violated the 1966 Covenant on Civil and Political Rights, signed by Spain. The facts that gave rise to the above-mentioned opinion are the result of complaint number 701/1996, filed by the legal representation of Mr. Cesáreo G. V., a Spanish national, and directed against the Kingdom of Spain, for violation of articles 14.5 and 26 of the Covenant.

We must start from a prior consideration that will determine the subsequent conclusions. This is based on the nature of the norms to which we refer, i.e., international norms arising from institutions that include numerous of countries (UN and Council of Europe). The purpose of these laws (fundamentally the ICCPR) is not to regulate how remedies should be configured in each legal system; these instruments are intended to establish minimum requirements, with no intention—because it is impossible—of establishing the content, the type of remedy and the particularized consequences of each one of them. Moreover, the right to criminal appeal that they advocate must be specified "as prescribed by the law" of each signatory country.[5] There can be no such provision when the criminal proceedings of each signatory state may differ diametrically.

Moreover, the ICCPR was basically inspired by the Anglo-Saxon American model, which is based on a sentence handed down by a jury court and where the right to appeal is a guarantee only for the convicted person, the content of which is

[5] See De Lucchi López-Tapia (2002), p. 334.

the review of the rules of due process and whether the sentence has been determined by applying an unconstitutional law, but not a new evaluation of the evidence.[6]

Thus, as a purely *subjective element*, the right to appeal is predicated only on the convicted person, which does not mean that it is prohibited to the prosecution. For this reason it would not be contrary to the Covenant to prohibit appeals to the prosecution. It would be a different matter if it were to pass through the filter of the principle of equality enshrined in the SC. Although this equality at the procedural level is merely illusory with regard to the Spanish Public Prosecutor's Office, which is far above the accused party in the proceedings. In our opinion, it is the fact that there is no monopoly of the prosecution that determines that the right of the prosecution to appeal should not be curtailed, although it is possible to limit it in terms of the grounds for filing it.[7] This has in fact happened, but, as we shall see, it has not been limited with a view to equalizing the procedural "weapons" between the prosecution and the defence, but as a measure to comply with the jurisprudential requirements of the ECtHR and, subsequently, of the SCC.[8]

On the same subjective level, the court that hears the appeal must be a higher court than the one that issued the appealed judgment. At present, although we will deal with this subject in greater depth later on, the competence to hear appeals against sentences is held by the following: The Provincial Court (matters not exceeding five years of imprisonment), the High Courts of Justice of the Autonomous Communities (matters exceeding five years of imprisonment) and, in the National High Court,[9] the Criminal Division (matters not exceeding five years of imprisonment) and the Appeals Chamber (matters exceeding five years of imprisonment). This superiority is not predicated of some courts, such as the Appeals Chamber of the National High Court, since it is not classified as a superior court, but rather as a hierarchically parallel one. And, even though it is common ground that the absence of administrative hierarchy is not an obstacle for us to consider that there is functional superiority and, therefore, the provisions of the Covenant and the Protocol would be saved, Spain should change it in order to avoid future condemnations in the event that the Committee or the ECtHR were to understand otherwise. This circumstance has not been tried to be corrected in the LECrim Preliminary Draft since it retains the same structure of jurisdiction in the area of the National High Court. The

[6]See Montero Aroca (1997), p. 167.

[7]See Lara López (2014), p. 195.

[8]In Spain, this opinion is not pacific and there are authors who, not without reason, defend that this limitation is contrary to the principle of equality of procedural arms. Calderón Cuadrado (2011), p. 394. And, more recently, and referring to the LECrim Preliminary Draft, Tomé García (2022), p. 1289. For a complete study of this limitation and the divergent opinions, see Lara López (2014), pp. 191–196.

[9]The National High Court is a court that has jurisdiction over very specific matters (mainly terrorism and large-scale drug trafficking) and has jurisdiction over the entire national territory. It is composed of certain investigating and prosecuting courts and an Appeals Division. For a more detailed description of the organization of this jurisdictional court, see, among others, Lara López (2017), pp. 78–80.

same does not happen in the rest of the jurisdictional courts since the creation of a different structure to the current one is foreseen, based on the so-called "Courts of First Instance" to hear cases in the first instance and the Appeals Division of the High Courts of Justice that will hear them, regardless of the length of the prison sentence.[10]

Regarding the *objective element*, that is to say, the scope of the full review of the judgment and sentence, researches have focused exclusively on the sufficiency of the cassation appeal to comply with this postulate. The Committee's opinions have exclusively addressed this sufficiency judgment, and in the aforementioned opinion, and many that followed it, considered that by limiting itself only to the analysis of legal and formal issues without the possibility of modifying the proven facts, it cannot comply with the full review of the judgment and the sentence postulated by the ICCPR.

Despite this, the SCC, with good judgment, has repeatedly ruled that the Pact is not sufficient to create non-existent appeals, and even less prescribes a second instance but a second pronouncement in which the conviction and sentence is submitted to a higher court, and that these prescriptions are fulfilled with the appeal in cassation.

I think that this is a reasonable position on the part of the SCC, but in order to comply with the postulates of the Covenant it should have made a broad interpretation of the grounds for the filing of the cassation appeal to allow for the control of the correctness of the judgment made in the first instance, reviewing the correct application of the rules that have allowed the finding of guilt and the imposition of the sentence.

This broad interpretation came about *through the extension of the plea* of art. 852 LECrim, i.e. the infringement of constitutional precept. Thus, by invoking art. 24.2 SC, fundamentally in its aspect of the right to a trial with all guarantees and the presumption of innocence, the appellant can question not only compliance with the legal and constitutional guarantees of the evidence, but also the declaration of guilt that the trial court deduced from its content. Therefore, access is gained not only to legal questions, but also to the factual questions on which the finding of guilt is based, through the control of the application of procedural rules and the assessment of evidence. With the reform of the LECrim of 2015, the grounds of art. 852 have been considerably reduced, as the judgments handed down in the second instance by the Provincial Courts and the Criminal Division of the National High Court cannot be appealed on the grounds of infringement of the constitutional precept of the art. 852 LECrim.[11]

---

[10] Tomé García (2022), p. 1281.

[11] See Agreement of the Non-Jurisdictional Plenary of the Second Chamber of the Supreme Court of 9 June 2016. Furthermore, this limitation on the grounds of appeal has been endorsed by the Constitutional Court in its First Section Order no. 40/2018, of 13 April 2018. In arguing in favour of the limitation of the grounds, the TC argues that the change in the situation brought about by the 2015 reform of the LECrim, generalising the second instance, means that it is not necessary to extend the grounds of art. 852.

With this broad interpretation, which denaturalized the appeal in cassation, our SCC considered it to be compatible with international postulates. In fact, this had been the understanding of the Committee in its opinions since 2005.

However although compatibility with international instruments could be saved, the appeal in cassation was distorted, which is why, albeit incompletely in our opinion, the appeal in cassation was generalized to all criminal cases. This corrected the asymmetry of our appeal system and, in theory, allows cassation to fulfil its primary functions, such as the unification of doctrine. Until the 2015 reform, cassation could only take place for the most serious types of crime, as the rest were interpreted by the Provincial Courts without the possibility of homogenization by means of a unifying appeal. Today, this issue has been rectified and for crimes with a custodial sentence of no more than five years, in addition to the appeal which, as we have pointed out, will be heard by the Provincial Courts and the Criminal Division of the National High Court, an appeal in cassation is provided for, which is the competence of the Supreme Court, but only on the grounds of infringement of the law (art. 847.1° letter b, LECrim), i.e. for the interpretation and unification of the jurisprudence of these criminal offences by the Supreme Court, thus correcting, with good criteria, the asymmetry we mentioned.

If this has been the core element of the compatibility of our appeals system with the postulates of the Pact, there are two other issues that have been criticized by the Committee. The first was the absence of an appeal when the court that handed down the sentence of first and only instance is the highest in the State, and the second was the possibility of the person acquitted in first instance being sentenced because of an appeal against his acquittal. Interestingly, these two issues constitute possible exceptions to the double degree of jurisdiction set out in Article 2(2) of Protocol 7 to the European Convention.

- *The absence of appeals in cases against persons with aforesaid status to the Supreme Court*: Although it is only for introductory purposes, it should be pointed out that in Spain, as provided for in the SC and certain Organic Laws,[12] certain persons (President of the Government, Ministers, Members of Parliament, Senators, Presidents of Autonomous Communities, etc.) by virtue of their position, have aforesaid status for their prosecution in criminal cases before the Second Chamber of the SSC.[13] Likewise, there are also privileges in other Chambers of the SSC, such as Chamber V and the special Chamber of Article 61 of the LO 6/1985 of the Judiciary. This "privilege" can also be extended by criminal connection to those persons who, although lacking the condition of "aforados", are subject to the jurisdiction of the SSC, although in this case we doubt that it is a privilege. Because they are judged by the highest court in the jurisdictional pyramid, both the original "aforados" and the related ones lack the right to appeal the criminal sentences that condemn them. The basis of

[12]Many have made provision for the President of the Autonomous Region to be subject to the Second Chamber of the Supreme Court, e.g. art. 117.5 of the Statute of Autonomy of Andalusia.

[13]For an exhaustive listing, see Gómez Colomer (2012), pp. 504–507.

the prohibition of this right has been refuted by the doctrine, which considers that this basis does not exist, since it is not contemplated in any legal text. [14] While it is true that there is no express legal prohibition,[15] it is true that it is indirectly considered that they do not have the right to appeal. The explanation is simple: there is no appeal foreseen for this, nor is there a higher court to which the appeal can be submitted, since it was the highest of all that handed down the first instance ruling.[16]

These privileges for the SSC have been continuously criticized by the UN Committee, the most significant being the Opinion in the *Segundo Marey case* in 2008. The response of the SCC has been invariable, and it has considered that the particular guarantees that the privilege of being judged by the highest court of the nation entails compensate or excuse the lack of appeal. The Committee's position is not surprising, as it takes the strict interpretation of the Covenant to its ultimate consequences. The SCC's position is also reasonable, due to the absence of a reservation to the Covenant by Spain, as other countries did in this respect. An attempt was made to address this issue in the 2005 Draft by instituting an appeal similar to the old appeal for review of the "Partidas" in which the same court with a different composition analysed the judgement under review. This option was discarded by the following Drafts, including the LECrim Preliminary Draft. The solution is not an easy one, as modern logic leads us to postulate the elimination of the "aforamientos". However, there is a legal solution, which is to make a reservation to the Pact on this matter and avoid sanctions by the Committee. The question is that the Committee, in an excess of obstinacy, continues to condemn Spain[17] for this reason without considering that what constitutes an exception in Protocol 7 of the ECHR cannot be used as an argument for condemnation, although it is not expressly provided for in Article 14.5 of the ICCPR.

- The *issue of the person acquitted at first instance and subsequently convicted* is based on similar conditions as the previous case. The Committee's position has been to interpret art. 14.5 of the Covenant strictly. Thus, in the absence of any reservation by our State and bearing in mind that it is inspired by a system such as the American one, in which appeals against acquittal are prevented because of the prohibition of double jeopardy,[18] the Committee's position is not surprising. However, we believe that a change in the Committee's position is necessary, even from within, since in a dissenting opinion to the Opinion in the Gomariz

[14] For all, see De Lucchi López-Tapia (2002), p. 346.

[15] The exception provided for in Article 2(2) of Protocol 7 cannot be considered to be an express prohibition.

[16] Let us remember that the Supreme Court is the "superior court in all orders, except for the provisions on constitutional guarantees" (art. 123. CE).

[17] The latest case has been Communication no. 2844/2016, in the case of Baltasar Garzón v. Spain. On this case see Lascuaraín López (2022).

[18] More on the institution, see López Barja de Quiroja (2010), pp. 1472 et seq.; De Llera Suárez-Barcena (2007), pp. 120 et seq.

Varela v. Spain case in 2005, this is considered appropriate, but for the time being it has remained there.

It is true that since SCC Ruling no.167/2002, of 18 September, the possibility of sentencing the acquitted in first instance because of an appeal against acquittal has been considerably reduced, but it is still possible to sentence in second instance the acquitted in first instance and, of course, this would be his first conviction and would therefore be without appeal.

Although it may be thought that this debate has been settled with the approval of Law 41/2015, of 5 October, reforming the LECrim, which introduces the right to criminal appeal of sentences handed down by the Provincial Courts, we still believe that the second instance has not become generalized, as it has turned the appeal into a quasi-extraordinary resource and it is left to the freedom of the second instance court to apply it in truth and without limitation, with the excuse of immediacy.

3.4 The Criminal Appeal in Spain and Its Configuration Problems

Before doing so, we must first summarize what constitutes the appeal and the conceptualization of the second instance in the Spanish legal system.

3.4.1 Characteristics of the Appeal

Traditionally, it has been accepted that the opening of the second instance should take place instrumentally by an appeal which, without specific legal grounds, allows the appellant to submit the dispute in its entirety to the competent higher court.

Regarding the analysis of the appeal to verify whether it fulfils the postulates to be the key that opens the second instance, we must first look at its nature.

Although, at the beginning, it would be pacific that parties at the proceedings can appeal the ruling of the court for any reason, the categorization itself deserves certain nuances, as we will state later on.

A different feature of the Spanish criminal appeal is its transfer of power to a different court. It is questionable, though, if we consider that the transfer of power should be done to a higher level court. It seems that this issue will not be fulfilled with the reforms introduced, which grant, as we have had the opportunity to point out, the competence to hear the criminal appeal to courts that do not enjoy hierarchical superiority with respect to the courts that have issued the final judgment that they are going to hear in the appeal phase.

Until the current 2015 regulation, this problem did not exist. As already mentioned, this is since the only appeal with the capacity to open a second instance in criminal cases was the one that can be lodged against the sentence issued by the

Criminal Judge (or central Criminal Court) and which is resolved by the Provincial Court (or Criminal Division of the High National Court), which can be considered superior courts. In 2003, the LOPJ was amended to grant jurisdiction to hear appeals against sentences handed down by the Provincial Court or the Criminal Division of the National High Court to the High Courts of Autonomous Communities and the new Appeals Chamber of the National High Court respectively. In the latter case, superiority is non-existent. This modification of the LOPJ for the generalization of the second criminal instance has already been given content by the new appeal that has been produced by the reform of the LECrim of 2015.

This question is easily resolved by applying the criterion that, in the case of a court made up of magistrates of equal rank, although they do not essentially have administrative superiority, we can consider that they have functional superiority. However, as we have already mentioned, we would not be exempt from possible control and sanction by the international courts that have already sanctioned us on other occasions, although not due to the issue of superiority.

As for the *ordinary* nature of the appeal, today it is an ordinary appeal as it does not generally depend on certain grounds of challenge determined by law to appeal the decision that is unfavourable to it and, therefore, neither, except for those determined by the parties, in accordance with the maxim *tamtum devolutum quantum appellatum*, for the superior at the time of sentencing.

However, it has been understood that a determining condition for considering an appeal to be ordinary is the existence or not of admissibility requirements or the need to allege the grounds or causes of appeal when lodging the appeal. Until the 2015 reform, it is true that the appeal did establish certain formalities, especially when indicating the grounds of challenge, but this did not mean that it was no longer ordinary.

Today, after the 2015 reform, we can consider that the appeal against first instance sentences lacks the ordinary character when it is the prosecution that appeals. This is because it establishes certain grounds (which do not go hand in hand with immediacy) for the prosecution to appeal. The LECrim Preliminary Draft further emphasises the extraordinary nature as it further restricts the grounds for appeals by the prosecution, as they cannot request a review of the facts proven at first instance and can only appeal on grounds of infringement of the law.[19]

3.4.2 *The Second Instance*[20]

The next aspect that we are going to deal with is how this double degree of jurisdiction is carried out, that is to say, what is the extent of this new knowledge

[19] See Tomé García (2022), p. 1286.

[20] A full survey of possible configurations of the second instance, of which this heading is a schematic summary, can be found at Lara López (2014), pp. 93–148.

of the matter by the higher court. In other words, how the second instance is configured.

The first thing to do is to differentiate between appeal and second instance. These concepts have usually been treated as if they were the same institution and in an undifferentiated manner, when, without denying that both concepts are linked by a causal nexus (the final judgment on the merits), they are completely different institutions. The second instance is the complex activity generated by the appeal. However, not every appeal gives rise to a second instance, but only that which is lodged against a final judgment on the merits.

But there is more to be said about this. Given the dual content of our appeal, in which defects *in procedendo* and in *iudicando* can be alleged, when the judgement is challenged on the basis of the former, the second instance is not opened. In fact, it is not possible to speak of a second instance when the court hearing the appeal does not rule on the merits of the case, i.e. it does not issue a new judgment to replace the previous one, but rather rules the nullity without going into the merits of the case, as it only orders that the proceedings be restored to the state they were in at the time the fault was committed, sending the case back to the court of first instance. This, however, provided that the defect cannot be remedied in the second instance, in which case, it will proceed to remedy the defect and will rule on the merits.

3.4.2.1 Single or Double Instance System

Having made the conceptual delimitation, another important question is whether or not it is advisable for criminal proceedings to be structured in a single or double instance system. As we know, the original Spanish criminal procedure system was structured as a single-instance trial in cases of serious crimes (which was the only procedure—with some exceptions—for crimes that existed).

Traditionally, there has been a certain tension between establishing a system of prosecution based on a single or double instance, regardless of how the second instance should be configured. A multitude of arguments have been offered for and against.

The process cannot be unaffected by the possible existence of errors and having the possibility of eliminating them strengthens the guarantees of a fair administration of justice. From this perspective, the double degree is seen as an increase in the possibilities of justice that no legislator should disdain and that represents more advantages than disadvantages (without being totally free of them).

This does not mean that the sentences of the second degree are infallible, as Ulpiano pointed out, "... nobody is unaware of how necessary the practice of appeal is, since it serves to amend the injustices and imperfections of the judges, although sometimes it serves to worsen sentences that are well issued, since the one who rules last is not always going to be better".

Even so, a second trial by a higher court is a guarantee of greater accuracy in the ruling and makes it possible to eliminate errors that may have occurred in the first instance.

A weighty argument worthy of consideration, and one which has determined our current system of a single instance in serious crimes, is that in those oral trials where immediacy is necessary for the presence and assessment of evidence, the second instance court lacks it. This argument may be only half valid, as there are ways of resolving it.

Firstly, by repeating all the evidence in the second instance, secondly, by limiting the appeal to aspects that do not require immediacy (e.g. the legal aspect, the inference judgement or non-personal evidence); thirdly, by recording the hearings so that the evidence can be assessed by the second instance court with secondary immediacy.

This brings us to the possibilities for the configuration of the second instance.

3.4.2.2 Full or Limited Appeal

The content, scope and configuration of the second instance have been defined according to the appeal that gives access to it. So, a distinction has been made between a full appeal and a limited appeal.

The *full appeal* represents a *novum iudicium*, i.e. a new and complete examination of the previous instance, it would be a second first instance and is specified with the possibility that before the higher court it is possible to alter the object of the proceedings, expand or change the claim, introduce new claims, apply all the means of defence not used in the first instance, use new evidence and re-examine the evidence taken in the first instance.

The *limited appeal* is a *revisio prioris instantiae*, the purpose of which is to review the procedural activity carried out by the court a quo and the correctness of the judgment on the merits. It is not possible to innovate either in the claims, the facts or the evidence, since what is passed on to the second instance is a kind of fixed photo of the same made in the first instance.

As with the double or single instance, the advantages or disadvantages of a system of full or limited appeal have been the subject of discussion, although it must be borne in mind that both models in their pure form only exist on a theoretical level.

We have no doubt that a system which closes off any possibility of innovation in the second instance conspires against the ascertainment of the truth and does not guarantee the accuracy and justice of decisions. But neither does it contribute to the proper administration of justice to completely allow evidentiary material if its novelty is not protected by the impossibility of its introduction in the first instance, either due to ignorance of its existence or for reasons not attributable to the party requesting it.

With these precautions, an intermediate or eclectic system is preferable, since both systems in their pure configuration do not fully satisfy the list of conditioning factors that we have set out.

Regarding the evidential material, it should be limited to what was introduced in the first instance, with the only exceptions of evidence that could not be provided by the proposing party for reasons not arising from their own fault.

The problem arises in relation to the court before which this evidence must be taken and which will assess it. Logic dictates that such evidence should be taken before the court *a quo* once the appellate court has determined its relevance and usefulness and, therefore, orders the proceedings to be reinstated so that it can be taken and a new judgment can be handed down by the court of first instance. In these cases, a second instance would not be opened since the judgment would be issued again by the court *a quo*.

This option undoubtedly benefits the immediacy of evidence as all evidence will have respected this principle because the other way round only the new evidence will be immediate and not the evidence taken in the first instance. On the other hand, this possibility does not benefit procedural economy.

Nowadays we can consider that the Spanish criminal appeal is limited with certain concessions to the practice of evidence in the second instance, like evidence that was not provided in the first instance for reasons not arising from their own fault. In other words, evidence that was already taken at first instance is not retaken, as is the case in Italy or Germany. This could determine that the scope of knowledge of the *ad quem* court should be limited by this circumstance, as it can re-evaluate evidence that it has not directly witnessed with immediacy.

Even so, the SCC has made it clear that, except for appeals against acquittals when the judgement has been based on the assessment of personal evidence, the appeal court has full capacity to make a discrepant assessment of the evidence held in the trial and reach a different conclusion to that of the judge *a quo*. This could be solved with good audio-visual documentation of the plenary. However, it is sometimes difficult to re-evaluate the evidence in the second instance, as the court may point out that it does not modify the proven facts, as it has considered evidence that requires immediacy and it has not had it.

We must point out that no matter how many proposals there have been, none of them have settled this issue, probably because it is impossible to solve.

It is absolutely impossible to equate the positions of the first and second degree courts in terms of immediacy in the presence of evidence in the oral trial, the cornerstone of the criminal process. None of the systems studied satisfies this comparison in a complete way.

A pure *novum iudicium* in the second instance, which could be associated to a full appeal, does not solve the problem because it undermines the first instance, turning it into a mere rehearsal of the second in which the losing party will be aware of the mistakes it may have made in the evidence in the first trial and will try to correct them in the second, leading to the distortion of personal evidence. A limited appeal with concessions to *ius novorum* in terms of facts and evidence does not in any way satisfy the guarantee of the immediacy of evidence, which will only be produced with the evidence taken in the second instance.

Therefore, there are only two options, the single instance or the recording of the evidence so that the whole of this material can be reviewed by the *ad quem* court.

Neither system is completely satisfactory. The first because possible errors *in iudicando facti* would be irremediable in the absence of a higher instance. The second because the recordings and their subsequent playback do not fully satisfy the principle of immediacy. Even so, the second would be the more correct one. But this has not been the position of our legislator.

As a corollary to the above, we must reflect what is stated by the SSP, in its ruling 358/2019, of 10 July, where it reviews the systems that regulate the double instance, and, after recalling that the two traditional ones are the full appeal and the limited appeal, it says that "these systems, however, have experienced in recent years a process of legislative rapprochement, so that at present it is not easy to find them pure", opting for ours. It adds that "as a consequence, a corrected limited model is necessary, such as the one recognized in our system, which partially admits and only in justified cases the taking of certain evidence in the second instance", and specifying, in particular, that "in short, the generalization of the double instance is compatible with the maintenance of the current limited appeal model which does not exclude the factual review within certain parameters that respect immediacy".

This limited model with few concessions to the taking of evidence in the second instance is maintained in the LECrim Preliminary Draft, which in its Explanatory Memorandum opts for this system using the following words:

> Thus, with regard to the question of whether a model of full appeal should be introduced in our criminal procedural system or whether the traditional system of limited appeal should be maintained, it is decidedly decided to maintain and perfect the latter. Procedural doctrine and the experience of the German double jeopardy system itself show that the disadvantages and disadvantages of the full system are greater than those of the limited system.
>
> The full appeal leads, on the one hand, to the parties reserving their real procedural strategy for the second instance, with the first trial serving to test or explore the possibilities of the opponent. On the other hand, in the second trial, the dynamic of the testimonies loses its spontaneity; the participants tend to reproduce - or reconstruct, according to their interests - what was narrated in the previous trial, ceasing to have as their main reference their direct perception of the facts. The virtuality of the oral proceedings as a way of clarifying the truth is reduced in both instances, in one case by the omission of relevant evidence and in the other by the devaluation of its content.
>
> There is no guarantee that the appellate court will be more correct in its direct assessment of the evidence. In fact, in order to ensure a more rational assessment of the evidence, it would be more effective if the entire trial at first instance were attributed to a collegiate court, which would require a smaller economic investment than the establishment of a generalized system of full appeal. For this reason, the meaning of the review of the merits in the appeal has to be different, more appropriate to its consideration as an instrument of control of the legality of the proceedings at first instance. In short, the text clearly opts for a model of limited appeal.

We are in favour of this limited appeal as it is more compatible with the Spanish legal tradition and minimizes the risks of a devaluation of the first instance which could become a mere rehearsal of the second instance if all the evidence can be repeated or new evidence is admitted which could be used in the first instance, but which the party reserved for itself. [21]

3.5 The Purpose of the Appeal in Our Legal System

The current regulation of the appeal and the second instance in our legal system and its harmonization with the requirements derived from the international instruments signed by Spain is another aspect that needs to dealt with.

The LECrim of 1882 configured these institutions from a clear point of view: in criminal cases, the system of a single instance with subsequent cassation was established, as it was based on the assumption that the configuration of the oral and public trial was incompatible with the second instance. This idea, which remained latent for years, was truncated, not because it was abandoned, but because it had to be overcome by the legislator who, departing from the classic conception that investigation and prosecution should be the competence of different courts, combined both functions in the same court in the interests of speed and to respond to situations of collapse. With the breakdown of the principle of the judge not being prevented, fundamentally in the *1967 Automobile Act and in Organic Act 10/1980 on the oral trial of intentional, less serious or flagrant offences*, the legislator had to establish an appeal against the sentence handed down in criminal cases by the examining magistrate to compensate for the loss of guarantees in these proceedings. Although this legal aberration was corrected with the arrival of the Criminal Court Judges and the abbreviated procedure in 1988, the appeal procedure in force today was retained, even though it continues to come up against the problem of the immediacy of evidence.

This initial provision, driven by respect for the aforementioned principles, does not fit in well with what is foreseen for the final judgement in the trial for minor offences, [22] for which, although it is also carried out orally and publicly, it does provide for an appeal for the analysis of the issue in the second instance. This difference is explained not from a technical-legal perspective but from a political one due to an issue that was a constant during the previous centuries and will continue to be so throughout the twenty-first century, that is, the distrust of the single judge is what motivates the existence of a second instance in the trial of minor offences.

Since then and until the 2015 reform, our procedural system, as we have already mentioned, has maintained an asymmetry that is difficult to understand, since in less serious cases there is an appeal that opens a limited second instance and, on the other hand, in more serious cases there is no appeal but an extraordinary appeal in

[21] In the same opinion, and for a development of the objections, see Tomé García (2022), p. 1280.

[22] The minor offences trial is a procedure that lacks an investigation phase and whose competence belongs mainly to the Courts of Instruction and the sentence that is passed can be appealed before the Provincial Court.

cassation. As has been said, our legal system offered greater guarantees for the defence of the right to property than for the right to liberty.

In this legislative state, with the continuous reforms that have taken place, the LECrim no longer responded to a coherent model or system of prosecution, which is even more evident in terms of the system of appeals against final sentences.

Until 2015, the legislator had been trying, with very little success, to generalize the appeal and the second instance in criminal proceedings.

In this sense, Organic Act 19/2003, of 23 December, reforming the LOPJ, which granted jurisdiction to hear appeals in cases involving serious crimes to two different courts, saw the light of day. The way to do this was the creation of an *ex novo* Chamber in the National High Court, the "Appeals Chamber", and the granting of jurisdiction to an existing Civil and Criminal Chamber (as a Criminal Chamber) of the High Courts of Autonomous Communities. It is true that in the years following the 2013 reform, there were certain attempts to generalise the second criminal instance, although some, such as the 2005 Preliminary Draft, rather eliminated it despite generalising the appeal, but none was at the end enacted. Given the impossibility of tackling a global reform of the LECrim (it seems that now in 2020 another attempt is being promoted, but it does not seem that it will be tried in a short period of time), the aforementioned reform of 2015 was carried out in order to try to generalise the second instance with the schematic regulation that we set out below.

3.5.1 Appeals and the Second Instance in Criminal Cases[23]

The recourse to appeal is the most common type of ordinary recourse aimed at challenging a sentence. It is a multipurpose recourse since it is used to challenge factual issues, such as errors in the assessment of evidence, material issues such as the incorrect application of criminal law, or formal issues, i.e., procedural issues. Appeals have suffered greatly at the hands of lawmakers, since they were not generalised. The reform of the Criminal Procedure Act by Act 41/2015, of October 5, brought about the generalisation of our previously asymmetrical system. As such, for cases carrying a prison sentence of more than five years there was no appeal, while for crimes carrying a lower sentence, including those without a custodial sentence, there was. We will not deal here with appeals against jury trial sentences, which is not a true appeal but a cassation, nor with appeals against sentences handed down by the Juvenile Courts.

[23] See Lara López (2022), pp. 267–272.

3.5.1.1 Appealable Decisions

Since the generalisation of the second criminal instance, all first instance judgements can be appealed regardless of the quantum of penalty (Arts. 790 and 846 b. Criminal Procedure Act), except those issued by the Supreme Court of Justice and the Supreme Court in cases against individuals with parliamentary immunity. Likewise, certain orders, such as those lacking jurisdiction or dismissal, may be appealed.

3.5.1.2 Jurisdiction

The following courts are competent to hear appeals:

For judgments handed down at first instance by examining magistrates and judges of violence against women (minor offences and speedy trials), the provincial court.

For judgments handed down at first instance by criminal and central criminal court judges, the provincial courts and the Criminal Division of the National High Court, respectively.

For first instance judgments handed down by the provincial courts and the Criminal Division of the National High Court, the High Court of Justice and the Appeals Chamber of the National High Court, respectively.

3.5.1.3 Grounds for Appeal

It has always been understood that the recourse to appeal was an ordinary recourse where no specific grounds for filing an appeal were required. While this is true, nowadays it cannot strictly speaking be considered as such, since there are different grounds for filing an appeal depending on the appellant's procedural position. As we have seen, an appeal can be based on different grounds, including an error in the assessment of evidence, a breach of procedural rules and guarantees, and an infringement of the rules of the legal system.

(a) Error in the assessment of evidence

This has always been the Achilles' heel for the generalisation of the second criminal instance. This is because the allegation of error in the assessment of evidence involves a discrepancy between the facts declared proven by the judge which form the factual basis of the judgment, and what is alleged by the parties. In the past, our lawmakers understood that if the court of the second instance had not witnessed the evidence with immediacy, it could not assess it correctly. Hence, the original system of the Criminal Procedure Act only provided for a single instance. The 2015 reform, which generalised the second instance in criminal matters, faced the difficulty of lodging an appeal when it was constrained by a doctrine of the Spanish Constitutional Court in its judgment 167/2002, which stated that a person acquitted at first instance cannot be convicted or have a sentence increased as a result of an appeal against their acquittal without hearing the accused. For this reason, a plea of error in the assessment of evidence differs according to whether it is alleged by the individual convicted or the prosecution. Thus, for the former there is no limitation, while for the latter, where the allegation pleads an error in the assessment of evidence to request nullity of the acquittal or an increase in the sentence, it is necessary to justify the insufficiency or lack of rationality in the factual reasoning, the manifest departure from the maxims of experience, or the omission of all reasoning on one or several of the pieces of evidence which may be of relevance or whose nullity may have been inappropriately declared. (Art. 790.2 para. 3 1 LECrim), i.e., aspects which do not require immediacy to circumvent the aforementioned constitutional doctrine.

(b) Breach of procedural norms and guarantees (art. 790.2 para. 2 LECrim)

If the appeal requests nullity of the judgment due to an infringement of procedural rules and safeguards which cause the lack of a proper defence for the appellant, in such terms that it cannot be rectified in the second instance, the legal or constitutional rules which are considered to be infringed will be cited and reasons stated for the inability to provide a proper defence. In addition, it must be proven that rectification of the error or infringement was requested in the first instance, except if it was committed at a time when it was then impossible to claim.

(c) Infringement of rules of the legal system

This plea alleges that the court of first instance infringed a rule of substantive criminal law (in the broad sense), i.e., that it could have interpreted it incorrectly or failed to apply it or applied it inappropriately.

3.5.1.4 Procedure

The procedure is initiated with a reasoned statement of the grounds of appeal, which must be presented to the court that issued the judgment being challenged within ten days of notification of the judgement Art. 790. 1 LECrim).

Because our appeal system, although limited, is generous in terms of the new law, it allows the taking of evidence in the second instance, but this must be requested in the formal writ. The taking of evidence in the second instance is limited to cases of evidence unduly denied in the first instance, evidence admitted but not taken, or evidence based on new or updated facts (Art. 790.3 1 LECrim).

After the appeal has been lodged, the other parties are notified (ten days) for their possible opposition or adhesion subject to the maintenance of the initial appeal. After the filing of these documents or when the deadline has expired, the proceedings are transferred to the court *ad quem*, which will admit or reject the proposed evidence and convene a hearing providing there is evidence to be heard or it is deemed necessary (Art. 791.1 1 LECrim).

The decision on appeal must be passed within five days or ten days (depending on whether or not there was a hearing), and its content and effects will vary according to the grounds put forward (Art. 792 1 LECrim). A cassation appeal may be lodged against it for an infringement of the law or breach of form when the judgment on appeal was handed down by the Civil and Criminal Division of the Supreme Court or the Appeals Chamber of the National Criminal Court (cases carrying a sentence of more than five years' imprisonment) and only for breach of procedure when the judgment on appeal is handed down by the Provincial Court or the Criminal Division of the National Criminal Court (cases carrying a sentence of less than five years' imprisonment).

3.6 Most Problematic Aspects of the Second Instance in Spain

3.6.1 Appeals Against Convictions

Until the reform of the LECrim operated by Law 41/2015, the appeal was only foreseen to challenge sentences handed down by Criminal Judges (and by the single Central Judge of the National High Court), in relation to crimes punished with a custodial sentence not exceeding 5 years, a fine or any other sentence not exceeding 10 years. In relation to other offences, only an appeal in cassation was possible.

The reform introduced by Organic Act 19/2003, of 23 December, on the reform of the LOPJ, generalized the second criminal instance, influenced to a large extent by various opinions of the UN Human Rights Committee in this regard, and to this end, the Criminal Chambers of the High Courts of Justice of the Autonomous Communities, became the second criminal instance for sentences handed down by the Provincial Courts. An appeal chamber was also created in the National High Court.

But the truth is that in these years the mandate to adapt the procedural rules provided for in this 2003 reform had not been fulfilled, something that was done with the approval of Law 41/2015, which provides for an appeal similar to the current one, but generalized.

As for the scope of the appeal, i.e. the review to be carried out, there is no provision in our system for a retrial, which is naturally possible in exceptional cases of nullity due to a breach of form that requires it, a possibility that has nothing to do with the configuration of the appeal.

In evidential matters, Article 790.3 LECrim only provides that evidence which could not be proposed in the first instance, due to ignorance of its existence, or which was already proposed, but was improperly denied, or which was not carried out for reasons not attributable to the proponent, can be requested on appeal by the accusations or the defence, always justifying the relevance of the evidence.

According to article 791 LECrim, a hearing may be held on appeal if the evidence has been admitted, and when the Court considers it useful or necessary for the correct formation of a well-founded conviction.

However, for a long time, despite not repeating the trial, the Courts had been carrying out a wide-ranging review of the first instance sentence, both of the legal and merits issues; it was understood that the appeal represented a *novum iudicium*, even without repeating the trial, without taking into account that it is not possible to form a conviction based on the testimony of witnesses who have not been seen or heard to testify (SCC Ruling no. 167/2002).

The Constitutional Court, in this important ruling, made it clear that immediacy is a constitutional condition for the assessment of evidence, which applies not only to the criminal judge but also to the court of appeal and, of course, to the court of cassation.

The Preliminary Draft of 2020 establishes a continuity regarding the appeal when it is the convicted person who appeals. Thus, he will be able to appeal, both for infringement of the law (whether procedural or substantive), and for error in the assessment of evidence (art. 728). And it establishes the novelty of developing in Article 733 the review of the assessment of evidence which can be extended to everything relating to the sufficiency, validity and lawfulness of the prosecution's evidence, and can also complain that guilt has been established without sufficiently refuting, in accordance with the rules of logic, science and experience, the more favourable alternative hypotheses which would have been the object of debate in the trial.

On the other hand, as we will develop below, the prosecution cannot appeal on the grounds of error in the assessment of the evidence as this is not covered by the aforementioned article.

3.6.2 Appeal Against Acquittals

It has been debated in the doctrine, and we have mentioned it before, whether the appeal should only be foreseen against convictions, or also against acquittals.

The truth is that appeals against acquittals can raise constitutional and practical problems, since, on the one hand, the principle of *non bis in idem* in procedural law does not seem to allow the possibility of a new danger of conviction. This possibility is what, as we have already seen, is known as the prohibition of "double jeopardy", i.e. the double jeopardy of conviction—contained in the 5th Amendment to the US Constitution—which, although not expressly included in our Constitution, is undoubtedly implicit in the idea and tradition of a trial with all guarantees, therefore as a fundamental right and, on the other hand, the right to submit the conviction and sentence to a higher court, makes it necessary in these cases to provide for a kind of "third instance" in the event of the second sentence being condemned.

Furthermore, the reiterated doctrine of the Constitutional Court, which dates back to Ruling 167/2002, requires that any conviction must be based on an evidentiary activity in which the judicial court has directly and personally examined the evidence, in a public debate, with the necessary possibility of contradiction, so that the Court of Appeal cannot convict without a repetition of the evidence, something that was ruled out in the 2015 reform. But, as we shall see, this provision is changing and the trend initiated by the Appeals Chamber of the High National Court to use the hearing of art. 701 LECrim to retake the statement of the accused in the second instance is being imposed.

The reform opts for an appeal against arbitrary acquittals, allowing the sentence to be appealed, but with the case being sent back to the court *a quo* so that it can correct the defect. This same solution had also been suggested by the Supreme Court itself in relation to cassation against acquittals for infringement of the right to effective judicial protection. Thus, the non-jurisdictional Plenary Agreement of 19 December 2012 considered that, as the law did not provide for the taking of evidence before the court or the summoning of the accused to a hearing, the Chamber could not rectify the declaration of proven facts, so the appropriate thing to do in such a case was to return the case to the court of origin to rectify the defect, which could be simply a matter of motivation or require a new trial with a different court.

The LECrim Preliminary Draft is more groundbreaking than the 2015 reform since, as we have seen, the latter allowed the appeal for error in the assessment of evidence, but limited it to aspects that did not require immediacy. However, as we have also advanced, the LECrim Preliminary Draft does not contemplate this motive for the accusations in its art. 728. This does not imply that they lack all possibility of appeal in which, in some way, the factual account or, rather, its motivation, can be subject to appeal, but by way of the infringement of procedural law of art. 730.2 to seek the nullity of the trial and not for the issuing of a new sentence. Specifically, the plea of irrationality, arbitrariness or manifest inadequacy of the reasoning of the judgement must be alleged and must be in accordance with the rules of Article 732.1.[24] Furthermore, section 2 of the aforementioned article states that, when lodging an appeal on this ground, the prosecution may not request the modification of the facts declared proven in the trial court judgement nor may they request a review of the assessment of the evidence. Nor can they ask the court of appeal to convict the defendant who was acquitted or to aggravate his situation if he had been convicted.

Essentially, what the draft bill does is to classify as a procedural infringement what the current and valid art. 790.2 LECrim states as a motive for error in the assessment of evidence and with similar limitations and consequences.[25]

[24] (a) Clearly identify those aspects of the factual reasoning which manifestly deviate from the application of rational parameters of argumentation or maxims of experience; (b) identify factual conclusions which have been reached arbitrarily because they are not supported by any evidence; and (c) identify evidence on which reasoning has been omitted, highlighting its relevance to the judgment.

[25] Although Tomé understands that the control that today the second instance court can carry out of the evaluation of the evidence that the first instance court has carried out is broader than the model established by the Preliminary Draft of 2020. Cfr. Tomé García (2022), p. 1289.

3.7 Immediacy and Evidence at Second Instance. Special Reference to Conviction in the Second Instance After Acquittal

Criminal appeals have undergone a profound change in their content due to the requirement of immediacy of evidence in order to be able to convict on appeal a person who had been acquitted in the first instance. Since SCC Ruling no. 167/2002, of 18 September, the possibility of convicting a person acquitted at first instance as a result of an appeal against acquittal has been considerably reduced. This change in doctrine, as we have pointed out, came about by accepting the case law of the ECtHR (Ekbatani v. Sweden, no. 10563/83, 26 May 1988; Constantinescu v. Romania, no. 28871/95, 27 June 2000), which considered that the conviction at second instance of a person acquitted at first instance when this was based on a re-evaluation of personal evidence requires that the second instance court must witness this personal evidence with immediacy and, therefore, this evidence must be repeated in its presence. Otherwise, not the right to appeal, but the right to a fair trial would be violated. Thus, the ECtHR has repeatedly condemned Spain for not respecting these principles, the most significant being Román Zurdo and others v. Spain, no. 28399/09 and 51135/09, 8 October 2013 and, more recently, Gómez Olmeda v. Spain, no. 61112/12, 29 March 2016.

In this regard, the SCC's doctrine on the immediacy of the tribunal *ad quem* and the presumption of innocence is limited to these two requirements:

(a) *The prohibition of the appellate court to review the assessment of personal evidence.*

The fundamental right to a fair trial also entails the right of the accused not to be further burdened in his conviction or not to be convicted, if he has been acquitted in the first instance, as a result of a new assessment of the evidence, carried out by the second instance court, which requires the immediacy of the court.

This fundamental right, established in application of the doctrine previously upheld by the ECtHR, was recognized by the TC, for the first time, in its SCC 120/1999, of 28 June, whose doctrine was subsequently set out in SCC 167/2002, of 18 September, having given rise to a very broad jurisprudence.

In accordance with this doctrine, the Court *ad quem* cannot review the assessment of evidence carried out by the court of first instance, which requires the principles of immediacy, publicity and contradiction to be in force.

Such evidence, the assessment of which (in order to form a conviction as to its veracity) requires the immediacy of the court, is of a personal nature and must be confined to the statements of the parties, witnesses and experts, without, in any way and as has been said, reaching the assessment of documentary evidence, which can be examined by the court of appeal or the court of cassation on the occasion of the application of the grounds of infringement of the law or error of fact in the assessment of the evidence, although the prosecution cannot now, in accordance with the doctrine upheld in SSC Ruling no. 892/2016, of 25 November, exercise against the defendant.

(b) *The prior hearing of the defendant whenever the court has to impose a heavier burden on the defendant than was the case at first instance.*

The doctrine of the SCC, issued in compliance with that of the ECtHR (Popovici v. Moldova, no. 289/04 and 41194/04, 27 November 2007; Bazo González v. Spain, no. 30643/2004, 16 December 2008), is not limited to establishing this prohibition on the assessment of personal evidence by the appeal court, but also requires that, when the appeal or cassation court has to pronounce a longer sentence for the defendant, it must, at the end of the hearing, give him or her a hearing.

The Act 41/2015 has not introduced this requirement, as the "right to the last word" is only provided for at the end of the oral trial (art. 739.1 LECrim). However, this manifestation of the general principle of law that "no one can be sentenced without having been previously heard" should be present in each and every instance, including cassation, and this, because Articles 6 ECHR and 24.2 EC are also directly applicable, with the TC having declared that the defendant's "right to the last word" in each and every instance is included within the fundamental right to defence (SCC Rulings no. 22/2013, of 31 January and 13/2006, of 16 January).

However, the TS, arguing that there is no provision in the LECrim that enshrines this right in cassation, remains reluctant to allow the exercise of this fundamental right. And so, since the agreement of the Plenary of the Criminal Chamber of 19 December 2012, in various resolutions it has repeatedly denied the exercise of this fundamental right and, what is more serious, it seems that the number of oral hearings in the Criminal Chamber of the SSC has decreased significantly, solely for this reason.

However, as we have already mentioned, this provision has undergone an important change in the understanding of the Appeals Chamber of the High National Court that it is not forbidden to take a statement from the accused on appeal and, therefore, with the aforementioned precautions, to convict the person acquitted in the first instance (or increase the sentence initially imposed) as a result of the appeal lodged by the prosecution. The basis of this tendency is that, based on the doctrine of not being able to convict the defendant acquitted at first instance on the basis of a re-evaluation of the personal evidence, the conclusion is reached that there is only one opportunity to establish a conviction, that of first instance, which has come to be called the "one-shot theory".[26] This tendency clashes with the fact that no provision has been made for a hearing for the accused acquitted at second instance. A limitation that the Appeals Chamber of the High National Court sees as perfectly legal by summoning the acquitted defendant to the hearing under art.791 on the basis of the need to hold a hearing for the correct formation of a well-founded conviction (Sentence High National Court no. 4/2018 of 10 July). In that case, an appeal in cassation was lodged against this judgement which convicted the defendant

[26] See Hurtado Adrián (2020).

acquitted at first instance and the SSC upheld this conviction, therefore, it is considered that there is no reproach to the use of the hearing at second instance in order to be able to take the acquitted defendant's statement.[27] The question was based on determining, without altering the proven facts, whether the inference was correct when determining intentionality as a subjective element of wrongfulness. It has always been understood that intentionality was a legal and not a factual question, and therefore, if there was no modification of the proven facts, it was not subject to the rules of immediacy or its absence in the second instance, which prevent its re-evaluation and subsequent conviction of the acquitted (or aggravation). However, the ECtHR has made it clear that this subjective element, if it involves contact with personal evidence for its assessment, requires that the acquitted defendant must be heard again for its assessment in the second instance (Atutxa Mendiola and others v. Spain, no. 41427/1413, 13 June 2017). This is what the high national court has done and what the SSC has confirmed. Although we agree with this opinion, we believe that if the reason for the prosecution's appeal is the error in the assessment of the evidence due to a lack of motivation of the inference judgement (art. 790.2.3° LECrim), the acquitted in the first instance could not be convicted, since the consequence of the assessment of this reason is the nullity of the sentence. However, if, it appears to be the case, the intentionality is a legal element and not a factual one, an appeal will be lodged in accordance with the infringement of the law and, therefore, a new sentence can be handed down convicting the person acquitted at first instance if, on appeal, a statement has been taken to save the doctrine set out by the ECtHR.[28] I understand that this is a very forced argument to avoid the "one-shot" theory.

On this issue, the LECrim Preliminary Draft does not contribute much since the prosecutors can appeal the sentence due to infringement of the law and, therefore, the situation would not change since the hearing will be held under the same conditions as in the current regulation (art. 737.1.2.2 LECrim Preliminary Draft) and, therefore, the acquitted defendant could be heard again.

3.8 The Recording of Trials and Their Assessment in the Second Instance

Our appeals system is determined by the lack of immediacy of the appeal court when assessing the evidence given at first instance.

The advance of technology and the availability of certain audio-visual media could help to alleviate this lack of immediacy which, although secondary, is a better tool than the handwritten notes of the Court Clerk.

---

[27] STS 185/2019, de 2 de abril (ECLI:ES:TS:2019:1070).

[28] See Hurtado Adrián (2020).

However, the possibility of using the recording of the hearing held in the first instance in the second instance is not currently regulated in a profuse manner. Furthermore, the Constitutional Court has ruled that the person acquitted in the first instance cannot be sentenced in the second instance using the recording of the hearing in the first instance as evidence because "strictly speaking, there is no immediacy" (SCC Rulings no. 2/2010, of 10 January and 30/2010, of 17 May), although it is true that this doctrine is only applicable to cases in which the conviction in the second instance of the person acquitted in the first instance, or the aggravation of a sentence as a consequence of the appeal, is raised, so in principle, it would be applicable to cases of acquittal or reduction of the sentence.

Currently, the regulation of the LECrim allows the request for the reproduction of recorded evidence in Article 791.1, but it will only be used when the court admits it. This line is maintained in Article 736.2 of the LECrim Preliminary Draft.

The legislator had several options to achieve the desired generalization of the second criminal instance, making the re-evaluation of evidence that the second instance must contain in order to be considered as such compatible with the absence of immediacy in the practice of this evidence and, above all, with the doctrine emanating from SCC Ruling no. 167/2002. These options involved eliminating the appeal for the accusations and thus the previously acquitted could not be convicted in the second instance as the aforementioned judgement advocates, or allowing them to appeal, but only on grounds which do not require immediacy in the second instance. In this way, the appeal for the prosecution would become non-existent (it could have problems of constitutionality due to the principle of equality) or extraordinary, as it would only be for certain specific reasons.

In essence, this is what is included in the new regulation provided for in the reform of the LECrim of 2015, as it introduces a new third paragraph to art. 790. 2 to establish that when the prosecution alleges an error in the assessment of the evidence to annul an acquittal or aggravate a conviction, it must justify the insufficiency or lack of rationality in the factual reasoning, manifest deviation from the maxims of experience or omission of any reasoning on any or some of the evidence that could have relevance or whose nullity has been improperly declared. In other words, it does not eliminate the appeal of the accusations, but limits it to aspects that do not require immediacy.

In the case of an appeal against a conviction, there should be no limitation on the opening of the second instance except for those referring to the immediacy of the evidence. At present, there are no legal or jurisprudential limitations, as the existing approach that the judge *ad quem*, when determining the facts through the assessment of the evidence, is in the same situation as the judge *a quo* and, therefore, can assess the evidence taken at first instance, and examine and correct the position of the judge *a quo*. The problem is that appellate courts are also reluctant to review the facts when they have not witnessed the evidence with immediacy; in fact, it has become general opinion in court to state that the declaration of proven facts made by the trial judge must be respected. Therefore, the review of the facts in the second instance depends on judicial voluntarism and this is not advisable.

In such a situation, there can only be a clear regulation of the limits of the reviewing court *ad quem* in line with the regulation of the grounds of the appellant's claim. If a full evidentiary re-evaluation is allowed, it must be clearly defined.

We believe that it is not advisable to restrict the appeal and the second instance, as it should not exclude the possibility that a correct recording in accordance with the current state of the art substantially brings the immediate positions of both courts closer, which, let us not forget, can never be put on a par in their entirety, but this does not mean that we should limit the possibility of the review of the facts in the second instance.

Cited Case-Law

ECtHR

hudoc.echr.coe.int

Ekbatani v. Sweden, no. 10563/83, 26 May 1988
Constantinescu v. Romania, no. 28871/95, 27 June 2000
Popovici v. Moldova, no. 289/04 and 41194/04, 27 November 2007
Bazo González v. Spain, no. 30643/04, 16 December 2008
Román Zurdo and others v. Spain, no. 28399/09 and 51135/09, 8 October 2013
Gómez Olmeda v. Spain, no. 61112/12, 29 March 2016
Atutxa Mendiola and others v. Spain, no. 41427/1413, 13 June 2017

SCC

Ruling no.120/1999, 28 June
Ruling no.167/2002, 18 September
Ruling no. 13/2006, 16 January
Ruling no. 2/2010, 10 January
Ruling no. 30/2010, 17 May
Ruling no. 22/2013, 31 January

SSC

Ruling no. 892/2016, 25 November
Ruling no. 185/2019, 2 April
Ruling no. 358/2019, 10 July

References

Calderón Cuadrado MP (2011) La encrucijada de una justicia penal tecnológicamente avanzada: sobre la grabación de las vistas, los recursos y la garantía de la inmediación. Editorial La Ley, Madrid

De Llera Suárez-Barcena E (2007) La apelación contra sentencias absolutórias. Estudios de Derecho Judicial 149:117–129

De Lucchi López-Tapia Y (2002) Nuevas consideraciones sobre el derecho al recurso en el orden penal (el Dictamen del Comité de Derechos Humanos y la jurisprudencia constitucional en el Caso Segundo Marey). Revista de Derecho Procesal 1–3:323–352

Gómez Colomer JL (2012) Sobre aforamientos y principio de igualdad. Revista de Derecho Procesal 1:499–503

Hurtado Adrián AL (2020) Apelación de sentencias (con mayor atención) absolutórias. Diario La Ley, 9638, 22 de mayo de 2020 (electronic resource)

Lara López AM (2014) El recurso de apelación y la segunda instancia penal. Editorial Aranzadi, Cizur Menor

Lara López AM (2017) La organización jurisdiccional española. In: Conceptos de Derecho Procesal Civil. Editorial Tecnos, Madrid, pp 63–90

Lara López AM (2022) Appeals and other remedies. In: The criminal justice system in Spain. Editorial Atelier, Barcelona, pp 259–281

Lascuaraín López JA (2022) El Dictamen Garzón del Comité de Derechos Humanos, en Almacén de Derecho, de 18 de febrero de 2020 (electronic resource), https://almacendederecho.org/el-dictamen-garzon-del-comite-de-derechos-humanos

López Barja de Quiroja J (2010) Tratado de Derecho Procesal Penal. Editorial Aranzadi, Cizur Menor

Montero Aroca J (1997) Los Principios del Proceso Penal: Una explicación basada en la razón. Editorial Tirant lo Blanch, Valencia

Tomé García JA (2022) El recurso de apelación contra sentencias en el Anteproyecto de LECRIM de 2020. In: Reflexiones en torno al Anteproyecto de Ley de Enjuiciamiento Criminal de 2020. Editorial Tirant lo Blanch, Valencia, pp 1277–1305

References

Chapter 4
The Recordings Model in Portugal: The Appeal Court's Perspective

Rita do Rosário

4.1 Introduction

The ECtHR has interpreted the *immediacy principle*[1] as demanding the *direct examination* of the facts by the Appeal Courts—re-listening to witnesses or the defendant at the hearing[2]—, since the mere analysis of the recorded evidence produced at the first instance trial does not meet the requirements set out in Article 6 § 1 of the ECHR.

The evaluation of the practical applicability of that perspective in the Portuguese courts requires a comprehensive review of the national Appeal Courts' case law, as its traditional approach to appeals concerning matters of fact is a conservative one.

[1]Cf. Dias (2004), p. 232: 'the relationship of communicative proximity between the court and the participants in the procedure, in such a way that the court can obtain its own perception of the material that will take as a base for its decision', free translation.

The immediacy that characterizes the first instance allows the judge to contact personally with the various means of evidence, assessing the credibility of statements of testimonies, considering multiple factors, such as verbal and non-verbal cues of the person giving the evidence, cf. Lisbon Court of Appeal (LCA) no. 238/17.1PKSNT.L1-5 (15 June 2021), *dgsi.pt*.

[2]Cf. European Court of Human Rights (2020); Fanego (2012), p. 172; ECtHR Dan v. Moldova, no. 8999/07 (5 July 2011), § 30, *hudoc.echr.coe.int*.

R. do Rosário (✉)
University of Lisbon School of Law, Research Centre for Criminal Law and Criminal Sciences (CIDPCC), Lisbon, Portugal
e-mail: ritaalexandredorosario@fd.ulisboa.pt

H. Morão, R. Tavares da Silva (eds.), *Fairness in Criminal Appeal*,
https://doi.org/10.1007/978-3-031-13001-4_4

4.2 The Audio Recordings Model

The 1998 reform of the Portuguese Criminal Procedure Code (PCPP) gave a broader scope to appeals on matters of fact—no longer limited to judgments that suffered one of the defects listed in the Article 410 § 2[3] or were dependent on the renewal of evidence—, extending the appeal court's competence to scrutinize matters of fact and matters of law (Articles 410 and 428) based on the evidence produced in the first instance, which was necessarily documented: the renewal of evidence [Articles 430 § 1[4] and 431 § c)] has become, at this point, limited to cases when the analysis of that previous data is not sufficient for this purpose. Nevertheless, most of the Portuguese case law restricts the review of the appealed decisions concerning facts to cases that present notorious errors in that assessment.

Furthermore, the Portuguese criminal procedure law prescribes the video or audio recordings of the oral statements presented in the first instance, which is, however, regarded by the ECtHR as an insufficient guarantee of fairness in the context of the criminal appeal (Gómez Olmeda v. Spain).[5]

There are two main avenues to challenge matters of fact while appealing: a limited appraisal of certain defects and a broader appeal on factual matters.[6]

On one hand, the appeal on a matter of law can be based on the mere invocation of the errors of judgment set out in Article 410 § 2 of the PCPP, pointing out the insufficiency of the proven facts for the contested decision [Article 410 § 2 a)],[7] on irremediable contradictions in the reasoning or between the reasoning and the decision [Article 410 § 2 b)],[8] or on a notorious error in the assessment of the

[3]This is: if there was an insufficiency of evidence for the decision concerning the facts established or unproven, an irremediable contradiction in the reasoning, or a notorious error in the assessment of the evidence.

[4]Cf. Albuquerque (2011) p. 1168, note n° 3.

[5]Cf. Gómez Olmeda v. Spain, no. 61112/12 (29 March 2016), §§ 33–40, *hudoc.echr.coe.int*.

[6]As explained in, for example, Cunha (2019a, b, c), Mata-Mouros (2020), and Silva (2020).

[7]That is, the facts proven are insufficient to support the decision of law, and the court, while being able to do so, failed to investigate or comment on facts relevant to the decision of the case, alleged by the prosecution or the defence, or that resulted from the hearing or should have been determined therein due to their relevance to the decision, cf. Supreme Court of Justice (SCJ) no. 1748/02-5ª (3 July 2002), 03P3566 (18 March 2004), 07P2268 (21 June 2007); LCA no. 207/18.4GALNH.L1-5 (12 October 2021), 1851/20.5PFLSB.L1-5 (9 November 2021), 346/08.0ECLSB.L1-3 (11 November 2009) and 1229/17.8PAALM.L1-5 (16 November 2021), all at *dgsi.pt*; and Santos and Leal-Henriques (2002), p. 69; Silva (2009), p. 340.

[8]Concerning a contradiction between the proven facts, but also between the proven and unproven facts, as well as between the evidentiary reasoning for the factual material or even between the reasoning for the decision and the factual decision (cf. LCA no. 1063/14.7IDLSB.L1-5, 26 January 2021, *dgsi.pt*; Santos and Leal-Henriques (2002), pp. 71–73), according to logic, on the basis of the text of the decision, either alone or in conjunction with the rules of common experience: those contradictions must be such that the appeal court concludes it does not support the decision contested, makes it fundamentally insufficient or even justifies the opposite decision (cf. SCJ 1748/02-5ª, 2 July 2002, *dgsi.pt*). This error constitutes a decision-making anomaly, at the level

evidence [Article 410 § 2 c)],[9] provided that the defect can be observed through the *simple examination of the text* of the contested decision,[10] alone or in conjunction with the rules of common experience. This appeal can result in the upholding of the appealed decision, a new decision based on the correction of that error [Article 431 § a)], the renewal of the evidence [Article 430 § 1 and, in case of modification of the contested decision, Article 431 § c)][11] or, faced with the impossibility to decide, in the referral of the case for a new trial (Article 426 § 1).[12]

On the other hand, the extended appeal on factual matters is grounded on errors of judgment detectable by the *reconsideration of the evidence* produced and evaluated in the hearing of the first instance, concerning facts considered incorrectly judged [Article 412 § 3 a)], discrepancies between certain facts and the contested decision [Article 412 § 3 b)],[13] or the necessity for the renewal of evidence [Article 412 §

---

of the drafting of the sentence, limited to the factual matter, cf. LCA no. 1851/20.5PFLSB.L1-5 (9 November 2021), 346/08.0ECLSB.L1-3 (11 November 2009) and 1229/17.8PAALM.L1-5 (16 November 2021), all at *dgsi.pt*; and Santos and Leal-Henriques (2002), p. 69.

[9] This error occurs when an average person, in view of the content of the contested decision, alone or in conjunction with common sense, easily realizes that the court, while analysing the evidence: violated the rules of experience; assessed the evidence in a manner that is manifestly incorrect, inappropriate, or based on illogical, arbitrary or even contradictory arguments; or infringed the rules of evidence or *leges artis*, cf. LCA no. 1851/20.5PFLSB.L1-5 (9 November 2021), *dgsi.pt*. The notorious nature of the error refers to the idea that the error would not go unnoticed by the common citizen, the average man, or, from another perspective, by the 'normal' judge due to their gross, ostensible, or evident form, cf. LCA no. 5972/08.4TDLSB.L1-3 (21 February 2018), 1063/14.7IDLSB.L1-5 (26 January 2021), 333/14.9 TELSB.L1-3 (24 November 2021) and 943/17.2JFLSB.L1-5 (21 December 2021); Porto Court of Appeal (PCA) no. 0342994 (12 November 2003), and 0413844 (2 February 2005); Guimarães Court of Appeal (GCA) no. 895/05-1ª (27 June 2005), and 625/06 (27 April 2006); Coimbra Court of Appeal (CCA) no. 26/16.2GESRT.C1 (10 July 2018); SCJ no. 98P930 (3 March 1999), 03P4043 (24 March 2004) and 230/10.7JAAVR.P1.S1 (29 October 2015), all at *dgsi.pt*; and Santos and Leal-Henriques (2002), p. 77; Rainho (2006), pp. 145 et seq.

[10] See, among many others, LCA no. 943/17.2JFLSB.L1-5 (21 December 2021), *dgsi.pt*: '(. . .) they are defects of the decision and not of judgment, not to be confused with the error in the application of the law to the facts, nor with the wrong assessment and assessment of the evidence or its insufficiency for the decision rendered in fact (. . .)', free translation. About this subject, see Gonçalves (2009), p. 873; Silva (2009), p. 339; Santos and Leal-Henriques (2002), pp. 77 et seq.; SCJ no. 06P3649 (5 June 2008), and 1182/06.3PAALM.S1 (14 May 2009), and LCA no. 207/18.4GALNH.L1-5 (12 October 2021), all at *dgsi.pt*. cf. LCA no. 9590/11.1TDLSB.L2-5 (1 June 2021), *dgsi.pt*.

[11] If the text of the contested decision is enough to sustain that, cf. LCA no. 9590/11.1TDLSB.L2-5 (1 June 2021), *dgsi.pt*.

[12] Cf. LCA no. 207/18.4GALNH.L1-5 (12 October 2021), *dgsi.pt*: 'it concerns the impossibility of allowing any decision according to the various plausible solutions to the issue. If the proven facts allow a decision, even if with a different orientation from the one pursued, we are not facing the insufficiency for the decision of the proven factual matter, but, eventually, in the face of an error in judgment and in the subsumption of the proven facts to the law', free translation.

[13] Cf. LCA no. 510/19.6S5LSB.L1-5 (26 October 2021), and 7/17.9PHFUN.L2-5 (23 November 2021), and SCJ no. 07P21 (14 March 2007), 07P1498 (23 May 2007), 08P1312 (3 July 2008), 07P1016 (29 October 2008), and 08P3269 (20 November 2008), all at *dgsi.pt*.

3 c)]. Here, the appeal court can decide, or not, to change the appealed decision [Article 431 § b)].[14] This is not, however, a second trial or a way to reconsider the entire body of evidence previously produced,[15] but rather a reappraisal of the contested factual matter, by listening to or analysing the evidence specifically indicated by the appellant,[16] even though the court of appeal is able to hear and view other passages than those indicated (Article 412 § 6). Even so, the generally accepted rule that the modification of the appealed decision regarding facts can only be achieved when the data at hand *imposes* a certain conclusion indicates that the second instance only aims to correct glaring, evident, and obvious errors in the assessment of the evidence produced in the first instance,[17] this is, to detect and

---

[14] Cf. LCA no. 947/10.6PEAMD.L1-5 (31 January 2012), *dgsi.pt*: 'The reassessment of the evidence is an adjective way that opens as a result of the challenge of fact operated in compliance with the respective legal ritualism, which in turn is one of the ways to legitimize its modification under the terms of Article 431', free translation.

[15] Cf. LCA no. 333/14.9 TELSB.L1-3 (24 November 2021), *dgsi.pt*: '(. . .) the guarantee of the double degree of the jurisdiction in matters of fact does not aim at the systematic and global reassessment of all the evidence produced in the hearing, but only at the detection and correction of specific and concrete errors of judgment, focusing on certain facts', free translation.

[16] These facts must be identified, along with the respective time excerpts of the audio recordings, in order to determine what, in the factual scope, the appellant intends to see reconsidered and thus assure the objective de limitation of the appeal and its motivation.

This does not always mean, however, that the lack of those specifications has an irremediably preclusive effect, when is still perceptible, from the content of the motivation, which points of fact are in dispute and the evidence that, in the applicant's view, would lead to a different decision from the defendant, as a preliminary rejection of the appeal, without being given the opportunity to the appellant to make up for such deficiency, as this would be unconstitutional, for violation of Article 32 § 1 of the Constitution of the Portuguese Republic. Indeed, the court of appeal 'is not prevented from knowing of its own motion all errors that do not imply *reformatio in pejus*, even those not specified, since in criminal proceedings rules the principle of material truth and, when the freedom of the citizen whose innocence is constitutionally protected until the conviction becomes final, there is no need to impose formal obstacles to avoid a miscarriage of justice', cf. SCJ no. 07P1397 (17 May 2007), *dgsi.pt*, free translation.

In the other hand, granting an opportunity to perfect the motivation if often refused, since the order for improvement would be equivalent to granting a new period to appeal, which is not comprised in the right to appeal (Article 417 § 4 PCPP).

About this constitutional problem, see Portuguese Constitutional Court (PCC) Rulings no. 320/02, 529/2003, 322/04, 199/2005, 357/2006 and 685/2020, all at *tribunalcostitucional.pt*; Ruling to Standardize Case Law of the SCJ no. 3/2012, in D.R. no. 77, Series I, 18 April 2012; SCJ no. 2263/01 (26 September 2001), 2374/01 (18 October 2001), 153/00 (10 April 2002), 1255/02 (5 June 2002), 3286/04-5 (7 October 2004), 4716/04-5 (17 February 2005), 2951/05-5 (15 December 2005), 185/06-3ª (8 March 2006), 3518/06-3° (10 January 2007), 3460/07 (5 December 2007) and 2894/08-3° (15 October 2008); PCA no. 579/08.9SJPRT.P1 (19 October 2011); GCA no. 159/11.5PAPTL.G1 (23 March 2015); LCA no. 288/09.1GBMTJ.L1-5 (29 March 2011), 220/15.3PBAMD.L1-9 (8 October 2015) and 1063/14.7IDLSB.L1-5 (26 January 2021); *dgsi.pt*.

[17] See, amongst many others, SCJ no. 07P21 (14 March 2007), 07P1498 (23 May 2008) and 08P1312 (3 July 2008); CCA no. 11/13.6PBCVL.C1 (28 January 2015); Évora Court of Appeal (ECA) no. 212/04.8TACTX.E1 (15 March 2011) and 441/10.5TABJA.E2 (19 May 2015); GCA no. 159/11.5PAPTL.G1 (23/03/2015); LCA no. 5972/08.4TDLSB.L1-3 (21 February 2018), 477/

correct errors of judgment, 'not to serve as means of replacing a plausible conviction with adequate probative support for another one, even if equally plausible and possible': the evidence must *impose*—not simply *permit*[18]—other decision than the appealed one, reached with the benefit of immediacy[19] and according to the rules of logic, science, and common experience.[20]

This observation must be confronted with the idea behind the audio recordings model, which is the intent to allow for a true appeal on matters of fact, enabling the court of appeal to compare the documented personal evidence with the conclusions on fact affirmed by the first instance: this provides the court with the data to fully analyse the issues of fact, safeguarding the rights of defence and fair trial.[21]

Consequently, the Portuguese Appeal Courts follow one of three main options: to conclude, employing reading the decision of the first instance, that there is no defect regarding the matter of fact and, therefore maintain its decision; to amend the appealed decision on the matter of fact, using the recordings as a form of attenuated immediacy;[22] or, to refer the case for a new trial to ensure the immediacy that characterizes the first instance process.

According to the ECtHR recent case law, the immediacy principle requires the second possibility to be based on the direct re-examination of the witnesses, which can only be attained through the renewal of the testimony.

As we'll demonstrate, Portuguese case law, following the 1998 legislator, treats the renewal of evidence as a residual solution, and carries out, in its place, an autonomous reassessment of the reasonableness of the decision taken by the court *a quo* regarding the facts that the appellant considers having been incorrectly judged, evaluating whether the evidence indicated by the latter imposes a different decision.[23]

This first impression is not, however, enough to draw a solid conclusion about its conformity, or lack thereof, with the ECtHR's interpretation of the immediacy principle. Indeed, a further investigation is necessary, regarding the acceptance of that idea as a generalized criterion, its possible different authority in appeals of

20.8PDAMD.L1-5 (2 November 2021) and 275/21.1PQLSB.L1-5 (3 May 2022), all at *dgsi.pt*. See also Dias (1989), p. 202; Cunha (2002), p. 37.

[18] The contested decision can only be changed if the evidence indicated obliges to another conclusion, thus excluding from the powers of the Court of Appeal the opportunity to choose when the evidence allows for two or more outcomes. Indeed, in these cases, the previous decision must be upheld by the court of appeal, provided that the first is duly substantiated and fits within the possible solutions consistent with the rules of common experience, as this ensures its compatibility with the impositions of the law (Articles 127 and 374 § 2 of the PCPP), cf. ECA no. 360/08-1.ª (1 April 2008).

[19] Cf. ECA no. 145/13.7GAMCQ.E1 (5 July 2016), *dgsi.pt*, free translation.

[20] Cf. PCA no. 250/12.7TAVFR.P2 (24 May 2017), *dgsi.pt*.

[21] Cf. SCJ no. 07P1397 (17 May 2007), *dgsi.pt*.

[22] Cf. Morão (2021), p. 188, and, as the Author mentions, Albuquerque (2011), p. 945; Brito (2008), p. 391; Brito (2013), p. 61.

[23] Cf. LCA no. 220/15.3PBAMD.L1-9 (8 October 2015), *dgsi.pt*.

convictions or acquittals, and its potential contending with the *in dubio pro reo* principle.

4.3 The Predominance of the Dismissal of the Appeal

Differently from what has been enforced by the ECtHR, a significant number of the Portuguese Courts of Appeals' case law appears, as mentioned, to adopt a conservative approach, only changing the facts considered proven or unproven by the previous courts when the evidence absolutely *imposes* a different decision.

There are three key factors—different conceptual ideas, but that are interconnected—to this tendency for dismissal: the principle of free assessment of evidence,[24] the limited scope of the appeal concerning factual matters, and the development of the audio recordings model, which derive from and contribute to the immediacy principle and its relevance on these appeals.

The free assessment of evidence principle (Article 127 of the PCPP) allows for a personal uptake of the evidence,[25] asserting the first instance as the true stage of the trial and the preferable decider of factual matters. This aspect lessens the space for disagreement regarding that assessment, provided that the ultimate decision is grounded in understandable and coherent arguments, respectful of the normality of life, delivering a logical and rational basis for the option taken from among the plausible solutions.[26]

The limited power of the Portuguese Appeal Courts is not merely a dogmatic choice, since it has, precisely, been attached to the lack of immediacy in the court of appeal, where it is not possible to fully replicate the experience of the testimony given at trial, characterized by orality and direct contact between the judge and the elements of the case evidence (whether they are people, things, places, sounds, smells, timbre, or intonation): this personal, face-to-face, direct and immediate interaction makes it easier for the judge to form his own free conviction.[27]

[24] Although, in some cases, the jurisprudence rejects the relevance of this principle for the limitation of the powers of cognition of the court of appeal, cf. LCA no. 8428/2007-3 (10 October 2007), *dgsi.pt*: '11. What, in our view, limits the powers of the court of the second instance in the appeal regarding the matter of fact is not the principle of free assessment of the evidence, but the lack of immediacy and orality that, after the 1998 reform, in most cases, occurs', free translation.

[25] Cf. Dias (2004), pp. 203–205.

[26] See, for example, the PCC no. 391/2015, *tribunalcostitucional.pt*, and LCA no. 275/21.1PQLSB.L1-5 (3 May 2022), 238/17.1PKSNT.L1-5 (15 June 2021) and 1851/20.5PFLSB.L1-5 (9 November 2021), all at *dgsi.pt*.

This rational and critical assessment follows the common rules of logic, reason, maxims of experience and scientific knowledge (cf. LCA no. 238/17.1PKSNT.L1-5, 15 June 2021, *dgsi.pt*), as it is a freedom for objectivity (LCA no. 7360/19.8T9SNT. L1-3, 24 November 2021, *dgsi.pt*).

[27] Cf. LCA no. 275/21.1PQLSB.L1-5 (3 May 2022), *dgsi.pt*, where is explained how 'the statements are also inseparable from the attitude and posture of the person who makes them, looks, gestures, hesitations, pauses and other behavioural reactions to the various questions and issues

Lastly, the adoption of mechanisms that facilitate the indirect re-examination of evidence[28] such as audio recordings (Article 364) creates an opportunity for the court of appeal to assess the process and reasoning by which the first instance materialized its decision on a factual matter. In such matters, 'it is only for the court of appeal to verify, and control, whether the court *a quo*, in forming its conviction, made good use of the principle of free assessment of the evidence, assessing the legality of the path followed to arrive at the factual matter considered proved and unproven, given that such an assessment must be based on the motivation elaborated by the Court of the first instance, on the grounds for its choice—that is, on compliance with the provided for in Article 374 § 2 of the Criminal Procedure Code'.[29]

These circumstances reinforce the aforementioned perspective upheld by the national Courts of Appeals,[30] although a more proactive stance can be found in some cases.[31] The immediacy principle is, therefore, associated with the appeal

addressed, isolated, or combined, as well as the rules of experience and common sense in the light of the normality of human behaviour. (. . .) observation takes due account of the community assessment and the individual examination of all those involved in the case, before the court and during the hearing, with all the relevant and intrinsic advantages to the immediacy, resulting, without any reservation, in factors that are impossible to control after the respective closure', free translation.

Additionally, see, amongst many others, SCJ no. 07P4729 (13 February 2008) and 08P3269 (20 November 2008); PCA no. 0314013 (21 April 2004); CCA no. 1019/05.0OGCVIS.C1 (18 February 2009), 9/05.8TAAND.C1 (2 June 2009), 2354/08.1PBCBR.C2 (10 November 2010), and 102/10.5 TAANS.C1 (9 January 2012); GCA no. 732/11.8JABRG.G1 (16 May 2016); and LCA no. 8428/2007-3 (10 October 2007), *dgsi.pt*: 'The 1st instance saw and heard the accused, the witnesses and the experts, appreciated their non-verbal behaviour, formulated the questions they considered relevant in the way they considered to be most convenient and confronted these people with the pre-constituted evidence indicated by the procedural subjects, all faculties that the court of appeal, at least when the renewal of evidence is not required, cannot benefit. (. . .) the court of the 2nd instance does not have the same powers regarding the appeal of matters of fact that the 1st instance had. It can only change the decision therein if the evidence provided by the appellant imposes a decision different from the one handed down [Article 412 § 3 (b)]', free translation.

[28] Not in a sense of full review of the body of evidence produced in the contested decision—not a retrial—, but only to verify whether the facts challenged are supported by its reasoning, cf. LCA no. 275/21.1PQLSB.L1-5 (3 May 2022), and SCJ no. 07P21 (14 March 2007), 07P1498 (23 May 2007), 08P1312 (3 July 2008), 07P1016 (29 October 2008), and 08P3269 (20 November 2008), all at *dgsi.pt*.

[29] Cf. LCA no. 275/21.1PQLSB.L1-5 (3 May 2022), *dgsi.pt*, free translation. These considerations have been repeated in most cases where factual matters are appealed. See also, as mere examples, SCJ no. 07P4375 (12 June 2008) and LCA no. 404/07.8GTALQ.L1-5 (1 March 2011), *dgsi.pt*.

[30] Dias (1989), pp. 140 et seq.

[31] In this sense, see SCJ no. 07P1397 (17 May 2007), *dgsi.pt*: 'in the control of matters of fact, the principles of free assessment of evidence and immediacy, which are at the heart of the decision of the first instance, should not be neglected, but such principles are not an insurmountable obstacle, rather one of the many factors that the court of appeal must consider when modifying or not the proven facts', free translation.

court's limitations in terms of the cognitive power to assess whether the evidence imposes a different decision from the one handed down by the appealed court.[32]

4.3.1 The Limited Appeal of Factual Matter (Article 410 § 2 of the PCPP)

Although the appeal based on defects mentioned in Article 410 § 2 of the PCPP is not primarily a true appeal on facts, but instead on the reasoning of the written decision, in most of the case law reviewed it's fairly common for appellants to try to base their disagreement on the interpretation of the evidence produced calling on one of those defects.

Much of the Portuguese court of appeal's case law on appeals concerning factual matters denies changing the previous decision, especially when the appellant doesn't require the renewal of the evidence.[33] In most cases, the appeal court considers that the appealed decision was based on consistent reasoning, respecting the rules of experience,[34] logic, and criteria related to the normality of life.

Moreover, the principles of orality and immediacy are expressly noted by the appeal courts as the basis of the idea that the decision regarding facts is unassailable unless its reasoning is completely beyond all the plausible solutions according to the rules of experience[35] or, despite all evidence collected, cannot surpass the standard

---

[32] Cf. LCA no. 4622/15.7TDLSB.L1-3 (22 May 2019), 1063/14.7IDLSB.L1-5 (26 January 2021) and 1851/20.5PFLSB.L1-5 (9 November 2021); and SCJ no. 4375/07-3.ª (12 June 2008), all at *dgsi.pt*.

[33] See, amongst countless examples, LCA no. 333/14.9 TELSB.L1-3 (24 November 2021), and 1229/17.8PAALM.L1-5 (16 November 2021), both at *dgsi.pt*.

[34] As general criteria based on life experience—arguments that help explain what is normal to happen, knowing, however, that the particular cases can fall outside the typical, cf. Mendes (2010), pp. 1002 and 1011.

See, also, SCJ no. 233/08.1PBGDM.P3.S1 (9 February 2012): 'The rules of experience or rules of life as empirical teachings that the simple fact of living gives us in relation to human behaviour and that is obtained through a generalization of several concrete cases tend to be repeated or reproduced as soon as the same facts that supported the generalization happen.

'These considerations facilitate the logic of judicial reasoning since it is based on the probable similarity of human conduct carried out in similar circumstances, unless something else results in the specific case being analysed, either because of the existence of something that points in the opposite direction is demonstrated or because experience or insight indicates a contrary conclusion', free translation.

[35] Cf. ECA no. 871/06-1 (4 July 2006) and LCA no. 275/21.1PQLSB.L1-5 (3 May 2022), both at *dgsi.pt*.

See also LCA no. 1063/14.7IDLSB.L1-5 (26 January 2021), *dgsi.pt*, in which it was emphasized the necessity, in other to apply Article 410 § 2 of the PCPP, to find a manifestly incorrect or inadequate assessment, based on illogical, arbitrary, or contradictory arguments. In this, the court of appeal ultimately followed the provision of Article 412 § 3 b).

of belief beyond a reasonable doubt, therefore nor can they be considered as proven.[36]

4.3.2 *The Global Appraisal of Facts Relating to the Guilt or Innocence of the Defendant (Article 412 § 3 of the PCPP)*

When the appeal proposes the reconsideration of the factual matter (Article 412 § 3 of the PCPP), the appellant indicates the evidence which supports that decision. Most appeals regarding this problem are dismissed, upholding the contested decision.

As explained in Part 1, this appraisal is limited,[37] since the appellant must comply with the aforementioned specification burden, restricting the re-examination to those facts—in the sense of being restricted to the inquiry, point by point, of the existence or not of the concrete errors of judgment of fact pointed out by the applicant, correcting it if necessary.

In addition, the Portuguese case law demonstrates, as mentioned above, the denial of the second instance as a place for an entirely new evaluation of the evidence as if it were a second trial, as well as the natural lack of orality and immediacy, limiting the 'contact' with the personal evidence to what appears in the recordings.[38]

Most significantly, the rule that when deciding an appeal of a factual matter the court of appeal cannot change the contested decision unless the evidence *imposes* that modification[39]—this is, the reversal of the first instance decision as the appealed decision is inadmissible under the rules of common experience[40]—exponentially increases the number of cases of dismissal. In these instances, the appeal court

---

[36]Cf. Dias (2004), p. 213; Monteiro (1997), p. 53; SCJ no. 07P4198 (10 January 2008), *dgsi.pt*.

[37]These limits have been consolidated since the SCJ no. 07P4375 (12 June 2008), *dgsi.pt*.

[38]Cf. LCA no. 1884/06.4TABRR.L1-5 (15 December 2009), *dgsi.pt*: although it is natural to have different versions of the facts from the defendant and the assistant, in the first instance the court weights all those elements, and assesses their greater or lesser likelihood, often trying to detect the reactions of the witnesses the very resonance of the truth and evaluating their credibility. The appeal court, however, does not have the opportunity to access the type of mimicry of a personal nature, unless those more personal reactions have a significant impact on the voice, which can then be heard through the audio recordings.

See, also, LCA no. 3802/20.8T9LSB.L1-3 (23 February 2022), 844/20.7PBOER.L1-3 (16 March 2022) and 275/21.1PQLSB.L1-5 (3 May 2022), *dgsi.pt*.

[39]Cf. LCA no. 8428/2007-3 (10 October 2007), 257/18.0GCMTJ.L1-3 (3 March 2021) and 1211/18.8T9TVD.L1-5 (11 July 2019); ECA no. 360/08-1.ª (1 April 2008); and SCJ no. 07P4375 (12 June 2008), all at *dgsi.pt*. Most of the decisions of appeal courts regarding Article 412 § 3 of the PCPP relate these limitations in such terms.

[40]Cf. LCA no. 1229/17.8PAALM.L1-5 (16 November 2021); PCA no. 0314013 (dared 21 April 2004); and CCA no. 1019/05.0OGCVIS.C1 (18 February 2009), 2354/08.1PBCBR.C2 (11 November 2010) and 102/10.5 TAANS.C1 (9 January 2012), all at *dgsi.pt*.

reconsiders the evidence for the facts disputed—namely by reading the verdict and listening to the recorded personal evidence[41]—, reflects on the arguments proposed by the appellant, and highlights the absence of the intended defects, like incoherence, contradictions, arbitrariness, or doubts about the veracity of the facts.[42]

The most common ground for the dismissal of the appeals regarding factual matters in the broad modality prescribed in Article 412 § 3 is related to the lack of detailed reasoning for the intended modification, as is the appellant's burden[43]—that is, the specific facts that are considered incorrectly judged [Article 412 § 3 a)], the concrete evidence that imposes a different decision than the contested one [Article 412 § 3 b)], and/or the evidence that must be renewed [Article 412 § 3 c)], as well as referring the exact excerpts from depositions or testimony that, in their opinion, require the change of the factual matter, transcribing them or indicating the segments of the audio recordings that support their assessment. Instead, appellants often limit their arguments to the presentation of a generic alternative narrative to the factual description provided in the judgment, based on their testimony.[44] This is, essentially, a problem of divergence between the personal conviction of the appellant about the evidence produced at the hearing and the one that the first instance court established, which encloses a question on the assessment of evidence, hence, answered by the provision of Article 127[45] and rarely called into question, as this appeal is conceived as a legal remedy for the correction of errors[46] duly identified by the parties, and not as an instrument of jurisprudential refinement.[47]

As a result, this review of evidence is constrained to controlling the decision-making process of the first instance and the application of the principle of free assessment of the evidence, always taking as a point of reference the motivation of the decision and evaluating whether the conviction expressed by the Court under appeal has adequate support in what the recording of the evidence (with the other elements existing in the case file) can show before.[48]

---

[41] Cf. LCA no. 1211/18.8T9TVD.L1-5 (11 July 2019), *dgsi.pt.*

[42] Cf. LCA no. 636/17.0GDALM.L1-5 (11 February 2020) and 9590/11.1TDLSB.L2-5 (1 June 2021), both at *dgsi.pt.*

[43] This burden can't be transferred to the appeal court by way of inviting the appellant to perfect it, as it is a problem regarding the structure of the motivation, equivalent to the total lack of motivation, affecting the scope of the appeal, cf. LCA no. 207/18.4GALNH.L1-5 (12 October 2021), 1229/17.8PAALM.L1-5 (16 November 2021) and 333/14.9 TELSB.L1-3 (24 November 2021); and SCJ no. 3286/04 (7 October 2004) and 04P4324 (17 February 2005), all at *dgsi.pt*; and also the PCC no. 259/2002 and 140/2004, both at *tribunalconstitucional.pt.*

[44] There is a multitude of examples, including LCA no. 7360/19.8T9SNT. L1-3 (24 November 2021), *dgsi.pt.*

[45] Cf. LCA no. 207/18.4GALNH.L1-5 (12 October 2021), *dgsi.pt.*

[46] Cf. SCJ no. 240/03-5 (20 February 2003), *dgsi.pt.*

[47] Amongst numerous examples, cf. LCA no. 257/18.0GCMTJ.L1-3 (3 March 2021), *dgsi.pt.*

[48] Along with others, cf. LCA no. 257/18.0GCMTJ.L1-3 (3 March 2021), SCJ no. 08P3978 (27 January 2009) and 08P3269 (20 November 2008, all at *dgsi.pt*; Santos and Leal-Henriques (2002), p. 105.

In the significant majority of cases, the appeal court concludes for the validity of the appealed decision, since it has been made by resorting to 'valid and justified intellectual operations and with respect for the procedural rules concerning the evidence'.[49]

4.4 The Grant of the Appeal on a Factual Matter

4.4.1 Based on the Analysis of the Written Contested Decision (Article 410 § 2 of the PCPP)

Although limited, there are some cases in which the mere analysis of the appealed reasoning about factual matters supported a change based on an error established in Article 410 § 2 of the PCPP,[50] with the resulting modification of the decision [Articles 428 and 431 § b)].

One of the most significant cases where a Portuguese Appealed Court adopted the bold solution to overturn the previous decision is the Lisbon Court of Appeal decision of April 26th of 2012,[51] which promoted a judgment against Portugal by the ECtHR, in Paixão Moreira Sá Fernandes v. Portugal,[52] for convicting the defendant for the first time at second instance, while not adducing the evidence directly.[53]

The first instance decision—in which the defendant had been acquitted—was criticized by the Lisbon Court of Appeal (under its scope, as provided for in Article 428 of the PCPP) and declared null and void, as incurred the defect of the notorious error in the assessment of evidence according to the provided for in Articles 374 § 2,[54] and 379 § 1, a), of the PCPP for lack of critical reasoning for the ruling of some facts as unproven—that the defendant had acted 'well knowing the prohibited and

[49] As it was found in the LCA no. 3793/09.6TDLSB.L1-9 (21 May 2015), *dgsi.pt.*

[50] One example is the LCA no. 339/14.8 PGLRS.L1-9 (21 May 2020), *dgsi.pt*, where the LCA noted that the court *a quo* had considered, against the defendant, evidence that was not actually in the case file, pointing out the notorious error in the assessment of the evidence, easily detectable by the analysis of a man of average education. Consequently, the appeal court stated that the situation in question required resorting to the *principle in dubio pro reo*, in order not to harm the defendant, since there is no evidence to overcome the existing reasonable doubt. As this fact was essential to ascertain the guilt of the defendant, he was then acquitted.

[51] Cf. LCA no. 914/07.7TDLSB.L1-9 (26 April 2012), *dgsi.pt.*

[52] Cf. ECtHR Paixão Moreira Sá Fernandes v. Portugal, no. 78108/14 (25 February 2020), *hudoc.echr.coe.int.*

[53] According to the ECtHR, the LCA violated, with this decision, the benefit of fair proceedings, as well as the required reasoning and impartiality principle (see point no. 107 of the sentencing).

[54] Regarding the requirement for a complete exposition of the reasons on which the decision is based, with an indication and critical examination of the evidence. About this topic, see, for example, SCJ no. 3063/01 (30 January 2002), *dgsi.pt.*

punished nature of his conduct'. The *ex officio* examination of the evidence was conducted under the provision of the Article 410 § 2 c), and the appeal court found that fact sufficiently substantiated by the evidence, with no need for a new hearing of the witness (provided for in the Article 430, §§ 1 and 3), as the conclusion about the referred fact to as proven was deemed as obvious—and, thus, included by the appeal court in the 'Proved matter of fact' list (as permitted in Article 426 § 1, *a contrario sensu*)—, whereas the first instance had concluded the opposite. The previous acquittal was, thus, revoked, and the defendant was convicted for unlawful recording, provided for, and punished in Article 199 § 1 a) and b) of the Criminal Code (CC).

In his submission to the ECtHR, the defendant put forward arguments relating to the fact that he had not been heard directly and, in this way, his right to a fair trial had been violated, particularly regarding his rights to defence and adversarial proceedings. The Portuguese Government, on the other hand, considered the direct re-examination of the evidence—this is, hearing witnesses or the defendant personally—unnecessary, given the obvious answer to the question regarding the knowledge of the unlawfulness of the recordings made by the defendant as positive, as he was a lawyer. As Helena Morão points out, the LCA not only dismissed that opportunity but also reversed the acquittal without listening to the audio recordings of the testimony produced at the trial hearing, basing, instead, this new conviction on the assumption that the defendant must have had, as a lawyer, awareness of the illegal character of his acts, even though this legality was disputed, having, inclusively, been rejected by the appealed court, due to necessity.[55]

Ultimately, the ECtHR condemned the Portuguese State for violating the principles of immediacy in the assessment of evidence and of the impartiality of judges—as in the Article 6 § 1 of the ECHR, citing several examples[56]—, given its failure to

[55] Cf. Morão (2021), p. 185.

[56] Cf. Paixão Moreira Sá Fernandes v. Portugal, *hudoc.echr.coe.int*, no. 59: '(. . .) *dans un certain nombre d'affaires, la Cour a considéré que, lorsqu'une instance d'appel est amenée à connaître d'une affaire en fait et en droit et à étudier dans son ensemble la question de la culpabilité ou de l'innocence, elle ne peut, pour des motifs d'équité de la procédure, décider de ces questions sans appréciation directe des témoignages présentés en personne soit par l'accusé qui soutient qu'il n'a pas commis l'acte tenu pour une infraction pénale (voir, parmi d'autres exemples,* Ekbatani c. Suède, *26 mai 1988, § 32, série A no 134,* Constantinescu c. Roumanie, *no 28871/95, § 55, CEDH 2000-VIII,* Dondarini c. Saint-Marin, *no 50545/99, § 27, 6 juillet 2004*, Igual Coll c. Espagne, *no 37496/04, § 27, 10 mars 2009, et* Zahirović c. Croatie, *no 58590/11, § 63, 25 avril 2013) soit, si elle renverse par une condamnation un verdict d'acquittement prononcé par une instance inférieure, par les témoins ayant déposé pendant la procédure (Găitănaru c. Roumanie, no 26082/05, § 35, 26 juin 2012 et Hogea c. Roumanie, no 31912/04, § 54, 29 octobre 2013)*'; and no. 65: '*Ainsi, la Cour estime que, puisque, dans son arrêt du 26 avril 2012, la cour d'appel de Lisbonne a infirmé le jugement du tribunal de Lisbonne et condamné le requérant pour la première fois au cours de la procédure pénale ouverte contre lui, il aurait fallu que la cour d'appel procède à une administration directe de l'ensemble des preuves qui avaient amené le tribunal de Lisbonne à acquitter le requérant (*Ekbatani, *précité, § 32,* Popovici c. Moldova, *nos 289/04 et 41194/04, § 72, 27 novembre 2007* et Júlíus Þór Sigurþórsson, *précité, § 42) ou qu'elle entende personnellement le requérant (*Gómez Olmeda c. Espagne, *no 61112/12, § 33, 29 mars 2016). La Cour considère*

directly evaluate de defendant's testimony to decide matters of fact and consider the conviction.

4.4.2 The Broad Appeal of a Factual Matter and the Use of Audio and Video Recordings (Article 412 § 3 of the PCPP)

The modification of the contested decision regarding matters of fact [Articles 412 § 3 and 431 § b) of the PCPP] is extremely rare but can occur in circumstances such as 'to take a fact as proven based on the testimony of a witness who said nothing about the matter; to take a fact as proven without any evidence about it having been produced; (. . .) to take a fact as proven based on evidence that has been assessed in violation of the rules of evidence about its force; to take a fact as proven based on a testimony or statement, in which the witness, the accused or the declarant did not state what they are said to have stated in the reasoning; to consider a fact to be proven based on a document which does not contain what has been proven; consider a fact as proven with recourse to judicial presumption outside the conditions in which it could operate'.[57]

As we previously explained (see part 1), the grant of the appeal concerning factual matters is related to unreasonable or even arbitrary judgments in the assessment of the evidence produced.[58]

For this change to take place, the appellant must specify the specific factual points that the appellant considers incorrectly judged [Article 412 § 3 a)], the concrete evidence that imposes a different decision than the contested [Article 412 § 3 b)],[59] and/or the evidence that should be renewed [Article 412 § 3 c)].[60] The appeal is not procedurally valid if the appellant is only seeking to undermine the previous decision, questioning the relevance assigned to certain testimonies rendered at the hearing, and choosing others that align with his interests, as a mere disagreement, without the necessary unequivocal demonstration of the infringement of the rules of

---

donc que le requérant n'a pas bénéficié d'une procédure équitable devant la cour d'appel de Lisbonne'.

[57]Free translation of an excerpt of the LCA no. 275/21.1PQLSB.L1-5 (3 May 2022), *dgsi.pt*, although deciding to uphold the contested decision. In the same way, cf. LCA no. 844/20.7PBOER. L1-3 (16 March 2022), *dgsi.pt*. See, also, Silva (2008), pp. 126–127.

[58]Cf. PCA no. 250/12.7TAVFR.P2 (24 May 2017), *dgsi.pt*.

[59]See for example LCA no. 8428/2007-3 (10 October 2007), 1851/20.5PFLSB.L1-5 (9 November 2021) and 1229/17.8PAALM.L1-5 (16 November 2021), all at *dgsi.pt*. the appellant must specify the content of each means of evidence and explain the reason why such evidence requires a different decision.

[60]This includes the defects provided for in Article 410 § of the CPP and the reasons to believe the renewal will allow avoiding the referral of the case (Article 430), cf. LCA no. 1229/17.8PAALM. L1-5 (16 November 2021), *dgsi.pt*.

experience and disrespect for the basic principles of evidentiary law[61] and the indication of the evidence that *imposes* a different decision than the one contested.[62]

It must be noted that in some cases the validity of appeal regarding factual matter does not, ultimately, cause the revision of the decision of conviction or acquittal, since certain alterations of points of fact may not affect the entire decision, not overturning the conviction or acquittal, but just some elements concerning, for example, the measure of penalty.[63]

4.4.2.1 From Acquittal to Conviction

The amendment of facts that impose a conviction for a crime for which the defendant had been acquitted in the first instance[64] is, understandably, less frequent than the reverse, given the difficulty of justifying a conviction without direct analysis of the evidence and inherent immediacy, unless there is the renewal of evidence.

Nevertheless, some cases can be found[65] in which the audio recordings model demonstrates satisfactory for a new conviction by the court *ad quem*[66] [Articles 428 and 431 § b)], provided there is documentation of the evidence produced, orally, at the hearing in the first instance, and that the appellant indicates the specific facts considered to be incorrectly judged, specifying the concrete evidence (and the concrete passages of the recordings, that is, minute and second) that imposes a different decision (Article 412 § 3 and 4).

On these occasions, the court of appeal listens to the recordings of the personal evidence, compares them to other available evidence and uncontested facts, and confronts the reasoning of the appealed decision with the rules of common experience,[67] as well as all other relevant factors—for example, the disregard of certain

[61] Cf. GCA no. 575/04-1 (28 June 2004); PCA no. 463/09.9JELSB.P1 (6 October 2010); LCA no. 275/21.1PQLSB.L1-5 (3 May 2022), all at *dgsi.pt*.

[62] Cf. LCA no. 275/21.1PQLSB.L1-5 (3 May 2022), *dgsi.pt*.

[63] Cf. CCA no. 232/10.3TACTX.E1 (18 May 2011); ECA no. 232/10.3TACTX.E1 (17 December 2020); LCA no. 698/05.3PDLRS.L1-5 (7 December 2010) and 5972/08.4TDLSB.L1-3 (21 February 2018); PCA no. 469/11.8JAPRT.P1 (15 October 2014), 245/14.6PAVFR.P1 (29 April 2020), 167/17.9T9AGD.P1 (10 March 2021), 901/19.2JAPRT.P1 (19 January 2022) and 613/20.4PDVNG.P1 (16 March 2022), *dgsi.pt*.

[64] On this subject, see Morão (2019).

[65] Cf. LCA no. 4622/15.7TDLSB.L1-3 (22 May 2019), *dgsi.pt*, convicting the defendant of the crime of disobedience [Article 348 § 1 b) of the CC].

[66] Cf. LCA no. 166/20.3PCLRS.L1-9 (11 March 2021), *dgsi.pt*.

[67] Cf. LCA 115/08.7TASPS.L1-5 (19 May 2015), *dgsi.pt*: 'Such facts would result, according to the appellant, from the other facts deemed to have been proven and, also, from the critical and pondered analysis of all the evidence produced at the trial hearing – personal and documentary evidence that he materializes in the respective motivation –, combine with each other and with the rules of common experience and normality of life [Article 412 § 3 b) of the PCPP]', free translation. Based on these factors, the appeal court established the circumstances that determine the *appropriation* as an element of the crime, that this appropriation had occurred, and convicted the defendant for the

facts,[68] problems concerning the credibility of certain witnesses,[69] or the unwarranted application of the principle *in dubio pro reo*,[70] or otherwise unexplainable conclusions.[71]

4.4.2.2 From Conviction to Acquittal

The acquittal of a defendant after being convicted in the first instance appears less problematic, even though the lack of opportunity to be questioned before the court of appeal and this court's ability to exercise immediacy while reconsidering the evidence are materially identical to cases of new convictions: 'the lack of orality and immediacy with the evidence produced in the hearing, the non-experience of the trial as the seat of the adversary, with deprivation of the possibility of intervening in the production of personal evidence, will be, so to speak, epistemological limits to which the Court of Appeal must attend to in its assessment, even though they are no insurmountable barriers to the weighting, specifically and independently, of the evidence call on by the appellant, which may lead to the conclusion that such evidence imposes a judgment different from that contained in the contested decision'.[72]

The limited perspective on the powers of the court of appeal characterizes, as previously mentioned, most of the Portuguese case law concerning the appeal on factual matters.

There are, however, some exceptions: in certain cases, the appeal court has expressed a different approach, arguing that the court of appeal has the 'power-duty to form its own conviction on the facts put in crisis by the appellant', using the principle of the free assessment of evidence to the full extent, without finding itself limited or conditioned by the reasoning that served as the basis for the contested decision, in order to assure the correct assessment of evidence and an effective

---

crime of embezzlement (Article 375 § 1 of the CC). In a similar case, see PCA no. 1771/18.3T9PRT.P1 (12 May 2021), *dgsi.pt*.

[68] Cf. GCA no. 481/17.3GAAMR.G1 (14 October 2019), *dgsi.pt*: 'the Court 'disregarded', in the analysis of the evidence produced, several elements that, according to the rules of experience and logic, it should have considered, in fact, analysing the evidence produced at the hearing, we have that the factual decision was not the correct one, imposing a different and opposite one. (...) Thus, we believe that there is reliable and sufficient evidence of the practice of the facts by the defendant, and there is no doubt – much less irremediable (...) on them, without having to resort to the principle of presumption of innocence to decide the case', free translation.

For another example, see GCA no. 250/20.3GEVCT.G1 (27 September 2021), *dgsi.pt*.

[69] Cf. CCA no. 65/06.1GHCTB.C1 (22 September 2010), *dgsi.pt*.

[70] Cf. CCA no. 79/07.4GCSRT.C1 (15 September 2010), *dgsi.pt*.

[71] Cf. CCA no. 173/11.7GAMMV.C1 (7 March 2012), *dgsi.pt*.

[72] Cf. LCA no. 3773/12.4TDLSB.L1-5 (22 September 2020), *dgsi.pt*, free translation.

double degree of jurisdiction protected by the Constitution (Article 32 § 1).[73] From this point of view, it does not seem sufficient to verify only whether the appealed decision has reasonable support in the testimonies contained in the recordings. According to LCA no. 432/08.6TASCR.L1-3 (17 December 2014), the immediacy is achieved by listening to the recordings, since 'the Court of Appeal is most often able to capture, namely, the pauses in the voice of the deponents, the witness, with their indecisions, inflections voice, lack of coherence in reasoning, understandable weakening of memory, prepared speech, excessive firmness in answers, interest in a certain outcome of the case, discursive contradictions, etc. Indeed, other less ostensible signs may not be captured by the Court of Appeal simply by listening to the recordings or viewing the depositions'.[74]

In another case, the SCJ recognized the ability of the court of appeal to evaluate, for example, the credibility of witnesses, as the assessment of credibility must always be rooted in maxims from common experience, and these can be scrutinized by the higher court.[75] Even though it did not go as far as to affirm a greater power than the mere reconsidering of the reasonability of the assessment of the appealed court, the SCJ acknowledged the need for the investigation to have a 'global view of the reasoning on evidence produced in order to be able to follow the entire deductive process followed by the contested decision in relation to the facts specifically contested'.[76]

The most frequent grounds for acquittal at this stage are the different interpretations of the rules of common experience[77] and the lack of arguments for certain presumptions.[78] Another one of the most common arises from *contradictions* among the multiple testimonies—with various levels of credibility—about central cores of

[73] Cf. LCA no. 432/08.6TASCR.L1-3 (17 December 2014), *dgsi.pt*. In this case the appeal concerning the factual matters didn't succeed, but the analysis made by the court proved a more active approach.

[74] Cf. LCA no. 432/08.6TASCR.L1-3 (17 December 2014), *dgsi.pt*.

[75] Cf. SCJ no. 07P4203 (19 December 2007), *dgsi.pt*: 'the fact that the appealed court has submitted its action to the rule of free conviction and within the limits proposed by those principles does not conflict with the possibility of the Court of Appeal to rule on the verisimilitude of the report of a witness or expert and other means and for to appreciate the emergence of direct or evidential evidence and to control the inductive reasoning there, since we will be facing a question of verisimilitude or plausibility of the conclusions contained in the sentencing', free translation.

[76] Cf. SCJ no. 07P4203 (19 December 2007), *dgsi.pt*, free translation.

[77] Cf. ECA no. 145/13.7GAMCQ.E1 (5 July 2016), *dgsi.pt*, claiming a reductive or oversimplified assessment of the facts. See also PCA no. 7067/15.5T9VNG.P1 (27 April 2022) and LCA no. 16/07.6S6LSB.L1-3, (9 February 2011), both at *dgsi.pt*.

[78] Cf. PCA no. 69/15.3GBMTS.P1 (28 October 2021), *dgsi.pt*: 'there is no objective relationship of normality, of cause and effect, between those indications and the presumption that is drawn from them. (. . .) The aforementioned premises, based on the referred evidential facts, do not allow this conclusion without a serious violation of the rules of experience, and even less without facing the rules for evaluating the evidential evidence and the principle of *in dubio pro reo*, provided for in article 32 of the Constitution, before what would always have to be recognized as an irremediable, reasonable and motivating doubt about that concrete [fact]', free translation.

factual matter, which are ignored or surpassed by the appealed court, rendering the decisions unplausible.[79]

The evaluation of the *credibility* of the testimony is, as previously stated, particularly difficult, given the lack of non-verbal cues that accompany the hearing in person, which is not revived through this mechanism of appeal. Nevertheless, the appeal court supersedes the credibility assessment made by the first instance court, if its basis is inadmissible under the rules of common experience,[80] or if the testimony in question is the only basis for the conclusion about the evidentiary value of a certain fact and is confronted with other factors—for example, other testimony, especially when coming from other defendants[81]—and the reasoning of the appealed court does not support a conviction about those facts beyond all reasonable doubt,[82] or depends on vague testimony.[83]

There are, in recent years, several cases of acquittals (that is, reversal of previous convictions) resulting from appeals on factual matters, frequently correlated with the

[79] Cf. LCA no. 635/17.2T9LRS-5 (23 June 2020), *dgsi.pt*: 'The version of the facts narrated in the indictment does not, therefore, find support in the evidence that was produced at the hearing and, no matter how 'circumscribed' and 'without hesitation' the testimonies were, they do not allow formulating, given the well-known existence of an error in the assessment of evidence, the conclusion reached by the court appealed against, based on a more than minimal requirement regarding the standard of evidence necessary for a criminal conviction, regarding the occurrence of the facts and their authorship by the defendant', free translation.

As another example, see LCA no. 18/14.6PFLRS.L1-5 (29 November 2016), *dgsi.pt.*

See also LCA no. 1623/12.0TACSC.L3-9 (26 January 2017), *dgsi.pt*: 'The reasoning (. . .) is, for the most part, contradictory in the assessment/valuation of the evidence, (. . .) the credibility on which the decision on the test was based has no logical justification and directly collides with the logic and rules of common experience', free translation.

[80] Cf. PCA no. 0314013 (21 April 2004) and LCA no. 168/11.0SNLSB.L1-5 (21 May 2013) and 18/14.6PFLRS.L1-5 (29 November 2016), all at *dgsi.pt.*

[81] Cf. LCA no. 1884/06.4TABRR.L1-5 (15 December 2009), *dgsi.pt.*

[82] Cf. LCA no. 7/17.9PHFUN.L2-5 (23 November 2021) and PCA no. 250/12.7TAVFR.P2 (24 May 2017), both at *dgsi.pt.*

[83] Cf. SCJ no. 07P4198 (10 January 2008), ECA no. 89/15.8GTABF. E2 (13 September 2016); LCA no. 1178/16.7GLSNT.L1-5 (19 October 2021), all at *dgsi.pt*: 'The statements of the offended BB were, in our view, vague on the matter in question, without the matter having been sufficiently questioned at a hearing, with the necessary detail, to define what one and the other - the accused and the offended - concretely said and did, and the offended party's attitude towards the accused (. . .). The matter would need, in our view, further development for us to acquire as a fact that (. . .). In other words: outside the limits of the notorious error in the assessment of the evidence, the appeal of the decision of fact, within the scope of the broad challenge, empowers the Court, which knows the facts, to reassess the evidence, to formulate its free conviction and to determine whether the court of 1st instance, regardless of whether it was subjectively confronted with the situation of doubt, judged a proven fact unfavourable to the defendant despite the fact that the available evidence does not allow it, in a rational and objective manner, in the light of the rules of the experience and/or legal rules or valid principles in matters of evidentiary law, overcome the state of doubt about the reality of the fact (. . .). In the present case, given that evidence beyond all reasonable doubt constitutes the parameter in terms of which the question of evidence must be resolved to allow conviction, it seems to us that there are serious and insurmountable reasons that cannot allow proving points 31, 32 and 42', free translation.

violation of the *in dubio pro reo* principle,[84] as the appeal court struggles to establish a belief about the facts at issue that is beyond all reasonable doubt.[85] Regardless of the availability of audio recordings, analysed in conjunction with other elements of evidence and the first instance reasoning regarding factual matters, the appeal court is faced with doubts that, it claims, should have been recognized by the first instance decision maker so that the court could discern, if any, the concordant or contradictory information. Despite the possibilities of renewal of evidence or resubmission to a new trial provided for in the PCPP—by which those doubts may be resolved, namely, through questioning the witnesses—, the court of appeal acquits the defendant. The connection between these decisions and concerns about immediacy is not clear, hence we can only speculate about the lesser uneasiness being tied to the beneficial effect these decisions have on the defendant—contrasting the problems related to a first conviction at the second instance without the direct examination of the relevant testimonies. This protection of the position of the defendant may be praised when there are legitimate doubts about the facts that sustained the previous conviction. Nonetheless, the material truth and immediacy principles appear to be disregarded in those decisions, as it is not clear whether the doubts at hand could be solved through the aforementioned mechanisms of renewal of evidence or resubmission to trial.

4.5 The Referral of the Case for a New Trial

The solution to refer the case for a new trial allows for a return to immediacy when the errors of the contested decision: it is created a new opportunity to properly evaluate de facts with all the advantages of orality and immediacy.[86]

Even though this solution does not evoke the problems of immediacy at the second instance stage evoked by the ECtHR, its mention is noteworthy, given that is a relatively commonly used tool.[87]

---

[84] Cf. LCA no. 464/10.4PEAMD.L1-5 (15 November 2011), 3773/12.4TDLSB.L1-5 (22 September 2020) and 761/14.0PAALM.L3-5 (11 November 2019), *dgsi.pt*: 'Even if the violation of the principle *in dubio* does not result from the text of the contested decision, alone or in conjunction with the rules of common experience, as a notorious error in the assessment of the evidence [Article 410 § 2 c) of the PCPP], it can be detected in the scope of a broad challenge to the decision rendered on the matter of fact. (...) in view of the reassessment of the evidence, the appealed court did not express doubts, as it should necessarily have, in view of the fragility of the evidence produced regarding the agent of the facts, in the terms mentioned above', free translation. Similarly, see LCA no. 1063/14.7IDLSB.L1-5 (26 January 2021), *dgsi.pt*.

[85] Cf. ECA no. 1164/18.2T9OVR.P1 (29 April 2020); GCA no. 604/12.9JABRG.G1 (5 December 2016), and LCA no. 691/14.5PDAMD.L1-5 (28 November 2017), all at *dgsi.pt*.

[86] Cf. LCA no. 288/09.1 GBMTJ.L1-5 (29 March 2011), *dgsi.pt*.

[87] Cf. ECA no.738/12.0GBABF.E1 (2 July 2013), *dgsi.pt*.

4.6 The Direct Evaluation of the Oral Evidence at the Appeal Hearing

The previously mentioned solution of the renewal of evidence is one way to secure observance of the immediacy principle by which the testimonies are repeated before the court of appeal, assuring the orality of the procedure and the opportunity to ask new questions to the witness that can help to clarify the facts at issue—correcting errors pointed out in the appeal[88]—without an entirely new trial[89] (Article 430 § 1 of the PCPP).

To grant the renewal of evidence, the court of appeal must verify the existence of, at least, one of the defects enshrined in Article 410 § 2 and decide whether the renewal allows avoiding the resubmission of the case for a new trial in the first instance (Article 430).[90]

This expedient 'obeys a fundamental political-criminal double aim: to extend the double degree of the jurisdiction in matters of fact, in addition to the control of the vices of Article 410 § 2, nevertheless, there is no officious renewal, always depending on the request of the appellant or the appealed an only in the case of allegation of the defects provided in § 2 of Article 410 and on the assumption that resorting to such an expedient avoids having the case referred back to the first instance'.[91] This means that the appellant cannot use this mechanism to request the production of evidence that he/she had not asked for in the initial trial.[92]

The limited scope of the renewal—which is restricted to factual matters contested for errors provided for in Article 410 § 2[93]—does not, however, allow for its use to solve problems regarding the broader challenge prescribed in Article 412 § 3, which impairs the immediacy at the appeal level[94] and was criticized by Helena Morão, as there is no valid reason to negate this mechanism in cases that suffer from a different error.[95]

[88]Cf. Albuquerque (2011), pp. 1180–1181.

[89]Cf. Morão (2021), p. 172.

[90]Cf. ECA no. 940/12.4TAABT.E1 (14 July 2020), *dgsi.pt*.

[91]Cf. PCA no. 1582/12.0JAPRT.P1 (25 February 2015), *dgsi.pt*.

[92]In the PCA no. 1582/12.0JAPRT.P1 (25 February 2015), *dgsi.pt*, for example, the appellant requested the questioning of a witness who had provided statements for future memory, in order to clarify what had been said, which was deemed unviable from the outset, as the statement was already known to the defendant/appellant at the time of the hearing in the first instance, the appropriate place to evoke such expedient (Article 340 PCPP).

[93]Cf. PCA no. 1582/12.0JAPRT.P1 (25 February 2015), *dgsi.pt*.

[94]Cf. Morão (2021), p. 174, citing ECtHR's Moreira Ferreira v. Portugal, 5 July 2011.

[95]Cf. Morão (2021), p. 186.

The renewal of evidence has been characterized by Portuguese scholars as a *rule with no application*,[96] with hardly any examples of its use.[97]

This limitation of the use of the renewal of evidence creates a larger difficulty in the fulfilment of the guidelines of the ECtHR, since its use allows for a greater perception of the evidentiary material than listening to the audio recording.[98] This does not mean, however, that our view of the fair trial principle is the exact same as the ECtHR: it is not entirely clear that the repetition of evidence after a significant period of time—at least, long after the moment when it was first produced—creates a better opportunity to assess the truth than the recordings of testimony provided shortly after the facts related.[99]

4.7 Conclusion

The ECtHR guidelines for compliance with the immediacy principle at the appeal level suggest a more interventionist approach regarding the examination of personal evidence relevant to the conviction or acquittal of the defendant. The PCPP allows for such intervention, per the renewal of evidence. This is, however, an untapped tool, giving precedence to the reconsideration of the evidence produced at the initial trial.

Even though the Portuguese case law seldom uses the appeal on factual matters (Article 412 § 3 of the PCPP) to reverse the entirety of the appealed decision, the cases listed in Part 3 uncover the most pressing issues, such as the blatantly disregard for the common rules of experience or different levels of credibility of the witnesses, for which the audio recordings provide sufficient elements.

This standpoint seems to ensure a balance between the need to guarantee a justice system based on material truth and a thorough assessment of the facts, on the one hand, and the need to avoid the inadequacy of solutions in which the appeal is materialized in a second trial, on the other hand.

---

[96] Cf. Morão (2021), p. 186, and, as cited by the Author, Albuquerque (2011), p. 1181; Alves (2009), p. 132; Ramos and Churro (2019), pp. 342–343.

[97] Helena Morão reports a case (LCA no. 29/15.4PAAMD.L1, 25 November 2020, not published) in which the renewal occurred: even though the court rejected this mechanism, since it had not been argued a defect provided in Article 410 § 2 of the PCPP, but heard witnesses at the hearing, in order to discover the truth and decide the appeal correctly, based on Article 340 of the PCPP. This was, indeed, a renewal of the *production* of evidence, cf. Morão (2021), p. 187, footnote no. 33.

[98] Cf. LCA no. 404/07.8GTALQ.L1-5 (1 March 2011), *dgsi.pt*.

[99] See Chaps. 7 and 8.

Cited Case-Law

European Court of Human Rights (ECtHR)

hudoc.echr.coe.int

Ekbatani v. Sweden, no. 10563/83, 26 May 1988
Dondarini v. San Marino, no. 50545/99, 6 July 2004
Igual Coll c. Spain, no 37496/04, 10 March 2009
Zahirović v. Croatia, no. 58590/11, 25 April 2013
Gómez Olmeda v. Spain, no. 61112/12, 29 March 2016
Paixão Moreira Sá Fernandes v. Portugal, no. 78108/14, 25 February 2020

Portuguese Courts of Appeal

dgsi.pt

Coimbra Court of Appeal (CCA)
No. 1019/05.0OGCVIS.C1, 18 February 2009
No. 9/05.8TAAND.C1, 2 June 2009
No. 79/07.4GCSRT.C1, 15 September 2010
No. 65/06.1GHCTB.C1, 22 September 2010
No. 2354/08.1PBCBR.C2, 10 November 2010
No. 2354/08.1PBCBR.C2, 11 November 2010
No. 232/10.3TACTX.E1, 18 May 2011
No. 102/10.5 TAANS.C1, 9 January 2012
No. 173/11.7GAMMV.C1, 7 March 2012
No. 11/13.6PBCVL.C1, 28 January 2015
No. 26/16.2GESRT.C1, 10 July 2018

Évora Court of Appeal (ECA)
No. 871/06-1, 4 July 2006
No. 360/08-1.[a], 1 April 2008
No. 212/04.8TACTX.E1, 15 March 2011
No.738/12.0GBABF.E1, 2 July 2013
No. 441/10.5TABJA.E2, 19 May 2015
No. 145/13.7GAMCQ.E1, 5 July 2016
No. 89/15.8GTABF. E2, 13 September 2016
No. 1164/18.2T9OVR.P1, 29 April 2020
No. 940/12.4TAABT.E1, 14 July 2020
No. 232/10.3TACTX.E1, 17 December 2020

Guimarães Court of Appeal (GCA)
No. 575/04-1, 28 June 2004
No. 895/05-1[a], 27 June 2005
No. 625/06, 27 April 2006
No. 159/11.5PAPTL.G1, 23 March 2015

No. 732/11.8JABRG.G1, 16 May 2016
No. 604/12.9JABRG.G1, 5 December 2016
No. 481/17.3GAAMR.G1, 14 October 2019
No. 250/20.3GEVCT.G1, 27 September 2021

Lisbon Court of Appeal (LCA)
No. 8428/2007-3, 10 October 2007
No. 346/08.0ECLSB.L1-3, 11 November 2009
No. 1884/06.4TABRR.L1-5, 15 December 2009
No. 698/05.3PDLRS.L1-5, 7 December 2010
No. 16/07.6S6LSB.L1-3, 9 February 2011
No. 404/07.8GTALQ.L1-5, 1 March 2011
No. 288/09.1 GBMTJ.L1-5, 29 March 2011
No. 464/10.4PEAMD.L1-5, 15 November 2011
No. 947/10.6PEAMD.L1-5, 31 January 2012
No. 914/07.7TDLSB.L1-9, 26 April 2012
No. 168/11.0SNLSB.L1-5, 21 May 2013
No. 432/08.6TASCR.L1-3, 17 December 2014
No. 3793/09.6TDLSB.L1-9, 21 May 2015
No. 220/15.3PBAMD.L1-9, 8 October 2015
No. 18/14.6PFLRS.L1-5, 29 November 2016
No. 1623/12.0TACSC.L3-9, 26 January 2017
No. 691/14.5PDAMD.L1-5, 28 November 2017
No. 5972/08.4TDLSB.L1-3, 21 February 2018
No. 4622/15.7TDLSB.L1-3, 22 May 2019
No. 1211/18.8T9TVD.L1-5, 11 July 2019
No. 761/14.0PAALM.L3-5, 11 November 2019
No. 636/17.0GDALM.L1-5, 11 February 2020
No. 339/14.8 PGLRS.L1-9, 21 May 2020
No. 635/17.2T9LRS-5, 23 June 2020
No. 3773/12.4TDLSB.L1-5, 22 September 2020
No. 3506/17.9T9LSB.L1, 23 September 2020
No. 29/15.4PAAMD.L1, 25 November 2020 (not published)
No. 1063/14.7IDLSB.L1-5, 26 January 2021
No. 257/18.0GCMTJ.L1-3, 3 March 2021
No. 166/20.3PCLRS.L1-9, 11 March 2021
No. 9590/11.1TDLSB.L2-5, 1 June 2021
No. 238/17.1PKSNT.L1-5, 15 June 2021
No. 1002/18.6PAMTJ.L1-5, 7 September 2021
No. 207/18.4GALNH.L1-5, 12 October 2021
No. 1178/16.7GLSNT.L1-5, 19 October 2021
No. 510/19.6S5LSB.L1-5, 26 October 2021
No. 477/20.8PDAMD.L1-5, 2 November 2021
No. 1851/20.5PFLSB.L1-5, 9 November 2021
No. 1229/17.8PAALM.L1-5, 16 November 2021

No. 7/17.9PHFUN.L2-5, 23 November 2021
No. 333/14.9 TELSB.L1-3, 24 November 2021
No. 7360/19.8T9SNT. L1-3, 24 November 2021
No. 943/17.2JFLSB.L1-5, 21 December 2021
No. 360/20.7JELSB.L1-5, 22 February 2022
No. 3802/20.8T9LSB.L1-3, 23 February 2022
No. 844/20.7PBOER.L1-3, 16 March 2022
No. 275/21.1PQLSB.L1-5, 3 May 2022

Porto Court of Appeal (PCA)

No. 0342994, 12 November 2003
No. 0314013, 21 April 2004
No. 0413844, 2 February 2005
No. 463/09.9JELSB.P1, 6 October 2010
No. 579/08.9SJPRT.P1, 19 October 2011
No. 469/11.8JAPRT.P1, 15 October 2014
No. 1582/12.0JAPRT.P1, 25 February 2015
No. 250/12.7TAVFR.P2, 24 May 2017
No. 245/14.6PAVFR.P1, 29 April 2020
No. 167/17.9T9AGD.P1, 10 March 2021
No. 1771/18.3T9PRT.P1, 12 May 2021
No. 69/15.3GBMTS.P1, 28 October 2021
No. 901/19.2JAPRT.P1, 19 January 2022
No. 613/20.4PDVNG.P1, 16 March 2022
No. 7067/15.5T9VNG.P1, 27 April 2022

Portuguese Supreme Court of Justice (SCJ)

dgsi.pt

No. 98P930, 3 March 1999
No. 2263/01, 26 September 2001
No. 2374/01, 18 October 2001
No. 3063/01, 30 January 2002
No. 153/00, 10 April 2002
No. 1255/02, 5 June 2002
No. 1748/02-5ª, 2 July 2002
No. 1748/02-5ª, 3 July 2002
No. 240/03-5, 20 February 2003
No. 03P3566, 18 March 2004
No. 03P4043, 24 March 2004
No. 0314013, 21 April 2004
No. 3286/04, 7 October 2004
No. 4716/04-5, 17 February 2005
No. 2951/05-5, 15 December 2005
No. 185/06-3ª, 8 March 2006

No. 3518/06-3°, 10 January 2007
No. 07P21, 14 March 2007
No. 07P1397, 17 May 2007
No. 07P1498, 23 May 2007
No. 07P2268, 21 June 2007
No. 3460/07, 5 December 2007
No. 07P4203, 19 December 2007
No. 07P4198, 10 January 2008
No. 07P4729, 13 February 2008
No. 07P1498, 23 May 2008
No. 06P3649, 5 June 2008
No. 07P4375, 12 June 2008
No. 08P1312, 3 July 2008
No. 2894/08-3°, 15 October 2008
No. 07P1016, 29 October 2008
No. 08P3269, 20 November 2008
No. 08P3978, 27 January 2009
No. 233/08.1PBGDM.P3.S1, 9 February 2012
Ruling to Standardize Case Law no. 3/2012, in D.R. no. 77, Series I, 18 April 2012
No. 230/10.7JAAVR.P1.S1, 29 October 2015

Portuguese Constitutional Court (PCC)

tribunalconstitucional.pt

Ruling no. 259/2002
Ruling no. 320/2002
Ruling no. 529/2003
Ruling no. 140/2004
Ruling no. 322/2004
Ruling no. 199/2005
Ruling no. 357/2006
Ruling no. 391/2015
Ruling no. 685/2020

References

Albuquerque P (2011) Comentário do Código de Processo Penal à luz da Constituição da República e da Convenção Europeia dos Direitos do Homem, 4th edn. Universidade Católica Editora, Lisboa

Alves R (2009) Os recursos como indicadores da saúde processual – Querem-se vivos ou mortos? In: Monte M, Calheiros M, Monteiro F, Loureiro F (eds) Que Futuro para o Direito Processual Penal? – Simpósio em Homenagem a Jorge de Figueiredo Dias, por ocasião dos 20 anos do Código de Processo Penal Português. Coimbra Editora, Coimbra, pp 127–134

Brito A (2008) Recursos em processo penal – A interposição do recurso – O recurso da matéria de facto. Revista do Centro de Estudos Judiciários, no. 9 (especial Jornadas sobre a Revisão do Código de Processo Penal – Estudos), pp 383–399

Brito A (2013) Os poderes de cognição das Relações em matéria de facto em processo penal. Terra de Lei. Revista da Associação de Juristas de Pampilhosa da Serra 3:56–64

Cunha J (2002) O caso julgado parcial: questão da culpabilidade e questão da sanção num processo de estrutura acusatória. Universidade Católica, Porto

Cunha J (2019a) Algumas questões do actual regime de recursos em processo penal. Revista Portuguesa de Ciência Criminal 2:261–301

Cunha J (2019b) Sobre o recurso de apelação em processo penal – Alguns pontos susceptíveis de crítica e de necessária reforma. Revista Portuguesa de Ciência Criminal 3:487–504

Cunha J (2019c) Recursos na área penal – a perspetiva académica. In: Centro de Estudos Judiciários (ed) Reforma do Sistema de Recursos. Centro de Estudos Judiciários, Lisboa, pp 73–84

Dias J (1989) Direito Processual Penal. Lições do Prof. Doutor Jorge de Figueiredo Dias, collected by Maria João Antunes, Professor at University of Coimbra School of Law. Faculdade de Direito, Coimbra

Dias J (2004) Direito processual penal, 2nd edn. Coimbra Editora, Coimbra

European Court of Human Rights (2020) Guide on Article 6 of the European Convention of Human Rights – Right to a fair trial (criminal limb), available at *www.echr.coe.int*

Fanego C (2012) The right to a double degree of jurisdiction in criminal offences (Art. 2 P7). In: Roca J, Santolaya P (eds) Europe of rights – a compendium on the European Convention of Human Rights. Martinus Nijhoff Publishers, Leiden/Boston, pp 153–165

Gonçalves M (2009) Código de Processo Penal Anotado – Legislação Complementar, 17th edn. Almedina, Coimbra

Mata-Mouros M (2020) Recurso em matéria de facto no processo penal. In: Albuquerque A (ed) Comentário da Convenção Europeia dos Direitos Humanos e dos Protocolos Adicionais, vol III. Universidade Católica, Lisboa, pp 2394–2422

Mendes P (2010) A Prova Penal e as Regras da Experiência. In: Andrade M, Antunes M, Sousa S (eds) Estudos em Homenagem ao Prof. Doutor Jorge de Figueiredo Dias, vol III. Coimbra Editora, Coimbra, pp 997–1011

Monteiro C (1997) Perigosidade de inimputáveis e 'in dubio pro reo'. Coimbra Editora, Coimbra

Morão H (2019) Sem apelo nem agravo – Sobre o direito ao recurso em matéria de facto em caso de primeira condenação em segunda instância. Revista do Ministério Público 159:155–167

Morão H (2021) Pela renovação da renovação da prova. Anatomia do Crime, Revista de Ciências Jurídico-Criminais 12:171–195

Rainho J (2006) Decisão da matéria de facto: exame crítico das provas. Revista do Centro de Estudos Judiciários, 1st semester, pp 145–173

Ramos V, Churro B (2019) Report on Portugal. In: Quattrocolo S, Ruggeri S (eds) Personal participation in criminal proceedings – a comparative study of participatory safeguards and in absentia trials in Europe. Springer, Cham, pp 305–360

Santos M, Leal-Henriques M (2002) Recursos em Processo Penal, 5th edn. Rei dos Livros, Lisboa

Silva G (2008) Curso de Processo Penal, vol II. Verbo, Lisboa

Silva G (2009) Curso de Processo Penal, vol III, 4th edn. Verbo, Lisboa

Silva S (2020) Direito a um duplo grau de jurisdição em matéria penal. In: Albuquerque A (ed) Comentário da Convenção Europeia dos Direitos Humanos e dos Protocolos Adicionais, vol III. Universidade Católica, Lisboa, pp 2372–2393

Chapter 5
The Recordings Model in Portugal: The Defendant's and the Victim's Perspectives

Tiago Geraldo and Nuno Igreja Matos

5.1 Introduction

Criminal immediacy[1] entails the judge establishing a relationship with the defendant, the facts, and the evidence gathered during the criminal proceeding. On this basis, immediacy, having its origins[2] in the overcoming of secret proceedings and during the reform of what were exclusively inquisitorial procedures, is traditionally conceived as encompassing both a formal (the judge responsible to contact with the evidence must also be the judge responsible for the final decision) and a material (the judge must contact the evidence in the most direct form) dimension.[3]

In obedience to its historic origins and its current core contents, immediacy demands, in its optimal implementation, the judge to have a direct and personal contact with all the relevant evidence—a contact that is usually seen as a guarantee that the judge is to decide only after being face-to-face with the most pertinent elements of the case in a publicly visible proceeding. Spatial proximity, as well as some degree of personal interaction, are thus elementary requirements for the maximum immediacy: they give assurance not only that the judge will have a robust

[1]On the immediacy principle, see Dias (2004), pp. 229–235; Ibãnez (2006), pp. 9–32; Summers (2007), pp. 47 et seq.; Ruiz (2016), pp. 249–268; Winter (2019), pp. 279–293; Silva (2020), pp. 697–713.

[2]For the origins of immediacy, see Summers (2007), pp. 47–50; an overview of German scholarship on the principle can be found in Selçuk (2012), pp. 7–10.

[3]A third dimension can also be laid out: a temporal dimension, according to which the evidence should be examined as soon as possible with relation to the moment of its production. Accordingly, da Silva (2020), p. 698, quoting Willimman (2016), p. 161.

T. Geraldo · N. I. Matos (✉)
University of Lisbon School of Law, Research Centre for Criminal Law and Criminal Sciences (CIDPCC), Lisbon, Portugal
e-mail: tgeraldo@mlgts.pt; nimatos@mlgts.pt

H. Morão, R. Tavares da Silva (eds.), *Fairness in Criminal Appeal*,
https://doi.org/10.1007/978-3-031-13001-4_5

cognitive and intellectual approach to the case (that the parties can discuss and influence), but also that the valuation of the evidence derives from intense and publicly visible contacts with both the personal and non-personal evidence of the case at hand—which will also, hopefully, reinforce the credibility and consistency of the final decision. In particular, when facing personal evidence—i.e., statements and testimonies from the parties and from witnesses—, immediacy also goes hand in hand with the orality principle, similarly a principle regarded as a tool to reinforce the publicity and deepen the intensity of the judge's relationship with the case.

Given its mentioned connection with publicity, orality, and the strengthening of the final decision, immediacy is currently seen as a principle contained within a more broad and fundamental right to a fair criminal trial. Under this light, immediacy is a principle to be shaped on a case-to-case basis and may ground a specific right of the defendants or the victims to immediacy concerning specific evidence—even at the appeal stage, which will be the main focus of this text.

However, immediacy is also perceived as being subject to a variable degree, including in its nature and consequences, at least to some extent. According to this view, immediacy can, in fact, be obtained at different levels and intensities, since there is no rule imposing—let alone defining the exact degree or methods necessary to achieve it—that immediacy necessarily demands a direct and personal contact with the evidence if an indirect and non–personal contact also solves a doubt arising from the relationship of the judge with the case. In this sense, immediacy may also be ascertained through indirect and impersonal acts of the judge, notably by applying some forms of 'mediate' or mitigated immediacy—for example, the analysis of a previous judicial decision on the evidence or other documents that summarize the evidence gathered and previously evaluated (instead of examining directly such evidence), or through an analysis centred on playing an audio or video recording of the evidenced being presented at the trial stage.

The discussions surrounding these forms and the sufficiency or insufficiency of mitigated immediacy are usually put forward vis-à-vis the definition of the appeals' procedure. It is not clear—and it is, in fact, an option with geographical and legal cultural differences—whether the appeal stage of a criminal procedure should require an immediacy as intense as the trial phase or if its differences to the trial stage allows the appeals stage to be compatible with mitigated forms of immediacy. Such discussion is particularly problematic under Portuguese law, due to the apparent preference for mitigated immediacy in the appeal phase, almost always materialised through the listening of audio recordings—which may be seen as detrimental to other rights and principles (that could probably be better attended through a more intense and more personal contact with evidence) within that phase. Not surprisingly, this is reprimand that has already been delivered by the ECtHR against the Portuguese courts.

The present chapter intends to face these doubts in light of the Portuguese experience, with the intent of understanding, first, how the appeal stage is designed and applied in the Portuguese Criminal Procedure Code (PCPP) on matters involving evidence (re)examination (Sect. 5.2); second, what is the immediacy standard for the appeal stage according to the ECHR and to the ECtHR (Sect. 5.3); and, finally, how the Portuguese case compares with this standard and what difficulties arise for both the defendants and the victims (Sect. 5.4).

5.2 Immediacy in the Appeal Stage: The PCPP in Law and in Action

The PCPP in force since 1987 originally intended to counter the lack of intervention and insufficient immediacy of the Appeal Courts that turned into a general practice in the previous years. With that in mind, the PCPP brought the idea of a more participatory procedure, notably by allowing and encouraging the holding of oral hearings before the appeals judges. As stated in the preamble of the PCPP, 'the Code establishes a framework in line with the idea of unitary appeals, in principle identical for the Appeal Court and the Supreme Justice Court and covering, to the extent possible and convenient, both the discussion of law and the discussion of the facts. With the same purpose of lending greater consistency to appeals, it seeks to respond the tendency to make them a merely routine task performed on paper, converting them into an authentic knowledge of real problems and conflicts, mediated by the motivated intervention of people. For this reason, appeals are subject to the general principle – which is, moreover, legally and constitutionally imposed! – of the accusatorial structure, with the consequent requirement of a hearing where the maxim of orality is respected'.

As we shall see on the next pages, notwithstanding this original proclamation, the version today in force of the PCPP has not, however, led to a significant maximization of evidentiary hearings before the Appeal Courts for two main reasons: on one hand, because the PCPP limits the cases in which the Appeal Courts are bound or even have the option of directly examine evidence; on the other hand, because, since 1998, taking advantage of the technological advances, the PCPP was amended to favour the use of audio recordings of the trial hearings as an easier alternative to grant and facilitate immediacy during the appeal phase.

5.2.1 The Legal Provisions Applicable to the Appeal Stage

To follow-up on the original intention to turn the appeal stage into a more comprehensive, interventive, and knowledgeable phase, the PCPP granted—and still grants today—the Appeal Courts the power to modify the decision of the trial court on the evidence of the case.

In fact, with some minor exceptions, the PCPP foresees, as a general rule, a double jurisdiction on criminal matters for both the revaluation of the facts and of the laws applied by the trial courts, irrespectively of the acquittal or conviction of the defendant. The facts established during the trial phase may therefore be revaluated and reformed in three situations, foreseen in article 431 of the PCPP: *(a)* when the case file contains all the evidence that supported the trial court's decision; *(b)* if the applicant (the defendant, the Public Prosecutor, or the assistant[4]) disputes the evidence of the case vis-à-vis the evaluation of the trial court's decision and the Court of Appeal agrees with the reasons and counter-evidence pointed out to sustain the dispute; *(c)* when the Court of Appeal proceeds to a renewal of the evidence, or, in other words, when the Court of Appeal directly and personally contacts with the evidence through an evidentiary hearing before its judges.

In these cases, a double degree of jurisdiction on the factual decision of the criminal offence is guaranteed. However, this does not translate into an appeal stage endowed with maximum immediacy. The main reason relates to the fact that the PCPP significantly limits the option to directly and personally renew the evidence brought before the trial court at the appeal stage. And the PCPP does it through a set of rules on the recording of the trial stage that are later useful to facilitate mitigated forms of immediacy and to exclude the need to make use of direct and personal acts of (oral and presential) immediacy. First, by setting, as a rule, that during the trial stage all the personal and oral statements (namely, from the defendant, the victim, and the witnesses) must be listed in a document and its content recorded (articles 363 and 364; also foreseeing that omission to record leads to the annulment of the trial). Second, by determining that the Court of Appeal may and should use the recordings to evaluate the trial court's decision [article 412(6)]. Third, the PCPP allows for a non-evidentiary hearing before the Appeal Courts where the lawyers of the defendant and of the assistant, as well as the Public Prosecutor, are entitled to present their arguments directly to the judges that will decide on the trial courts' analysis (article 423), which is to function as a sort of alternative to the need to present the evidence under dispute at the appeal stage that also serves as a middle ground solution that prevents risks of neglect or omission to consider any key aspect of the case (that will—or should—normally be highlighted by the lawyers and prosecutors during the hearings) while at the same time saving the Appeal Courts from the need to order evidence presentation before themselves.

All these legal provisions—regarding the recording of the evidence presented during the trial and the option of a non-evidentiary hearing—are designed to allow a mitigated form of immediacy in the appeal stage without making mandatory the need for repeating and renewing all the evidence, even the evidence relating to the statements and testimonies presented in the trial. In fact, the Court of Appeal, according to these provisions, when in need to examine this personal evidence, should do it by playing and listening to the recording of the trial. For the PCPP, the use of the documents, the use of the recordings, or the scheduling of non-evidentiary

[4]Under Portuguese Criminal Procedural Law, the assistant serves as a supporting entity (offering, therefore, *assistance*) to the Public Prosecutor due to a personal interest in the success of the criminal proceeding. In some cases, depending on the criminal offence at stake, the assistant may even be responsible for deciding whether to prosecute the suspect. Given its personal connection to the case, the victim may in general request to be granted with such formal assistant role and status during the procedure.

hearing with the parties habilitates the Court with a sufficient overview of the evidence of the trial, making its repetition unnecessary.

In light of the above, and since its relevant provisions guarantee that the evidence presented before the trial court is always recorded, the PCPP afterwards adopts more strict rules on the option to renew evidence before the Appeals Courts. In particular, the renewal will only be available to control a possible 'error of assessment' in the trial court's decision that the Appeal Courts cannot judge without being face-to-face with the evidence—therefore ordering, in these cases, the evidence's renewal to avoid sending the case back to the trial stage [articles 410(2) and 430]. This means that the Appeal Courts cannot demand for the repetition of evidence (notably, the hearing of the defendant, the victim, or any witness) unless the trial court's decision incurs in such an 'error of assessment'. According to the PCPP, an 'error of assessment'—that paves the way for this theoretical chance of renewing the evidence—occurs only on the following situations: when the decision is flawed because of a defect within its text, i.e., a contradiction, an inconsistency or an insufficiency between the evidence cited by the court and its final judgment; or when the decision is at fault due to manifest error in the assessment of the evidence. Direct renewal of the evidence is apparently not viable in any other situation—making it impossible, for instance, to bring evidence to the Appeal Courts when the applicant challenges, in his appeal, the trial court's decision on different grounds (when the causes of the challenge do not amount to an error of assessment), such as a disagreement with the court's evaluation of the evidence, or when the applicant intends to present new evidence that was not put forward in the trial stage.

5.2.2 The Portuguese Case-Law on the Immediacy Required at the Appeal Stage

Not only the PCPP contrasts the original intention to promote a direct immediacy with rules that seemingly—and effectively—favour forms of mitigated immediacy, but also the case law of the Portuguese's Appeal Courts supports this option and further restricts direct immediacy by practically rejecting to ever proceed to the renewal of evidence[5] and sometimes even by dismissing the need to scrutinize the documented evidence or recordings of the trial's evidence (the mitigated forms of immediacy).

The reasons generally summoned by the Appeal Courts to refuse a more direct immediacy (i.e., the renewal of evidence) and even mediate forms of immediacy (i.e., the analysis of recordings of the evidence presented in the trial stage; the holding of a hearing for the presentations of the arguments of the parties, etc.)

[5] To a point where specialized scholars have already stated that article 430—that foresees the possibility to present evidence directly before the Appeal Courts—is a provision lacking legal enforcement. *Ipsis verbis*, Albuquerque (2011), p. 1179.

vary from more abstract arguments concerning the nature and philosophy of the appeal stage and procedural constraints to its powers, to more specific justifications revolving around the preference and suitability of examining only documentation and recordings and a selective interpretation of the abovementioned legal provisions.

These are three of the more recurrent arguments laid out by the Portuguese courts to minimize or entirely dismiss the immediacy options from the appeal stage: *(a)* the renewal of evidence before the Appeal Courts can be rejected if there is a recording of the same evidence from the trial phase; *(b)* even when faced with recordings of the trial, the Appeal Courts are not forced to—nor have the power to—examine all the documental evidence and recordings of the personal evidence; *(c)* the Appeal Courts, even when assessing the evidence presented to the trial court, should nevertheless still favour the decision of the trial court.

An example of the first type of reasoning can be seen in a recent decision taken by the Supreme Justice Court in July 2021. This decision summarizes an argument frequently made by the Appeal Courts to reject the renewal of the evidence (i.e., the most direct and personal form of immediacy in the appeal stage enshrined in the PCPP). The Supreme Justice Court wrote in it: 'if there is an appeal alleging the existence of the errors in assessment as set out in article 410(2) of the PCPP, the Court will decide whether to renew the evidence, and this decision is final [see article 430(2) of the PCPP]. The scholarship on this matter has already considered that there is never a renewal of evidence when the evidence produced in the hearing is recorded, because in this case the renewal is useless. As such, taking into account that renewal of evidence only takes place when the above-mentioned decisional defects occur [see art. 430(1) of the PCPP] and that there was a record of the trial stage, the Court decided in accordance with the provisions of art. 430, no. 2 of the PCPP, and no nullity has occurred'.[6]

In sum, the Supreme Justice Court supports the common understanding that the Appeal Courts are not required to renew evidence if there is a record of the evidence. This is a solution which favours—even in the face of possible error of assessment—mitigated immediacy to a personal and direct immediacy. With an argument that is more definitive than it shows at first, because it actually gives way for a more extreme consequence: the exclusion of the option of renewal of evidence in virtually all appeals: as stated above, since documentation and recording of the trial is mandatory [articles 363 and 364(1)], the Appeal Courts can always resort to those elements to virtually refuse all chances of evidence's renewal.

An example (among many) of a reasoning that rejects a full examination of all the evidence, even under a mitigated immediacy procedure—to focus instead only on a partial analysis—, can be found in a decision taken by the Évora's Appeal Court in October 2020. It states the following: 'the very common idea that the existence of recordings of oral evidence implies that the existence of an appeal is enough for the court of appeal to have to examine this recorded evidence plus the documents, without any effort on the part of the appellant, is deeply flawed. The appellate

[6]Supreme Court of Justice, no. 147/13.3JELSB.L2.S1, 15 July 2021, *dgsi.pt*.

court does not have to re-examine the case and all the evidence that has been produced in the records! The appellate court only has to examine the appeal in the manner in which the appellant places it (apart from the defects of ex-officio knowledge, naturally) [...]. In short, an appeal is not a sum of arguments that, as interesting as they may be, do not follow the above-mentioned routes and by demonstrating obvious or demonstrable errors by evidence that has to be laboriously prepared and presented by the appellant'.[7]

This decision shows a different but equally general argument to dismiss even mitigated forms of immediacy under the justification that a comprehensive analysis of the evidence through the documents and the recordings of the trial would go beyond the purpose and powers of the Appeal Court. The general idea is that the Appeal Courts should only consider the arguments of the applicant provided they are already sufficiently densified and individualized as to the matters the applicant wishes to be reassessed. This suggests a formal conception of the appeal stage, entirely attached to the content of the appeal, which thus indicates that evidence may be ignored for procedural reasons even if material justice and the intent of truth-finding demand an examination of said evidence.

Finally, even when the Appeal Courts admit and proceed to revaluate the trial's evidence, one common outcome of that revaluation is the holding of the trial court decision on the basis of its more direct and personal contact with the evidence.

For instance, in a decision dated from September 2017, the Supreme Justice Court wrote: 'As has been understood, the re-examination, based on evidence with non-binding probative force, of the 1st instance decision on the matter of fact should be carried out with the necessary care and consideration, given the principles of orality, immediacy and free appraisal of evidence, since there are countless relevant factors in assessing the credibility of testimony that can only be understood by the judge through direct contact with the deponents at the hearing. Notwithstanding the fact that the review of the facts, as far as the appeal court is concerned, is also subject to the principle of free assessment of evidence and without limitation – with the exception of binding evidence – in the process of forming its opinion, it must be taken into account that the aforementioned principles result in aspects of indisputable relevance – reactions of the deponent himself or others, hesitations, pauses, gestures, expressions – in the evaluation of personal statements that are better perceived by the first instance [court]. The appeal court will be responsible, bearing these limitations in mind, for analysing the process of formation of the judge's conviction, assessing, on the basis of the evidence produced and other elements of proof in the case-file, whether the given answers contain an obvious error and/or are reasonably supported by the evidence and the rules of logic, experience and common knowledge'.[8]

---

[7] Évora Court of Appeal, no. 243/18.0GDFAR.E1, 10 November 2020, *dgsi.pt*. Also, using the same argument, word by word, Évora Court of Appeal, no. 214/17.4IDFAR.E1, 17 December 2020.

[8] Supreme Court of Justice, no. 959/09.2TVLSB.L1.S1, 7 September 2017, *dgsi.pt*.

In a similar sense, a recent decision from the Lisbon Court of Appeals dated February 2021 goes as follows: 'It is important not to forget, as it is the current jurisprudence of our Higher Courts, that the appeal court can only revert the decision of the judge, based on his or her free conviction and founded on immediacy and orality, if it becomes clear that the solution chosen, from among the various possible ones, is illogical and inadmissible in the light of the rules of common experience. If the decision on the matter of fact of the judge, duly founded, is one of the plausible solutions according to the rules of experience, it will be undisputable, since it was given in obedience to the law that requires him to judge according to his free conviction'.[9]

In other words, even when reassessing evidence, the Appeal Courts tend to limit their assessment to the logic, the syllogism premises, and the possibility of evidential inference of the trial court's final decision. The Appeal Courts are not concerned, therefore, with obtaining the best interpretation from the evidence, because it is widely understood that the assessment made at the appeal stage, due to its (also self-) diminished immediacy, will always be less valuable than a distinct but still more credible interpretation made directly by the trial court.

From this brief overview of the PCPP and the case-law of the Supreme Justice Court and other Appeal Courts, it is now clear that the Portuguese procedural system of double jurisdiction in criminal cases fell short of its original intention to bring a maximization of orality and a broader intervention to the appeal stages.

PCPP is nowadays primarily devoted—both in legal and in practical terms—to mitigated forms of immediacy, in particular through the examination of the recordings made of the trial stage above any other more personal forms of renewal or repetition of the evidence.

The case-law shows that the reasonings usually put forward by the second and third jurisdiction courts go even beyond the PCPP: on the one hand, because they have practically eliminated the option of evidence renewal, and, on the other hand, because even when faced with the need to scrutinize the evidence through mitigated forms of immediacy (typically, recordings and documents), the higher courts tend to validate the decision of the trial court in tribute to its greater achievable degree of immediacy.

These legal and judicial options not only distance Portugal from the provisions now in force in other countries with similar criminal procedures, namely Italy,[10] where the applicable legal regimes demand that at least in some, more serious cases, such as the reversal of acquittals, evidence needs to be brought—directly and personally—to the Appeal Courts, but also give cause to risking the violation of the ECHR, as discussed in the following Section.

---

[9]Lisbon Court of Appeal, no. 10684/18.8T9LSB.L1-5, 2 February 2021, *dgsi.pt*.

[10]See Chap. 2. Also, on the immediacy principle under Italian law overview, Negri (2014), pp. 213–237. Comparing the Italian solution with the Portuguese case, Morão (2020), p. 181; Morão (2021), p. 661.

5.3 Immediacy in the Appeal Stage: The ECHR and ECtHR Standard

The principle of immediacy has earned its place in the ECHR as an extension or a development of the right to a double jurisdiction explicitly set out in Protocol No. 7 to the ECHR.

Before briefly listing the ECtHR main decisions on the matter, it is therefore necessary to provide an outline of Article 6 of the ECHR on this specific perspective, as well as an overview of said Protocol No. 7, dated 1984 (as amended by Protocol 11 in 1998) and its Explanatory Report to the Protocol No. 7, also from 1984.[11]

Article 6 established a right to a fair trial within criminal procedure, not explicitly foreseeing nor mentioning a right to appeal or to double jurisdiction: only article 2 of Protocol No. 7 provides, in explicit terms, the right of appeal in criminal matters. This Protocol states that 'everyone convicted of a criminal offence by a tribunal shall have the right to have his conviction or sentence reviewed by a higher tribunal'—even though simultaneously accepting that in some cases the right may be dismissed, specifically 'in regard to offences of a minor character, as prescribed by law, or in cases in which the person concerned was tried in the first instance by the highest tribunal or was convicted following an appeal against acquittal'.

Article 2 of said Protocol does not, however, go further on the terms and scope of the appeal. Also, it does not provide any light as to the immediacy rules applicable in the appeals. In fact, it explicitly lays out that 'the exercise of this right, including the grounds on which it may be exercised, shall be governed by law'.[12]

Additional light on this right to appeal can be obtained by reading the Explanatory Report on Protocol No. 7. The §§ 17 and 18 of the Explanatory Report clarify that the right 'does not require that in every case he [the applicant] should be entitled to have both his conviction and sentence so reviewed'. It is subsequently added in those paragraphs that 'different rules govern review by a higher tribunal in the various member States of the Council of Europe. In some countries, such review is in certain cases limited to questions of law, such as the *recours en cassation*. In others, there is a right to appeal against findings of facts as well as on the questions of law. The article leaves the modalities for the exercise of the right and the grounds on which it may be exercised to be determined by domestic law'.

Even though the ECHR, its Protocols, and Explanatory Reports do not take a stand on the immediacy requirements in the appeal stage, the ECtHR has nonetheless been establishing the need for the States' Appeal Courts to comply with an immediacy principle, in line with its case-law on the immediacy requirements in the trial stage.

---

[11] On these, Fanego (2012), pp. 168–172.

[12] It is worth mentioning that Portugal, when incorporating said Protocol No. 7 into its own legal system, issued a reservation by which it stated that 'criminal offence' and 'offence', pursuant articles 2 and 4 of the Protocol, would be construed according to the set of facts that are qualified as criminal offence according to the Portuguese law.

Even before the entry into force of Protocol No. 7, in *Ekbatani v. Sweden*[13] the (at the time known as) European Commission of Human Rights had already put forward an understanding of the right to a fair trial that could, in some cases, and depending on the terms of the appeal at the national level, demand a court of appeal to be presented with direct evidence, at least to conduct a hearing of the defendant.

In *Constantinescu v. Romania,*[14] the ECtHR followed the line of arguments previously expanded in *Ekbatani v. Sweden* case and decided that 'where an appellate court is called upon to examine a case as to the facts and the law and to make a full assessment of the question of the applicant's guilt or innocence, it cannot, as a matter of fair trial, properly determine those issues without a direct assessment of the evidence given in person by the accused'.

In *Destreheim v. France,*[15] the ECtHR declared a violation of the right to a fair trial by a Court of Appeal that reverted an acquittal based on a different evaluation of witnesses that were not present in the appeal stage, even though their presentation had been requested (§ 45).

It is also important to mention the cases *Hanu v. Romania*[16] and *Dan v. Moldova,*[17] not only for being recent but also because of their widely spread recognition. In both cases, the defendant was initially acquitted by the trial court and then convicted by the Court of Appeal without directly hearing any evidence. The ECtHR concluded that the relevant States had violated the defendant's right to a fair trial because of their omission to hear the witnesses in person, failing to allow for the 'possibility for the accused to confront the witnesses in the presence of a judge who must ultimately decide the case'.

Similar rulings were laid out in identical cases such as, among others, *Almenara Álvarez v. Spain*, *Serrano Contretas v. Spain* and *Lazu v. Republic of Moldova.*[18]

Particularly interesting for its connection with the recording models of immediacy in the appeal phase of criminal proceedings is the *Gómez Olmeda v. Spain,*[19] in which the ECtHR also had to take a position on the use of video recordings as a possible form of immediacy for the appeal stage. In this case, the Court was once again faced with a criminal proceeding where a defendant was partially acquitted from the criminal charges made against him and was later convicted (for the same crime regarding which he was initially acquitted) by the Spanish Court of Appeal on the grounds of a re-examination of the evidence via the screening of the video recording of the trial.

---

[13] *Ekbatani v. Sweden*, no. 10563/83, 26 May 1988; namely its §§ 34–47, *hudoc.echr.coe.int.*

[14] *Constantinescu v. Romania*, no. 28871/95, 27 June 2000; namely its § 55, *hudoc.echr.coe.int.*

[15] *Destreheim v. France*, no. 56651/00, 18 May 2004; namely its § 45, *hudoc.echr.coe.int.*

[16] *Hanu v. Romania*, no. 10890/04, 4 June 2013, namely its § 40, *hudoc.echr.coe.int.*

[17] *Dan v. Moldova*, no. 57575/14, 10 November 2021, namely its § 30, *hudoc.echr.coe.int.*

[18] *Almenara Álvarez v. Spain*, no. 16096/08, 25 October 2011, namely §§ 47–50). *Serrano Contreras v. Spain*, no. 49183/08, 20 March 2012, namely §§ 35–40. *Lazu v. Republic of Moldova*, no. 46182/08, 5 July 2016, namely §§ 38–44; *hudoc.echr.coe.int.*

[19] *Gómez Olmeda v. Spain*, no 61112/12, 29 March 2016, namely §§ 32–39, *hudoc.echr.coe.int.*

The defendant had not requested to be heard (nor requested any other evidence to be presented) before the Court of Appeal because he had been acquitted and didn't anticipate the need to renew the same evidence. Once again, the ECtHR decided that 'the appellate court was under a duty to take positive measures to this effect, notwithstanding the fact that the applicant had not expressly requested a hearing to be held' (§ 32), while noting additionally that 'failure to hear the accused in person is even more difficult to reconcile with the requirements of a fair trial in the specific circumstances of this case, where the court of last resort was the first court to convict the applicant in the proceedings brought to determine a criminal charge against him', concluding for the violation of article 6 of ECHR.

On the matter revolving around the immediacy that the Court of Appeal was able to obtain by viewing the video-recording of the trial, the ECtHR stated the following: 'contrary to what the Government contended, the Court considers that the viewing of the video-recording by the *Audiencia* did not compensate for the lack of a hearing because rather than responding to the applicant's right to address the *Audiencia*, it merely represented part of the *Audiencia*'s review of the first instance proceedings. The Court notes that the Spanish Constitutional Court, in ruling on similar cases, has found that the viewing of a video recording of the first-instance trial does not enable an appellate court to assess personal evidence [...]. Consequently, it may not be considered that the viewing of the video-recording placed the *Audiencia Provincial* in the same position as the first-instance judge for the purposes of Article 6 § 1 of the Convention' (§ 37–39). In sum, for the ECtHR, it seems that the video recording is not always necessarily nor can be deemed as a sufficient alternative for meeting the requirements of the principle of immediacy at the appeal stage.

Even though the cited case-law shapes the majority viewpoint of the ECtHR on immediacy in the criminal appeal phase, it should be highlighted that there are also some decisions taken by the Court that turn in the opposite direction.

In cases such as *Bazo González v Spain*[20] and *Kashlev v. Estonia*,[21] the ECtHR has stepped back in construing article 6, repeating that it is not mandatory for the defendant to be heard or have evidence be presented before the Court of Appeal, even if acquitted by the trial court. In all these cases, the ECtHR has based its reasoning on grounds related to the case at hand, the fact that the defendant had not requested the presentation of the evidence, and/or on reasons connected to the immediacy previously obtained during the trial.

The same can be said so as to the more general argument, also adopted by the ECtHR, that leaves to the States and its domestic courts the assessment of the 'credibility of witnesses and the relevance of evidence to the issues in the case'.[22]

Although in all these cases the ECtHR is careful as to not directly contradict its previous case-law, namely by mentioning that there is a degree of immediacy required in the appeal stage that depends on a case-to-case assessment

[20] *Bazo González v Spain*: no. 30643/04, 16 December 2008, *hudoc.echr.coe.int*.

[21] *Kashlev v. Estonia*: no. 22574/08, 26 April 2016, *hudoc.echr.coe.int*.

[22] *Kashlev v. Estonia*, § 47.

(an argument broad enough to allow the inference that in the other cases the ECtHR concluded the assessment with a different view), the contradiction between some of the decisions referred inevitably come up—which gives cause to uncertainty in view of the lack of clarity on the criteria that allows the appeal courts to deny the presentation of the evidence before its judges.

Even though the ECtHR has already ruled on the victim's guarantees of immediacy at the trial stage, neither the ECHR,[23] its Protocol and Reports, nor the case-law of the ECtHR hint that such guarantee is to applicable to the victims also in the appeal stage. As referred, Protocol No. 7 expressly limits the right to double jurisdiction only to 'everyone convicted of a criminal offence'.

The ECtHR has never taken a principled stand on the immediacy requirements in appeals that revert a previous conviction or deny victims' requests (when legally allowed to appeal an acquittal) to present evidence before Appeal Courts. The reason for this may be traced back to an idea that the rights of the ECHR on criminal matters are aimed exclusively or predominantly at protecting the defendant, based on the understanding that the defendant is the 'weak party' in the relationship established in the criminal proceedings vis-à-vis the State.[24] An idea that has, so far, resisted to the recent trends of victimology in substantive and procedural criminal law.

Although there is no judicial background on the immediacy rights of the victims in the appeal stage of a criminal procedure, a comparable discussion concerning the rights of the victims in civil claims within criminal proceeding has already been subject to ECtHR decisions and is owed a brief reference.

In this specific context, the ECtHR has been repeatedly stating that all requirements of Article 6 are less onerous in the civil limb than in the criminal charges, even when the civil claim is part of a criminal procedure.

In *Mihail Mihalescu v. Romania*,[25] and *Victor Laurentiu Martin v. Romania*,[26] also from April 2021, the ECtHR was called to decide if a pre-trial judge could dismiss a criminal claim filed by the victim without being confronted with evidence and through a decision that extinguished any possible criminal liability in definitive terms (i.e., without appeal to a higher court). In both cases, the ECtHR found no violation of article 6, arguing that the rights provided therein have less weight within the scope of civil claims, even if they are integrated in criminal proceedings, and that a criminal judgment with civil effects is not a decision that definitively rejects civil liability, since the victim may still argue for the civil liability in a purely civil (and autonomous) proceeding.

[23] See Chap. 6.

[24] Fanego (2012), pp. 168–170.

[25] *Mihail Mihalescu v. Romania* (no 795/15), April 2021.

[26] *Victor Laurentiu Martin v. Romania* (no 75614/14), April 2021.

5.4 The ECHR Standard in Portugal: The PCPP at a Crossroads

The mapping of the PCPP and of the ECHR rules on immediacy in the appeal stage made visible some divergences between both frameworks.[27] These differences are even more striking in the criminal cases that were brought before the ECtHR on matters concerning the right to a fair trial in the Portuguese Appeal Courts, notably *Moreira Ferreira v. Portugal*,[28] *Pereira Cruz et al. v. Portugal*,[29] and *Paixão Moreira Sá Fernandes v. Portugal*.[30]

In *Moreira Ferreira v. Portugal*, the defendant (also applicant in the appeal stage) saw a conviction upheld by the Court of Appeal without the renewal of evidence on the defendants' alleged legal disability, even though a hearing had been directly requested to the Court. The ECtHR stated that 'where an appellate body is called upon to hear a case on the facts and the law and to consider the question of guilt or innocence as a whole, it cannot, for reasons of fair trial, decide these issues without a direct assessment of the evidence presented in person by the accused in support of his or her claim'.[31] Eyeing the PCPP, the ECtHR noted that in the case at hand the issues raised in the appeal made it relevant to renew the evidence to better determine whether a legal disability existed, since that could lead to the reversal on the conviction determined by the trial court,[32] concluding at last that the omission of gathering new evidence from the Court of Appeal actually infringed article 6 of the ECHR.

In *Pereira da Cruz et. al. v. Portugal*, among other allegations, the ECtHR was confronted with a case where three defendants were denied the right to present new evidence (not assessed in the trial phase by the trial court) before the Court of Appeal. The ECtHR once again turned its attention to the PCPP's appeal system enshrined and the interpretation held by the Portuguese court in the sense that the PCPP didn't allow for the analysis of evidence unseen by the trial court (and therefore was not used to support its decision). ECtHR specified that the new evidence could undermine the conviction held by trial court, since the facts under discussion were also contradicted by the evidence effectively examined in the trial stage. The ECtHR also rejected the idea that adducing new evidence was only possible through a different type of appeal, because the need to start a new formal procedure would be 'an excessive burden on any convicted person'.[33] Therefore, the

---

[27] A thorough and detailed overview on the ECtHR case-law confronted with the appeal phase designed by the PCPP can be found at Mata-Mouros (2020), pp. 2394–2422.

[28] *Moreira Ferreira v. Portugal*: no. 19808/08, 5 July 2011, *hudoc.echr.coe.int*.

[29] *Pereira Cruz et al. v. Portugal*: no. 56396/12, 26 June 2018, *hudoc.echr.coe.int*.

[30] *Paixão Moreira Sá Fernandes v. Portugal*: no. 78108/14, 25 May 2020, *hudoc.echr.coe.int*.

[31] *Moreira Ferreira v. Portugal*, § 30.

[32] *Moreira Ferreira v. Portugal*, §§ 32–34.

[33] *Pereira da Cruz et. al. v. Portugal*, § 230.

ECtHR decided that article 6 had been violated due to the rejection of new evidence by the Court of Appeal.

Finally, in *Paixão Moreira Sá Fernandes v. Portugal* the ECtHR faced a case like those mentioned above in Sect. 5.3: an acquittal being reversed by a Court of Appeal that, although basing the decision reversal on a disagreement upon a fact relating to the knowledge (*mens rea*) of the defendant, decided not to hear the defendant nor any witnesses about that same fact. To the ECtHR, the PCPP allowed the Court of Appeal to examine the evidence through a direct and personal hearing.[34] By omitting these acts, article 6 was once again disrespected, since the defendant was not able to present his defence against the new fact that was considered only by the Court of Appeal.

These three cases are especially relevant because they can be used to illustrate the two most noticeable flaws in the PCPP appeal system.

First, the fact that, under the PCPP appeals' regime, evidence cannot be—or, in practical terms, usually is not—renewed before the Appeal Courts for purely procedural and formal reasons, even when the presentation of the evidence before the appeal judges is clearly advisable (if not utterly necessary) in light of the applicant's claims. As seen above, the PCPP apparently discourages the production of direct evidence before the Appeal Courts outside of restrict situations described as 'errors of assessment'. Which means that evidence may be declined even when its presentation is the obvious solution to ascertain the justice of the trial court's decision and to determine whether the applicant is right in its challenge of that decision.

Second, the fact that it is not mandatory (at least considering the terms that the PCPP's rules are construed in practical cases) to renew any evidence even when the Appeal Courts are inclined to reverse an acquittal for reasons resulting from a disagreement of the appeal judges on a given and crucial fact of the case—a flaw that directly contradicts the dominant case-law of the ECtHR on the legal requirements of immediacy in the appeal stage resulting from article 6 of the ECHR.

But the flaws pointed out in the *Moreira Ferreira v. Portugal*, *Pereira Cruz et al. v. Portugal*, and *Paixão Moreira Sá Fernandes v. Portugal* cases are the product of what one can say to be a deeper problem in the whole architecture of the appeals stage system under Portuguese criminal procedural law.

As above noted, since its entry into force the PCPP seems to exist in contradiction with the eloquent proclamations it initially announced. The promise of a more interventive appeal phase is inconsistent with legal provisions that, in fact, point towards mitigated forms of immediacy over the renewal of the evidence and that allow the Appeal Courts to avoid a full reassessment of the evidence and to limit themselves to uncritically rely on the previous decision taken by the trial courts. In fact, the PCPP not only favours the use of audio recordings, but also virtually extinguished the chance of bringing (new or renewed) evidence before the Appeal Courts.

[34] *Paixão Moreira Sá Fernandes v. Portugal*, § 67.

The philosophy underneath these options and decisions is very clear: to put it simple, the Appeal Courts are acting under an understanding according to which they are not to be primarily guided by justice and truth purposes; Appeal Courts see (and self-limit) their intervention as one that is aimed only at checking whether the trial court's decision achieved one valid and logic conclusion under the light of the existing evidence, even if other conclusions could also be reasonable or even more likely if additional evidence had been put forward.[35]

As a result of all these interpretations—which (self-)create a sort of *capitis diminution* upon the Appeal Courts, significantly limiting the broadness of their power in handling and reviewing facts and evidence—, it is therefore comprehensible that the Appeal Courts feel uncomfortable in promoting hearings for the presentation of evidence or in deciding based on new evidence which was not available to the trial court. Which leads to a case-law excessively formalistic and focused, not on the merits of the case, but on procedural issues. And therefore, more occupied with the terms of the appeal and the overall inferences of the trial court and at the same time (willingly) more and more distanced from the facts and the evidence of the criminal cases.

All this becomes almost ironic to realize when we see that the decisions of the Appeal Courts, in addition to not directly assessing the evidence, often even refuse to draw any consequences from their indirect analysis of recordings under the argument that their examination cannot be seen as *more valuable* than the examination of the trial court, due to a lack of direct immediacy. In a word, Appeal Courts first refuse direct and personal immediacy and then shy away from ruling differently based on their own lack of immediacy.

From the defendant's standpoint, the reality we have been describing gives cause to a material restriction to the defendants' right to a fair trial, namely to the right to double jurisdiction and to immediacy in the appeal stage. The Portuguese defendants are usually at the risk of facing an unbalanced appeal stage vis-à-vis the standard of the ECHR and of the ECtHR, because of the difficulties they face when trying to bring evidence before the Appeal Courts (even evidence not before seen nor therefore considered by the trial court) and because of the Appeal Courts bias to simply validate the trial courts' reasoning, in obedience to a principle not mentioned by name, but that we see being applied, which could be designated as a sort of an *in dubio pro trial court* principle.

As one could expect, all these features of the practical enforcement of the PCPP far decrease the chance of reversing a conviction or of reducing the penalty determined by the trial courts. The most discernible practical consequence of it all is therefore to create a disincentive to appeal—or at least to appeal already with a complaint to the ECtHR in mind when the production of new evidence, or its renewal, is mandatory in the appeal's economy.

[35] Sustaining this approach, on the grounds that in any case the contact made with the evidence in the trial stage is always non-repeatable, see Ibãnez (2006), pp. 23–27.

On the converse perspective, victims also face the same disincentives and overall disbelief in the appeal stage, with identical practical consequences. Perhaps facing even an aggravated disincentive and disbelief since the victims cannot anticipate—as the defendants today can—that the ECtHR may in the future declare an infringement of article 6 of the ECTHR in case of refusal to produce their evidence before the Appeal Courts.

In this respect, it seems that there is a complete lack of correspondence between the rights granted by Portuguese law to victims of crimes and the case-law of the ECtHR. In Portugal, victims may request to become 'assistants' (as mentioned before) and, once they have been recognised with procedural status, enjoy the same rights as defendants at the appeal stage. However, since the ECtHR does not equalise victims with defendants on the requirements of immediacy at the appeal stage, victims are always seen in a disadvantaged position.

Having done this course, it is now time to face the subsequent question: should the PCPP be amended in line with the ECtHR requirements? Although the Portuguese Appeal Courts are clearly below the line of the ECtHR standard, the transformation of the said standard in national law could nevertheless entail new difficulties and excesses, possibly perverting valuable aspects of the global procedural regime.

First, it seems that the ECtHR case-law is at hands with an unsolved dilemma concerning immediacy in the appeal stage. The ECHR simultaneously wants to leave the appeal stage to the dimension of legal nationalism—as inscribed in the Protocol No. 7 and in its Explanatory Report, which clearly indicate that the States may freely decide on the terms and scope of criminal appeals—but, at the same time, the case-law from the ECtHR apparently intends to establish a universal standard on the need to hear evidence, at least when the Appeal Courts are inclined to revert an acquittal. This poses a risk of paradox: the States may freely deny the right to appeal to challenge the evidence evaluated by the trial court but cannot, however, allow that challenge and then determine that the challenge of the evidence is to be assessed only through mitigated immediacy acts, such as recording analysis—since that solution would probably be rebuked by the ECtHR on the basis of a violation to article 6.[36]

Second, even if it is to be understood that the appeal stage cannot be considered fair unless it guarantees direct and personal immediacy, at least when there is a reasonable chance of reversing an initial acquittal, this position of the ECtHR is not entirely convincing and may even be seen as even technologically outdated.[37] In fact, why should evidence always be directly brought before the Appeal Courts, even in the face of a possible reversal? This may prove excessive in those cases where the evidence being challenged in the appeal is not necessarily better examined in a direct and personal hearing (for instance, if there are other, non-personal, means of

[36] Even the infringement is not entirely clear. The abovementioned cases *Bazo González v Spain* and *Kashlev v. Estonia* cast doubts on whether direct immediacy is to be considered as indispensable to a fair trial (in the appeal stage) and on what should the criteria be to decide if mitigated immediacy is to suffice in a given case.

[37] Morão (2020), p. 187.

evidence that are sufficiently consistent to give the Appeal Courts the needed certainty to change the trial court's decision). Also, in other cases, the viewing of recordings, namely video-recordings, could suit the needs of the Appeals Courts, for example, if the challenge of the applicant concerns only something that was said by a witness that was wrongly not considered by the trial court. In sum, the ECtHR appears focused in determining as a rule that the Appeal Courts need to personally see and hear the personal evidence of the case, even if not requested by the parts; but it probably would be more advisable—even for the sake of procedural economy and to avoid abuses in the appeal phase with senseless evidence requests—if the ECtHR defined a clear criteria and detailed guidelines so as to distinguish the situations in which the exam of recordings may still be seen as a reasonable solution to comply with article 6.[38]

Third, the transposition of the case-law of the ECtHR into Portuguese law on the victims' different standard of immediacy before the Appeal Courts could disfigure the status of the 'assistant' (encompassing all the procedural rights of the victims) in the appeal stage, for the reasons already mentioned above.

How, then, should the PCPP, in the future, balance its insufficiencies without incurring in these paradoxes and difficulties that arise from the ECtHR case-law?

Aside the need to start a broad debate on the future architecture of the Portuguese appeal stage, it seems that the time has come to at least study the introduction of some key changes to Portuguese criminal procedural law.

In order to avoid increasing the violations of article 6 of the ECHR, it seems urgent, first and foremost, to study an amendment to the PCPP in order to enable a wider renewal of evidence at the appeal stage, notably when the Appeal Courts feel inclined to reverse an acquittal or a conviction—and to do it through a rule that privileges direct and personal immediacy when the doubts of the Appeal Courts result from personal evidence that can be actually brought before its judges. Even though the PCPP could also gain from updating its rules on the use of technology during criminal trials—for instance, by demanding a video recording of the trial instead of only audio engraving, as it is the general rule—, when facing a decision reversal, direct immediacy should be always privileged. A rule of this sort would be highly advisable not only to comply with the ECtHR standard, but also because limiting immediacy to video-recordings in these situations would still give way to suspicions on its reliability and fairness. In fact, the viewing of a video recording does not allow the Appeal Courts with to have the same level of 'comfort' of the trial courts—and could therefore still lead to decisions in which the Appeal Courts, albeit recognizing other possible interpretations of the evidence, nevertheless maintain the trial courts' decision under a reasoning highlighting the 'preference-rule' for the immediacy of the trial judge. Moreover, a recording keeps the Appeal Courts at a distance (chronologically, spatially, and psychologically)[39] and faced with possible technical complications that make it difficult to fully grasp all the verbal and

[38] Offering specific criteria for such distinction, see Carrón (2013), pp. 167 et seq.

[39] Carrón (2013), p. 179.

non-verbal languages[40] of the parties and the witnesses. Finally, mitigated immediacy does not guarantee any adversarial moment,[41] since the defendant, the victim, and its lawyers are not able to influence the outcome of the Appeal Courts video analysis. For these reasons, video recordings should be introduced to the PCPP but are not to be privileged to the scheduling of an evidentiary hearing where all the necessary evidence (new or to be renewed) can be produced. In short, there is no reason to accept that the reversal of a trial court decision—that desirably will only occur when there is sufficient certainty that the first decision was wrong—could be made based on indirect (and therefore less prone to form judgements of certainty) assessments of personal evidence.

For all of the above, one can say that the time has come for thoroughly evaluation and sketching an amendment to the PCPP's regime on criminal appeals. In doing so, the appeal phase would certainly have much to gain, namely by moving closer to the ECtHR standard—but also by doing it with a critical sense, aiming at a more convincing balance between the economy of the appeal phase, the technological developments, and the pursuit of the truth as well as material justice.

Cited Case-Law

ECtHR

hudoc.echr.coe.int

Ekbatani v. Sweden, no. 10563/83, 26 May 1988
Constantinescu v. Romania, no. 28871/95, 27 June 2000
Destreheim v. France, no. 56651/00, 18 May 2004
Bazo González v Spain, no. 30643/04, 16 December 2008
Almenara Álvarez v. Spain, no. 16096/08, 25 October 2011
Moreira Ferreira v. Portugal, no. 19808/08, 5 July 2011
Serrano Contreras v. Spain, no. 49183/08, 20 March 2012
Hanu v. Romania, no. 10890/04, 4 June 2013
Gómez Olmeda v. Spain, no. 61112/12, 29 March 2016
Kashlev v. Estonia, no. 22574/08, 26 April 2016
Lazu v. Republic of Moldova, no. 46182/08, 5 July 2016
Pereira Cruz et al. v. Portugal, no. 56396/12, 26 June 2018
Paixão Moreira Sá Fernandes v. Portugal, no. 78108/14, 25 February 2020
Dan v. Moldova, no. 57575/14, 10 November 2020
Mihail Mihalescu v. Romania, no. 795/15, 12 January 2021
Victor Laurentiu Martin v. Romania, no. 75614/14, 12 January 2021

[40] On the relevance of non-verbal language for a better examination of personal evidence, see Ibãnez (2006), pp. 10–11; Pérez (2020), pp. 278–280.

[41] Pérez (2020), pp. 273–274.

Portuguese Courts

dgsi.pt

Supreme Court of Justice, no. 959/09.2TVLSB.L1.S1, 7 September 2017
Supreme Court of Justice, no. 147/13.3JELSB.L2.S1, 15 July 2021
Évora Court of Appeal, no. 243/18.0GDFAR.E1, 10 November 2020
Évora Court of Appeal, no. 214/17.4IDFAR.E1, 17 December 2020
Lisbon Court of Appeal, no. 10684/18.8T9LSB.L1-5, 2 February 2021

References

Albuquerque P (2011) Comentário do Código de Processo Penal à luz da Constituição da República e da Convenção Europeia dos Direitos do Homem, 4th edn. Universidade Católica Editora, Lisbon

Carrón CF (2013) La inmediación en la segunda instancia penal y civil: ¿resulta razonable que su significado y alcance vaíe en función de la naturaleza del proceso? In: Deu TA (ed) La convergencia entre proceso civil y penal: ¿una dirección adecuada? Marcial Pons, Madrid, pp 163–184

Dias F (2004) Direito Processual Penal. Coimbra Editora, Coimbra

Fanego CA (2012) The right to a double degree of jurisdiction in criminal offences (art. 2 P 7). In: Roca JG, Santolaya P (eds) Europe of Rights: a compendium on the European Convention of Human Rights. Martinus Nijhoff Publishers, Leiden, Boston, pp 161–176

Ibãnez PA (2006) Valoração da Prova e Sentença Penal. Lumen Juris, Rio de Janeiro

Mata-Mouros F (2020) Recurso da matéria de facto no processo penal. In: Albuquerque PP (org) Comentário da Convenção Europeia dos Direitos Humanos e dos Protocolos Adicionais, vol III. Universidade Católica Editora, Lisbon, pp 2394–2422

Morão H (2020) Pela renovação da renovação da prova. Anatomia do Crime 12:171–195

Morão H (2021) Reformando o recurso em processo penal. In: Albuquerque PP, Cardoso R, Moura S (eds) Corrupção em Portugal. Avaliação legislativa e proposta de reforma. Universidade Católica Editora, Lisbon, pp 655–663

Negri D (2014) Das Unmittelbarketisprinzip in der italienischen Strafprozessordnung kulturelle Hintergründe, Umwege der Rechtsprechung, verfassungsrechtliche Ergebnisse. Zeitschrift für die gesamte Strarechtswissenschaft 126(1):214–238

Pérez FO (2020) La inmediación en el proceso penal. Justicia: revista de derecho procesal 1:255–284

Ruiz FL (2016) El principio de inmediación en el processo penal: una crítica epistemológica. Justicia: revista de derecho procesal 1:221–268

Selçuk H (2012) The actual role of the principle of immediacy in the Dutch Criminal Procedural. Tilburg University, Tilburg

Silva LD (2020) Processo eletrónico e conexão à distância. In: Gomes CA, Neves AF, Serrão T (eds) Comentários à legislação processual administrativa. AAFDL Editora, Lisbon, pp 683–714

Summers SJ (2007) Fair trials. Hart Publishing, Oxford

Willimman M (2016) Der Unmittelbarketsgrundsatz im Zivilprozess. Mohr Siebeck, Tübingen

Winter LB (2019) Principio de inmediácion y confrontation: paralelismos, diferencias y tendências en la prueba testical. In: Ambos K, Malarino E (eds) Fundamentos de derecho probatório en material penal. Tirant lo Blanch, Valencia, pp 279–332

Part III
Immediacy in Criminal Procedure Theory and Cognitive Sciences

Chapter 6
Immediacy at the First Instance Trial

Mafalda Moura Melim

6.1 The Immediacy Principle at Its Origins: *Code d'Instruction Criminelle* (1808)

As judicial systems evolved from its primary forms of private settlements to punishments imposed by the community and finally to an undeniable competence of modern liberal states, multiple questions arose. Especially in criminal procedures, important choices had to be made, in order to assure that former abuses of absolute monarchies were definitely set aside. The origins of the immediacy principle are traditionally found in the *Code d'Instruction Criminelle* of 1808.[1] Its article 317 prescribed that 'the witnesses' testimony is to be presented orally before the judge',[2] a provision that was followed by a series of formal requirements. As noted by

[1]However, according to Chmiel (2016), p. 2, 'already in the Republic period, testimony given personally by a witness before the court was preferred to testimony in the form of a document. (...) In the Empire period, the Roman criminal procedure was also dominated by the immediacy principle. The fact that the principle was adhered to is explicitly confirmed by the rescripts issued by Emperor Hadrian, expressing the demand that direct evidence be taken before the court, the reform of the irenarchae's office implemented by Antoninus Pius, as well as a ban on legal assistance in criminal cases, confirmed by Justinian. Certain exceptions to the immediacy principle were allowed, such as submitting at a trial written *laudationes* prepared out of court and reports on interrogation of witnesses compiled during the proceedings, as well as admissibility of circumstantial evidence'.

[2]Article 317 du Code d'Instruction Criminelle (1808): *'Les témoins déposeront séparément l'un de l'autre, dans l'ordre établi par le procureur général. Avant de déposer, ils prêteront, à peine de nullité, le serment de parler sans haine et sans crainte, de dire toute la vérité, et rien que la vérité. Le président leur demandera leur nom, prénoms, âge, profession, leur domicile ou résidence, s'ils connaissaient l'accusé avant le fait mentionné dans l'acte d'accusation, s'ils sont parents ou alliés,*

M. M. Melim (✉)
University of Lisbon School of Law, Research Centre for Criminal Law and Criminal Sciences (CIDPCC), Lisbon, Portugal
e-mail: mafaldamouramelim@fd.ulisboa.pt

H. Morão, R. Tavares da Silva (eds.), *Fairness in Criminal Appeal*,
https://doi.org/10.1007/978-3-031-13001-4_6

H. Selçuk,[3] the Code was highly influenced by English procedural principles, which favoured the open and public discussion of criminal causes, in opposition to the confidentiality and obscurity of civil law systems. However, this nineteenth century French law preserved a clear boundary between the pre-trial phase and the trial stage. The former, to be held secretly, in written form, by the judge *(juge d'instruction)* and the attorney general (*procureur général*), without the defendant being present or represented, and no information being provided to him or her in most cases; the latter, consisting of a public trial, characterized by oral discussion and the possibility of questioning the opposing witnesses.

Since the roots of this principle are to be found in the spirit of the French Revolution, it is essential to highlight that it was intended to be used as a trump granted to the individuals that enabled them to control and react against the (likely) unfairness of a secret written trial.[4] This historical intention hints that this principle served primarily the interests of the people involved in a conflict against the State. It was not, thus, a prerogative offered to the judge—or the court—to be weaponised against the accused or the victim. Nevertheless, gains went and still go beyond the defendant. As Hélie noted, by confronting the accused with the witnesses, the path for uncovering the truth was significantly shortened, and the *conviction intime* of the judge was much strongly moulded.[5] Furthermore, the information gathered by the judge was simultaneously made available to other parties, enabling them to build their own perception of the evidence being offered. In addition, when contradicting the statements, the defendant could actively take part and be more influent in the process of convincing the court of his or her innocence.

6.1.1 The Immediacy Principle in Early European Criminal Procedure Codes

The inspiration of the French *Code d'Instruction Criminelle* of 1808 to the early European Criminal Procedure Codes is unequivocal. Around this period, the immediacy principle was being abundantly discussed in Germany and, in 1877, the Criminal Procedure Code adopted the principles of orality and immediacy (§ 188). Although the criminal procedure was also structured in two different phases—the investigation and the trial—no reading out in court of earlier statements or written

soit de l'accusé, soit de la partie civile, et à quel degré ;il leur demandera encore s'ils ne sont pas attachés au service de l'un ou de l'autre: cela fait, les témoins déposeront oralement'.

[3] Selçuk (2012), p. 4.

[4] Pérez (2020), p. 265; Winter (2019), p. 293.

[5] Hélie (1866–7), p. 488.

explanations was allowed,[6] differently from what occurred in the French model.[7] As stated in the referred paragraph, the preliminary phase was directed at determining whether a trial should take place and was presided by an investigating judge. At this stage, examinations of the accused, witnesses or experts were to be led by the judge in the presence of a court writer, responsible for recording all evidence heard. Furthermore, whereas the accused was to be questioned in the absence of both the prosecutor and defence counsel, witnesses or experts were to be examined before them. The trial took place in the uninterrupted presence of the judge, the accused being assisted by counsel at every stage of the procedure. Moreover, the judge was entitled to ask supplementary queries, following the questioning by both parties. Another interesting feature of the German example refers to the possibility of an expert, witness, or co-accused provide further explanations if and when needed.

Several aspects of the immediacy principle were studied by German scholars during the years surrounding its inclusion in the Criminal Procedure Code. However, each author chose to address its content in a particular way. For instance, Holtzendorff highlighted that the immediacy principle and the principle of oral procedure both demand that the judge be provided with the live testimonial of the accused and the witnesses, and not to experience them through reading written statements.[8] Feuerbach, on the other hand, emphasised that the evidence sustaining the verdict should always be presented before the accused, allowing him or her—as well as his or her defence—to challenge such testimonials. According to the author, in its initial implementation the principle was being infringed, since the evidence collected in earlier phases of the proceedings was still copiously used to determine the charge.[9] Sharing some of these concerns, Mittermaier added that the immediacy principle should determine that the judge pronouncing the verdict be able to see and hear the witnesses so that he/she could ask supplementary questions, enabling him/her to assess the reliability of the witnesses' testimonies.[10] More recently, the risk of distortion carried by the transfer of information has also been reckoned as a relevant element of the immediacy principle. It ended up with the formation of the

[6]Exceptions made to dying declarations, mental illness and untraceable witnesses, as explained by Summers (2007), p. 53.

[7]Articles 318 and 341 of the French Criminal Procedure Code determined, that 'the president shall cause a note to be taken by the clerk of the court of the additions, changes, or variations which may exist between a witness's deposition and his previous statements. The attorney-general and the accused may require the president to have notes take on these changes, additions, and variations' and 'the president puts the written issues before the jury in the presence of the foreman of the jury; he adds thereto the indictment, the official reports establishing the offences, and the documents of the action other than the written depositions of the witnesses'.

[8]Holtzendorff (1879), p. 63.

[9]Summers (2007), p. 55.

[10]Mittermaier (1845), p. 246. Consequently, the use of statements obtained during the investigative phase constituted a violation both of the notion of immediacy and of the requirement that the proceedings take place orally. In order to rectify this he favoured a solution whereby the evidence collected during the preliminary phase could be used only to assist in the decision whether or not to prosecute—Summers (2007), p. 56.

idea that a witness testimony in front of the judge is preferred to a written witness testimony.[11] Additionally, and to sum up, Goldschmidt's vision of this principle was widely diffused and still remains an important reference. Combining all previous suggestions, Goldschmidt distinguished between the objective content of the immediacy principle—the need to choose and prefer direct and immediate sources of evidence—and its subjective implications—concerning the direct rapport to be established between the judge deciding the cause and the evidence to be offered.

In Italy, the Criminal Procedure Code of 1865 was inspired by its French companion, stating the rule of orality in articles 281 (3), 304 and 310. The Code determined that the witnesses and experts were to be heard, demanding them to testify orally. However, the underlying risk of the judge having read the witnesses' testimonials at the secrecy of *camera di consiglio* (council chamber) remained present and was seen as a risk that could undermine the oral debate and the understanding of sound and visual details absorbed during the trial. The Italian Criminal Procedure opted for a mixed approach, through a preliminary investigation phase and a trial—*il dibattimento*. Consequently, the deciding judge was prevented from casually disposing of evidence repeatedly filtered by colleagues—namely, the investigating judge and the council chamber or the prosecution section.

Furthermore, multiple exceptions to this orality clause were legally conceived, allowing previous statements to be read in trial. As explained by M. Miletti, it was possible to read minutes and reports 'relating to the case' (article 281(2)) and to discuss at trial 'documents and objects' potentially relevant 'in conviction or exculpation' (Art. 287(7)).[12] As a consequence, although some progress was undeniable, this Code did not meet neither the immediacy requirements set out by English criminal procedural law, nor the spirit of the revolutionary rulings that inspired its publication. For that reason, some changes were in need and the discussion was fertile. As described by G. Martyn and R. Sontag, after a first group of scholars consider immediacy a non-negotiable principle of liberal justice, the Italian positivist school feared that the rule could favour popular and emotional interferences in the trial. Still, a bright discussion was intertwined on this topic, aiming at determining the immediacy principle implications in criminal procedures.[13]

In 1913, following a series of heated debates influenced by German and French models, the Italian Criminal Procedure Code restrained, as far as it was possible, the cases in which it was legitimate to read depositions and written statements of witnesses. This fact is generally considered to be the victory of the 'orality movement', led by Lucchini, Manzini and Chiovenda, who envisioned the immediacy principle as an unfailing complement to oral procedures. According to them, the idea of immediacy was included in the 'orality principle', and had to be perceived altogether with the notions of concentration of the trial and identity of the judges.

[11] Maas (1907), p. 13.

[12] Miletti (2021), p. 851.

[13] Martyn and Sontag (2021), p. 716.

Finally, another important contribution of the Italian authors consisted of associating these principles with *l'intimo convencimento* (the intimate belief or the intimate conviction of the judge). In their words 'by virtue of orality, (. . .) all evidence was unfolded in the presence of judges, not only because of the 'conflict of testimony' but also by 'the demeanour of the witnesses and the accused, by the emotions they feel, by the gestures and disturbances that reveal their intimate feelings, and together by all those signs that speak eloquently to the eyes, and which it is not possible to portray exactly with words'.[14]

The Spanish *Ley de Enjuiciamento Criminal* (Criminal Procedure Code) published in 1882, stated, at its initial remarks, that the actual criminal procedure would not start until the opening remarks were made before the court.[15] It did not mention, throughout its articles, the immediacy principle or the need for an oral contradictory debate during the trial phase. However, its article 741 declared—and still does—that the court is to assess the 'evidence presented at the trial' according to its conscience, which implies, at least, that the evidence is to be preferably presented before the court.

As suggested by Ortego Pérez, the immediacy principle—duly integrated in the 'immediacy, publicity and orality triangle'—unveiled itself as a solid alternative to the system of legal proof. In fact, the free assessment of evidence according to the rule of conscientious evaluation was seen as only feasible if the judge was in direct contact with the sources of each evidence. Since the immediacy principle imposed that all evidence be presented before the judge who would later examine it, it ensured that the person analysing all evidence witnessed its presentation. Thus, and gradually, those principles acquired a constitutional relevance, and started to be treated as a procedural warrantee of criminal trials.

At last, it is important to recognise that the historical reasons for implementing the immediacy principle were not connected to the need to cross-examine the evidence. As a matter of fact, such prerogative was initially conceived as a lawful weapon to be used against inquisitorial defiance and secret criminal procedures.[16] It was meant to bring some publicity and transparency into the criminal procedure. But it was perfectly possible to adopt the immediacy rule for criminal hearings without providing the participants with the chance of interacting with witnesses or experts.

In Portugal, the immediacy principle is typically considered as a characteristic of the rapport established between the court and the evidence to be presented. In fact, during the nineteenth century, jury trials started to take off in the Portuguese criminal system[17]. With them came the need of an oral debate to be openly held in order to determine the defendants' guilt or innocence. In fact, the direct contact established between the court and witnesses in these cases became therefore a need before it was seen as a principle. It represented the proper—and only—way of providing the jury

---

[14] Miletti (2021), p. 851.

[15] Winter (2019), p. 286.

[16] Winter (2019), p. 293.

[17] Mesquita (2015), p. 125.

with the available data concerning the facts, enabling them to get in touch with all relevant evidence. The criminal procedure system implemented in 1929 upheld the differences between the pre-trial stage and the criminal hearing and adopted immediacy as a general requirement of criminal trials. Although the evidence gathered in the primary phase could be imported to trial, immediacy and oral debate became essential features of the hearing itself, in order to allow the judge to shape his conviction regarding the defendant's criminal liability[18].

In 1932, a procedural reform held by Manuel Rodrigues and Alberto dos Reis highlighted that the immediacy principle also referred to the 'direct contact to be established between the judge and the parties, witnesses, experts, briefly, with all those who can help uncover the facts'. Another step was taken into favouring a real debate between the parties and the court. Consequently, as the second quarter of the twentieth century approached, immediacy had already established itself as the preferential vehicle of judicial knowledge in the Portuguese inquisitorial and authoritarian model[19].

The Anglo-American criminal procedure has always trusted the jury with the task of finding the relevant facts sustaining the final verdict to be held. As a consequence, early on became imperative to expose juries to all available data relating to those facts, which implied that all evidence had to be presented directly at trial. This was an uncontroversial requirement in Scottish and English law.[20] In Scotland, all evidence was to be presented not only before those determining the charge, but also before the accused (Statute of 1587 cc 91 and 92). Moreover, as stressed by R. Vogler, juries tended to be illiterate people with very little time for the performance of decision-making in criminal justice. That is why the trial had to be swift, entirely oral and touch on all available evidence within the shortest period of time. For that reason, written evidence was found to be useless.[21] In England, it was a firm rule that evidence collected during pre-trial investigations (such as in the course of magistrates' hearings) could not be introduced in written form at trial.[22]

In this context, the immediacy principle itself had very little meaning, as it still does today, due to its connection with continental types of criminal procedures. In fact, the concerns of Anglo-American scholars addressing this topic are limited to cross-examination and hearsay rules. The former, determining that the accused is entitled to question the prosecution witnesses and experts, which demands that statements be taken before the accused and the court, during trial;[23] the latter, asserting, at its primary stage, the inadmissibility of declarations other than the ones given orally in the proceedings.

[18] Mesquita (2015), p. 127.

[19] Mesquita (2015), p. 127.

[20] Summers (2007), p. 56.

[21] Vogler (2014), p. 240.

[22] However, in some cases the assize never actually saw the witness, Summers (2007), p. 53.

[23] Winter (2019), p. 294.

6.1.2 Final Remarks

All things considered, it is clear that the immediacy principle presents an undeniable historical component of criminal procedures. In fact, in most European countries, it emerged as a reaction to the unfairness of ancient judicial systems—namely, criminal procedure codes.

As mentioned, the continental tradition was marked by the secrecy of pre-trial investigation, carried in written form, and associated with the system of legal proof. According to this structure, the trial judge was only to verify whether the collected evidence would meet the legal requirements. Should that be the case, a conviction was in order. It is then accurate to assert that this principle reflects a political option to reform this system and to submit the judicial system to public scrutiny, evolving from secrecy to publicity and from written statements to oral debates. Furthermore, judges became responsible for directly analysing the evidence presented before them, so that they could reach their own personal conclusions as to the verdict to be held. That being said, no strict instructions were to be followed when assessing the evidence gathered—as it used to be the case with the systems of legal proof. The judge was therefore only under the duty to present his or her reasoning when explaining the verdict, describing his or her conclusions regarding the evidence presented. All in all, the immediacy principle appeared, for these countries, has a triumph of the French Revolution.

Much opposingly, the Anglo-American criminal procedure had always involved an oral debate, the jury being offered all evidence in their presence. This means, as noted above, that the immediacy requirement was understood in other terms. Here, the spotlight was set at cross-examination demands and the hearsay rule. As a result, the immediacy principle came to represent a relevant component of the right to a fair trial.

It is also clear that the immediacy principle is associated with several other features of criminal procedures. For instance, the need of an oral debate. As German and Italian scholars explained, demanding all evidence be led directly at trial was pointless if the judge was prevented from submitting further queries and shaping his/her conviction regarding the facts. Besides, the imposition of a contradictory debate—also known as the cross-examination requirement—ensured that both the court and the parties took part in the procedure, meeting the purpose of publicly enacting the law. Moreover, it began to be seen as strange and unwanted that the person deciding the charge had not been present at trial—which led to the rule that all evidence was to be presented successively and in the briefest period of time. Finally, the immediacy principle enabled the judge to decide freely, according to his or her *intime conviction*, granting him or her direct access to all relevant evidence, and offering him the elements to substantiate the verdict.

In general, the main implications of embracing the immediacy principle were: the court's conviction concerning the accused's responsibility had to be formed according to evidence led in trial; a preference for personal sources of evidence, ideally obtained during an oral debate; and the right of all parties to direct access to sources of evidence presented in trial. Some exceptions were gradually introduced and are still today accepted, but restricted to those cases involving dying declarations, mental illness or untraceable witnesses.[24] This means that, as a rule, pre-trial statements provided by witnesses who later refuse to talk before court should not be admissible.

On the one hand, it represents a tool provided to the judge, enabling him or her to shape his or her perception of the relevant facts, allowing doubts to be solved, questions to be asked and contradictions to be detected. In this context, we can ascertain that the immediacy principle consists of a legal tool with two main purposes: (*i*) provide the court with the required factual elements to analyse the case through its own perception; (*ii*) offer a solid basis when substantiating the final decision. Here, it is obviously associated with the need to assure that the person deciding the charge is duly aware of the facts involved in the cause, having had the possibility to develop some further *field* investigation. That being so, the verdict to be announced will reflect a thorough analysis led by a judge possessing all available information. This aspect of the immediacy principle relates to its European origins: as a matter of fact, countries abolishing the system of legal proof needed to provide the judge with an alternative tool of assessing the evidence. With that purpose, direct access to all evidence was given to judges, imposing it be led in trial.

On the other hand, and more importantly, the immediacy principle also appears as a prerogative granted to the parties—namely the accused—providing him or her direct access to all evidence, and allowing him or her to challenge such evidence before the court responsible for determining the charge. Here, the Anglo-American root of the principle is clearly dominant, since it is regarded as an essential characteristic of fair trial, a prerequisite that has to be met in order to lead to a righteous decision.

Accordingly, the immediacy imposed on criminal procedures implies that parties shall present their evidence in court, that such evidence can be challenged before the judge, and that all evidence not meeting these requirements will not be used to sustain the verdict. Furthermore, it also enables a more accurate appeal, since all evidence had to be analysed under the same conditions by all subjects. That is to say that the accused is duly aware of the facts presented in court, and thus can more easily challenge the judge's decision.

At this point, we can establish that the immediacy principle demands for the implementation of cross-examination rules and hearsay legislation.

[24] Summers (2007), p. 53.

6.2 The Evolution and Development of the Immediacy Principle Requirements

The second part of our study aims at determining whether the immediacy principle is still a relevant component of modern criminal procedure systems in Europe. Specifically, we will compare its primary forms with the current implementation of such principle in multiple countries. Pursuing that goal, we will emphasise some recognised exceptions to the immediacy requirement, in order to assess its evolution and development throughout the decades. In that regard, thoughtful attention should be given to the possibility of using videoconference statements and adjourning trial sessions.

Oral contradictory debates held before the court, during a public audience, are still the most common form of pursuing criminal justice in the European continent. In fact, Portugal,[25] Spain,[26] France,[27] Germany,[28] and Italy,[29] all rely on the immediacy principle as a fundamental characteristic of criminal hearings. At the same time, keen importance is given to the possibility of challenging the evidence presented by the opposing party or the prosecutor, allowing participants to react to unexpected developments and to request adjournments in order to adapt their strategy.

Alongside the more common exceptions to the immediacy principle—dying declarations, mental illness and untraceable witnesses—, several criminal procedure systems have also admitted in certain situations bringing pre-existing evidence into trial. In this context, the most relevant topic concerns the reading or reproducing of former statements given by the defendant. At the time being, most countries have accepted this model, even though submitted to strict requirements and conditions to ensure that the accused is duly aware of the potential implications of his or her declarations.[30]

[25] Article 355 of the Portuguese Criminal Procedure Code.

[26] Article 229 (1) of Ley Orgánica del Poder Judicial.

[27] As noted by Leblois-Happe (2014), p. 186, French criminal procedural law does not foresee a direct legal provision on immediacy or orality of the trial, although its application is present throughout the Criminal Procedure Code. Publicity is guaranteed under article 306. The defendant as a right to be orally informed of the charges brought against him (article 327). The witnesses are to provide their statements through oral evidence (article 331).

[28] Immediacy is also not expressly included in a legal provision under German law; however, it is widely understood that the StPO intends, through different legal provisions, to maximize immediacy during the trial (see Dumitrescu 2014, p. 109). The main legal provisions from which an immediacy principle is usually obtained and applied in the trial stage are articles 250 (principle of examination in person at the main hearing) and 261 (principle of the judge's free evaluation of the evidence presented in the hearing) StPO.

[29] Articles 525 and 526 of the Italian Criminal Procedure Code.

[30] Article 357 of the Portuguese Criminal Procedure Code; articles 714 and 730 of LECrim; article 251 of the StPO; articles 513 and 514 of the Italian Procedure Code.

Our study, however, wishes to focus on different exceptions to the immediacy requirements, namely those interfering with the possibility of direct contact being established between the court and the available sources of evidence. For that reason, we will examine three possible threats to the immediacy principle, according to European legislation: *(i)* the impact of a change to the court's composition; *(ii)* the consequences of the trial being suspended for an indefinite period of time; *(iii)* the validity of using recordings and videoconference as an alternative source for examining statements.

6.2.1 Variations to the Court's Composition

We have previously mentioned that the immediacy principle entails that the court examining the evidence must also be the one determining the destiny of the charge. In fact, by establishing a direct contact with the sources of evidence, the judge collects crucial data that will form his or her judgment regarding the defendant's criminal liability. Additionally, by submitting further questions, the judge may unveil hidden information that might be crucial for defining the outcome of the proceedings. Consequently, in order for that understanding to be reflected into the judgment, the identity of the court has to remain unblemished until the case is decided. Bearing this in mind, it is clear that any transformation in the court's composition may represent a threat to this feature of the immediacy principle.

On this subject, the Italian Criminal Procedure Code states that 'the same judges who took part in the hearing shall take part in the deliberations, on pain of absolute nullity. If deputy judges are to take part in the deliberations in place of judges prevented from attending, the measures already pronounced shall remain in force unless they are expressly revoked' (article 525, no. 2). Likewise, article 111 of the Italian Constitution determines that 'in criminal law proceedings, the formation of evidence is based on the principle of adversary hearings'. However, according to Italian scholars the immediacy principle has been repeatedly attacked by unlawful decisions, which have contributed to its progressive degradation.[31] Thereupon, an increasing discrepancy is observed between law in books and law in action.

Recently, the Italian Supreme Court (*Corte de Cassazione*) issued a decision concerning the immediacy principle—specifically, on the matter of the identity of judges composing the court.[32] In that context, the Court ruled that the immutability clause emerging from the immediacy principle entails exclusively the identity of the judge before whom the evidence was taken and the judge of the decision, excluding from the scope of the principle the previous measures on the admission of evidence. As a matter of fact, the latter are to be understood as confirmed unless expressly revoked by the new panel. In other words, the Court considered that although the

[31] Manfrini and Sartori (2021), p. 4.

[32] ICCass Joint sections, 30 May 2019, no. 41736, Bajrami.

judge who had admitted the evidence was not the one issuing the verdict, article 525, no. 2 of the Criminal Procedure Code was not at risk, since those decisions were not comprised in the immediacy clause. Furthermore, the *Corte di Cassazione* asserted that the change in the composition of the court entitles the parties to request either new evidence, or the renewal of evidence taken by the court otherwise composed, pursuant to articles 468 and 493 of the Criminal Procedure Code. Should the party choose the renewal option, a specific indication of the reasons requiring such renewal has to be presented, the judge being able to deem such request manifestly superfluous (articles 190 and 495 of the Criminal Procedure Code).

As foreseen, the decision was highly criticised by Italian experts, who found the Supreme Court to be unlawfully tampering with the requirements of the immediacy principle, because the principle also related to decisions on the admissibility of evidence. Under the pretext of hasty justice, the Court has progressively tightened the essence of this principle, neglecting its role as a component of a fair trial. Moreover, it challenged the understanding adopted by the same Supreme Court in *Iannasso*,[33] according to which 'following a change of the judicial body, the trial should be entirely renewed which entails the need for the repetition of the procedural sequence consisting of the declaration of the opening of the hearing (Art. 492), the requests for the admission of evidence (Art. 493), the measures relating to admission (Art. 495), the taking of evidence that has been admitted under Articles 495(1), - 190(1), - 190-bis according to the rules laid down in Articles 496 et seq. in Articles 496 et seq. of the Code of Criminal Procedure'.

From our standpoint, the immediacy principle should not be treated as an immutable feature of criminal procedures. In fact, the conclusive test consists of determining whether its main purpose remains uninjured following the disputed choice.

In Portugal, article 328.°-A, no. 2 of the Criminal Procedure Codes determines that 'if during the discussion and trial by a collective court one of the assistant judges dies or becomes permanently incapacitated, the acts already performed shall not be repeated, unless the circumstances make it advisable to repeat one or more of the acts already performed, which shall be decided, in a reasoned order, by the judge who is to preside over the continuation of the hearing, after hearing the substitute judge'. This means that, in general, a modification to the composition of the court does not claim for the renewal of the evidence already presented, unless the new judges so decide. In this spirit, the Proposal behind Law no. 27/2015 (Proposal no. 263/XII) clarified that 'the loss of all procedural acts carried out up to that moment is difficult to understand, given the collegiate functioning of the decision-making body, as well as the current obligation to record hearings'. By affirming this, it becomes clear that recordings are considered to be, as a rule, a legitimate way of compensating for the lack of immediacy regarding the new member of the court.

This option also suggests that the Portuguese legislator considers that the majority of the judges integrating the panel being present during all trial is enough to fulfil the

[33]ICCass Joint sections, 15 January 1999, no. 212395, Iannasso.

immediacy requirement. As a consequence, if changes occur but do not affect the majority, this principle will still be respected.

Another threat to the trial's immediacy is the passing of a long period of time. Generally speaking, time poses various risks to the integrity and value of the evidence—and even to the trial itself. For example, all evidentiary principles recommend that the evidence is to be collected and presented in the shortest possible time, in order to guarantee its quality and greater reliability. The importance of this practice may in certain cases even justify a restriction on the immediacy of the trial, specifically in cases where criminal procedural laws allow for the valuation of statements made specifically at an earlier stage of the proceedings with an intent of a future use during the trial phase. Another example, more directly related to immediacy in the trial, is the risk that arises from an excessively long judgment. When a trial goes on for many days or months—either because of the intrinsic length and complexity of the case at hand or because there is a long break or a suspension between trial sessions—disturbances begin to happen. It becomes harder for the judge (and to all other parties) to remember all the evidence that was previously presented. It also makes it more challenging to compare all the testimonies with the statements made earlier on the same subject, with prejudice for the desirable critical and reciprocal approach to evidence. The harms that these effects, all related to the passing of time, may cause in the fairness of the trial are so relevant that today the material prerequisites of the immediacy principle are understood to also encompass a time limit.[34] On this subject, let's consider the cases of both Spain and Portugal to see how these States deal with the loss of immediacy due to the course of time.

In line with the recommended time limit for the evidence and for the duration of the trial, LECRIM establishes a rule of consecutive sessions for the trial (article 744). However, its legal provisions also foresee the possibility of suspending an ongoing trial[35] in certain situations revolving around the lack of conditions to proceed with the trial.[36] In these situations, the Court must, if possible, determine the maximum duration of the suspension (article 747)—a rule that also aims to contain the harms to immediacy. But even more relevant is the rule that establishes that if the trial remains suspended 'for too long', the part of the trial already held (namely, the evidence brought before the court) shall be declared void (article 749). This extreme solution is only applicable to cases of illness and unexpected revelation and leads to the need to restart all the trial once the cause of the suspension ends. Even though limited to

[34] The establishment of a rule that all evidence should be produced in the shortest possible time during the trial also follows from one other evidentiary principle, the concentration principle.

[35] On the suspension of the trial, see Zamora (2015), p. 57 et seq.

[36] Article 746 LECrim details some causes for the said suspension: the need to solve an incidental issue that cannot be immediately determined; the need to move outside the court for reasons foreseen in Spanish law; when witnesses do not appear and the Court decides that the trial cannot move forward without them; when a judge, a prosecutor, a lawyer or the accused falls ill and cannot continue to take part in the trial; if unexpected revelations make it necessary to start a new investigation and to bring new evidence to the trial.

these cases, this legal consequence is one of the most extreme legal solutions on attempting to safeguard the immediacy of the trial.

The PCPP also includes a similar rule on the continuity of the sessions of the trial (article 328 (1)) and used to establish an even more broad consequence for the loss of immediacy arising from an excessively long trial that was, however, removed from the PCPP in 2015. Before 2015, under article 328 (6), if between two sessions of the trial elapsed a period of more than 30 days, the evidence would 'lose its effectiveness'. Portuguese scholars[37] used to converge in limiting the loss of effectiveness to personal evidence (statements and testimonies from the parts, experts, or witnesses) since only personal evidence was subject to a time-limit under the immediacy principle.[38] The consequence of this violation was the need to repeat all personal evidence. If the court decided not to repeat the evidence, the whole trial could be annulled under article 120 (2) (d) of the PCPP (since such decision could be seen as an 'omission of an essential act for the purposes of truth finding'). In 2015, however, even though the principle of continuity remained, Law no. 27/2015 amended the PCPP to erase the 'loss of effectiveness' of the evidence after 30 days without a session of the trial. According to the Proposal behind Law no. 27/2015, the technological advances of the past years had outdated the need for that legal provision, since evidence is nowadays more easily preserved (namely, via recordings). This change of perception on the importance of the course of time shows that the immediacy principle is constantly being updated and renewed, sometimes even generating discontinuities between different countries in the face of the same threats.

Times are changing and so are the once insurmountable boundaries of immediacy. This is particularly visible regarding the technological developments and their effects on immediacy, including at trial stage. On this topic, we will scrutinise the French and Spanish legislation issued on the theme, since these are two countries to have expressly included this option in their Criminal Procedure Codes. More explicitly, we will discuss the admissibility of statements given through videoconferencing mechanisms under the immediacy principle requisites.

Since 2001, the French Criminal Procedure Code has contained a section named '*on the usage of telecommunication means during proceedings*', composed of articles 706-71 and 706-71-1. This amendment was implemented on behalf of efficiency reasons, and enabled the court to question any participant and ensure cross-examination procedures via alternative means of communication, namely videoconferencing. According to these rules, all statements to be given (witnesses, civil parties, experts and defendant, even if imprisoned) could be carried out online. Nonetheless, as underlined by J. Bossan, article 706-71 clearly suggests that the

---

[37] For all, Albuquerque (2011), p. 852.

[38] This position casted some doubts on whether personal evidence already documented (for example, oral statements from witness that had meanwhile been transplanted to a written support) could be exempted from the loss of effectiveness rule—doubts that were, however, solved with a 'judgment for the uniformity of jurisprudence' taken by the SCJ that determined that the loss of effectiveness was also applicable in these situations (Decision to Standardize Case Law no. 11/2008, case no. 4822/07-3, 11 December 2008).

employment of such alternative means is exceptional, and will only be admissible under special circumstances, that must be duly summoned and demonstrated by the court.[39] In fact, some guidelines have been issued in 2019, mentioning the importance of the judge's initiative, the need for the party to accept and the relevance of the lawyer's choice. Similarly, J. Leborne clarifies that 'if the legislator has now largely enshrined the use of videoconferencing, it is because it reduces costs and increases the speed of the procedure'.[40]

Taking all this into consideration, it is undisputable that the French legislator did not intend to tarnish the immediacy principle and to deny direct contact between the court and all personal evidence to be obtained. This urge to implement alternative paths of immediacy originated from the daily life at courts, that were unable to provide proper Justice to its citizens. Amid other explanations, geographical distance, security concerns, and updating the justice administration were the main reasons for implementing this reform—and not, therefore, a change in perception on the importance of immediacy.

Concerning this matter, the French Constitutional Council (*Conseil Constitutionnel*) recently issued three decisions,[41] underlining the importance of the defendant's presence before the court. All rulings addressed the possibility of using videoconferencing in the context of provisional detention: the first one considered it to be inadmissible to eliminate the need for obtaining the defendant's consent regarding the usage of such means of communication in proceedings relating to the extension of a pre-trial detention measure; the second and third ones found it illegitimate to determine that the accused could not object to audio-visual means of communication when the hearing referred to an application for release. In order to validate such conclusions, the Constitutional Council stated that particularly in the context of pre-trial decisions, the direct contact between the defendant and the court is essential to assure his or her proper defence.

Around the same topic, the French Conseil d' État[42] determined the suspension of the emergency sanitary measures implemented in 2020, enabling videoconferencing in criminal procedures, regardless of the parties' consent, after the investigation phase was concluded. According to the ruling, 'the seriousness of the penalties incurred and the role given to the intimate conviction of magistrates and jurors give a specific place to the oral proceedings. During the closing arguments, the physical presence of the civil parties and the accused is essential, especially when the accused speaks last, before the end of the proceedings'. It further stressed that 'in the balance of the interests involved, given the conditions under which these means of telecommunication are used (. . .), the requirements of the proper functioning of justice are not sufficient to justify the infringement of the founding principles

[39] Bossan (2011), p. 807.

[40] Leborne (2021), p. 95.

[41] Decision no. 2019-778 DC (21 March 2019), Decision no. 2019-802 QPC (20 September 2019) and Decision no. 2020-836 QPC (30 April 2020).

[42] Order dated 27 November 2020—*Ordonnance du Conseil d'État du 27 novembre 2020.*

of the criminal trial by the contested provisions and the rights of the people involved in the trial, whether they are rights of (...) parties to the trial, whether they are accused or victims'.

Corroborating our initial perception, it now became explicit that the French legislator was not eager to abandon the immediacy principle heritage. On the contrary, the exceptions to its requirements were constantly disputed before the highest judicial institutions of the country, that were assertive on affirming its importance in criminal procedure. It is beyond doubt that, to this system, the immediacy principle remains a founding value.

Spain emerges, in this context, as the most vivid example of the debate on the technological adaptation of immediacy.

Under Spanish Law, all judicial proceedings, including those of a criminal nature, are subject to legal provisions requiring a public and adversarial stage in every procedure of immediacy and orality between the court, the parties in dispute and the evidence (article 229 (1) of *Ley Orgánica del Poder Judicial* ('LOPJ') and 744 LCRIM). Since 2003, following a modernization of justice plan (the 2001 *Pacto de Estado para la Reforma de la Justicia*), Spanish law has incorporated provisions for the use of live videoconferencing as another means of communication and evidence at the disposal of its courts, including in criminal cases, in both LOPJ (article 229 (3)) and LCRIM (for the preliminary stages of the criminal procedure, under article 325 LCRIM, as well as the trial phase, under article 731bis LCRIM). 'Videoconference', for the purposes of the mentioned legal provisions, is curiously defined by law not only by its technical features, but also in line with some immediacy's typical requirements: according to article 229 (3) LOPJ, videoconference is a 'system that must allow for two-way and simultaneous communication of image and sound, auditory and verbal interaction between two geographically distant persons or groups of persons, ensuring in any case the possibility of contradiction of the parties and the safeguarding of the rights of defence'.

Not long afterwards a dispute began over whether the use of videoconferencing could be made compatible with the principle of immediacy at the trial.[43] The problem arose—and still arises—due to the content of article 731bis LCRIM, according to which the use of videoconference to hear parties, witnesses, or experts on a given case is to be limited to situations justified under utility, security or public order reasons. A limitation that is usually seen by both the Spanish scholars and the Spanish courts as intending to allow for the use of videoconferencing only in situations where waiting for the person to be physically present before the court would cause serious procedural harm.[44] In other words, as an exceptional solution. The reasons for limiting the use of this communication system relates directly to a

[43]For an overview of the debate, including the main court decision on this matter, Jiménez (2015)—(https://noticias.juridicas.com/conocimiento/articulos-doctrinales/10122-el-principio-de-inmediacion-penal-y-la-prueba-por-videoconferencia-relacion-entre-los-arts-229-lopj-y-731-bis-lecrim-/, 2015).

[44]Barrenengoa (2019), pp. 36–37. An example of such a situation would be, according to a case in which the Spanish Supreme Court discussed the use of videoconferencing, the occurrence of

preference for direct and personal immediacy. Many reasons are put forward to sustain this legal preference for a direct and personal contact with the person to be presented to the court, namely reasons concerning the better observation of the verbal and non-verbal language, as well as a better control of the respondent's freedom. Notwithstanding these arguments, still argued by the Spanish courts, videoconferencing is gradually gaining more supporters and attempts are being made to reconcile its utilization with the essential core of the immediacy principle. After all, videoconferences also bring some advantages to the table in relation to physical and more traditional forms of immediacy, such as a better conciliation with the economical and concentration principles.[45] Whether videoconference will evolve to be seen as an intrinsic form of direct immediacy or whether it will be the legal provisions that will extend their criteria on the use of videoconferencing is something that the next few years will certainly clarify. But one thing is already certain: the technological advances are today the most relevant topic of immediacy at the trial stage and undoubtedly the subject that most urgently needs reflection and legal review.

6.2.2 Final Remarks

All in all, the immediacy principle endures as an important component of most criminal procedural systems in Europe. As we have seen, criminal procedure codes conceive the public, oral, and contradictory trial as the main phase of the proceedings, where all the evidence has to be presented, discussed and examined. In other words, immediacy is the rule. Consequently, any exception to be implemented concerning its requirements undergoes a thorough reflexion process, often calling upon superior courts and constitutional jurisdictions. These institutions, in general, carefully weigh the implications of such changes to the defence, recalling that immediacy consists of a component of fair trial.

Throughout the decades, some restrictions have been imposed on its core, mainly due to objective constraints and effectiveness needs. For instance, the possibility of importing previous statements from the defendant into trial depends on a series of conditions being met, recalling the *Miranda* spirit. In fact, the Anglo-American perspective on the immediacy principle has been finding its way into continental law, enabling a less theoretical vision of it to develop. At the same time, ECtHR case law has built an integrated concept of immediacy, that has undoubtedly influenced the understanding of several national criminal law.

As far as we are concerned, it remains undisputed that the immediacy principle is a primordial feature of European criminal procedure law. Its development and

'eternal circumstances, that could cause serious disruption of the trial sessions due to mass gatherings of people around the courthouse'.

[45] A list of those advantages can be found in Barrenengoa (2019), pp. 34–35.

evolution has consisted more of an adaptation to modern societies, its dilemmas and technologies than an abandonment of its main purpose. To sum up, it would be accurate to state that immediacy is still legally required, even if the means of attaining them are subject to some, slowly building, variations.

6.3 The Immediacy Principle: State of the Art According to ECtHR Case-Law

At this point of our endeavour, we have gone through the historical origins of the immediacy principle and the challenges it has faced in many countries. In that regard, we have concluded that European legislators are strongly reluctant to relinquish to its requirements, fighting any attempts to restrain its role in criminal procedures. That said, we are now fully equipped to analyse ECtHR case-law regarding this matter, hoping to anticipate the upcoming trials to be faced by the immediacy principle, as well as the solutions at the disposal of scholars and jurists of the future.

As stated by R. Vogler 'English hearsay and the continental immediacy principle have different origins and different purposes, while the right to confrontation under Article 6(3)(d) of the ECHR seeks to span both traditions'.[46] The ECtHR has been pursuing the strenuous mission of combining multiple facets of this theme under the right to a fair trial. Consequently, no exact match can be found between the European immediacy principle, the English hearsay rule and the right to a fair trial, pursuant to articles 6(1),(3)(d) of the ECHR.

That said, it is our firm conviction that the basic content of the immediacy principle, as defined by the ECtHR under article 6(1) of the ECHR, is closer to the European definition raised in the aftermath of the French Revolution, focusing on the presentation of all evidence before the court. In P.K. v. Finland[47] ECtHR has held that an important element of fair criminal proceedings is also the possibility of the accused to be confronted with the witness in the presence of the judge who ultimately decides the case'. To our understanding, this means that for the ECtHR this principle determines that the accused must be able to gather the same information as the court, to personally observe the witness when giving the statement, to perceive the incoherence and hesitations shown to the judges. As further explained by ECtHR in the same ruling, 'the observations made by the court about the demeanour and credibility of a witness may have important consequences for the accused'—namely, in the event of an appeal being filed. According to this structure, it would be possible to sustain that the immediacy principle does not necessarily claim for the defendant's right to examine witnesses. In fact, it would still represent an important guarantee of fair trial to simply assure that the defendant has direct access to the evidence being presented in court.

---

[46] Vogler (2014), p. 246.

[47] P.K. v. Finland, no. 37442/97, 9 July 2002, *hudoc.echr.coe.int.*

However, article 6(3)(d) of the ECHR seems to be closer to the Anglo-American perspective on the immediacy principle, commonly identified as the hearsay rule. In this context, the ECtHR has clarified that 'article 6 §§ 1 and 3 (d) of the Convention contains a presumption against the use of hearsay evidence against a defendant in criminal proceedings'.[48] Therefore, the European idea of a contradictory oral debate is detached from the immediacy principle itself, since it has become an independent prerogative of the defence. It is thus perceived in accordance with the English hearsay rule and related to the possibility of cross-examining witnesses. On ECtHR's own words:

> Article 6 § 3 (d) enshrines the principle that, before an accused can be convicted, all evidence against him must normally be produced in his presence at a public hearing with a view to adversarial argument. Exceptions to this principle are possible but must not infringe the rights of the defence, which, as a rule, require that the accused should be given an adequate and proper opportunity to challenge and question a witness against him, either when that witness makes his statement or at a later stage of proceedings.[49]

In light of the above, it is clear that the right to a fair trial emerging from article 6(1) of the ECHR is seen as including also the immediacy principle as a general requirement of criminal procedures. Therefore, fair trial is to be seen as requiring specific procedural guarantees—namely, the right to examine witnesses, as set out by article 6(3)(d) of the ECHR. And since a combined vision of continental immediacy and Anglo-American hearsay rule is proposed by the ECtHR, case-law on both aspects must be shortly analysed.

6.3.1 ECtHR Case-Law on the Immediacy Principle: Article 6(1) ECHR

As previously explained, the immediacy principle is perceived by the ECtHR as concerning the rapport established between the court and the evidence to be presented. This means that fairness of criminal proceedings will be guaranteed once 'the accused is confronted with the witness in the presence of the judge who ultimately decides the case'.[50] The crucial element being, evidently, that the person participating in the proceedings is the one deciding the charge. Therefore, the main topic brought to the ECtHR's attention on this subject relates to the hypothesis where a change to the composition of the trial court has occurred. And whether that change infringes the immediacy principle.

---

[48] Thomas v. The United Kingdom, no. 19354/02, 10 May 2005, § 3, *hudoc.echr.coe.int.*

[49] Al-Khawaja and Tahery v. the United Kingdom [GC], nos. 26766/05, 22228/06, 15 December 2011, § 118; Hümmer v. Germany, no. 26171/07, 19 July 2012, § 38; Lucà v. Italy, no. 33354/96, 27 February 2001, § 39; Solakov v. the former Yugoslav Republic of Macedonia, no. 47023/99, 31 October 2001, § 57—*hudoc.echr.coe.int.*

[50] P.K. v. Finland, § a.

First of all, it is clear under ECtHR case-law that not all variations to the composition of the trial court affect immediacy and fair trial to a point to demand for the rehearing of witnesses. In Cutean v. Romania[51] the ECtHR indicated that 'measures can be taken to ensure that the judges who continue hearing the case have the appropriate understanding of the evidence and arguments, for example, by making transcripts available where the credibility of the witness concerned is not at issue, or by arranging for a rehearing of the relevant arguments or of important witnesses before the newly composed court'. Likewise, no breach of article 6(1) is to be found when although the presiding judge had changed, the three lay judges remained the same throughout the proceedings, especially if the new presiding judge had had at his disposal the minutes of the session at which the witness had been heard to a large extent [to] compensate for the lack of immediacy of the proceedings'.[52]

Another central criteria applied by the EctHR in limiting problems surrounding changes to the court's composition concerns the credibility of the witness and the relevance of his or her statement to the decision. In P.K v. Finland, it was noted that the credibility of the witness in question (not heard by the court that later judged the case) had at no stage been challenged, nor was there any indication in the file justifying doubts about her credibility. Similarly, in Graviano v. Italy[53] and Škaro v. Croatia,[54] the Court stressed that the applicant's conviction had not been based solely on the evidence of the witness in question, which assured the fairness of the proceedings. Finally, in Iancu v. Romania[55] the fact that the decision had been signed by the president of the court on behalf of the retired judge who had taken part in the examination of the case was not deemed enough to affect article 6(1) of the ECHR.

Opposingly, violations of the immediacy principle generating the breach of article 6(1) were found in cases where the judges deciding the cause had no previous contact with relevant evidence. In Cutean v. Romania,[56] the ECtHR recalled that 'according to the principle of immediacy, in a criminal case the decision should be reached by judges who have been present throughout the proceedings and evidence-gathering process', which meant that if 'the applicant's and the witnesses' statements constituted relevant evidence for his conviction which was not directly heard by the District Court single judge (...) the availability of statement transcripts cannot compensate for the lack of immediacy in the proceedings'. This understanding was subsequently adopted in Beraru v. Romania,[57] and in Cerovšek and Božičnik

[51]Cutean v. Romania, no. 53150/12, 2 December 2014, § 61, *hudoc.echr.coe.int.*

[52]P.K. v. Finland, § a.

[53]Graviano v. Italy, no. 10075/02, 10 February 2005, §§ 39–40, *hudoc.echr.coe.int.*

[54]Škaro v. Croatia, no. 6962/13, 6 December 2016, §§ 22–31, *hudoc.echr.coe.int.*

[55]Iancu v. Romania, no. 62915/17, 23 February 2021, §§ 52–60, *hudoc.echr.coe.int.*

[56]Cutean v. Romania, § 61, § 70.

[57]Beraru v. Romania, no. 40107/04, 18 March 2014, § 66, *hudoc.echr.coe.int.*

v. Slovenia[58] the Court found the 'two judges lack of involvement in the evidence-gathering process' and the fact that the previous judge had not left any written grounds to imply a violation of the immediacy principle: 'in conclusion, the Court considers that the applicants' right to a fair trial was breached because of the failure of the judge who conducted their trial to provide written grounds for her verdict and because of the absence of any appropriate measures compensating for that deficiency'. More recently, in Chernika v. Ukraine,[59] the Court seemed to admit that besides a written document to be provided for the new member for the court, a video recording would equally suit the immediacy requirements under the ECHR. It explained that 'the trial judge who eventually convicted the applicant had no opportunity personally to examine any of the three key witnesses for the prosecution. Neither did he have at his disposal a video recording of their statements even though domestic law envisaged a possibility of such video recording (. . .) and the latter may have provided an important additional safeguard'.

In the same way, in Svanidze v. Georgia[60] the relevance of the evidence in question, as well as the absence of compensating measures led to the following verdict:

> the statements of the applicant's co-defendants, the witnesses, and the experts constituted key evidence for the applicant's conviction. None of those individuals were directly heard by Judge P.S. He also refused to allow two other defence witnesses to be interviewed in his presence. In addition, as indicated in paragraph 35 above, the background of the case was factually complex and Judge P.S. examined the case as a single judge. In these circumstances, the availability of transcripts of witness statements could not compensate for the lack of immediacy.

Considering these elements, it is safe to establish that the ECtHR finds it essential that the judges deciding the case take part in the proceedings. This implies that, if no previous contact at all was established between the final judge and the collected evidence, the proceedings are seen as not compliant with the fair trial that encompasses the immediacy requirement, leading to an infringement of article 6(1) of ECHR. Nonetheless, the ECtHR has presented some criteria to help determine whether the immediacy principle is respected in cases of change to the composition of the court trial, when no rehearing of the witness was determined. Firstly, the relevance of the evidence for the decision; secondly, the credibility of the witness who was not heard by the deciding judge; thirdly, the availability of written documents able to replace the lack of immediacy.

All in all, no doubt should remain that the main concern of the ECtHR, in his context, is to verify whether the proceedings, as a whole, respected the immediacy requirements. Thus, no narrow vision should be adopted when examining a potential

---

[58] Cerovšek and Božičnik v. Slovenia, nos. 68939/12 68949/12, 7 June 2017, § 42, §47, *hudoc.echr.coe.int.*

[59] Chernika v. Ukraine, no. 53791/11, 12 March 2020, § 73, *hudoc.echr.coe.int.*

[60] Svanidze V. Georgia, no. 37809/08, 25 July 2019, § 37, *hudoc.echr.coe.int.*

breach of such principle. All stages of the proceedings must be considered and all details should be examined.

6.3.2 ECtHR Case-Law on the Right to Examine Witnesses: Articles 6(1)(3)(d) ECHR

It is now time to address the more specific procedural guarantee of the immediacy principle: the right to examine witnesses, as set out by article 6(3)(d) of the ECHR. As noted before, this independent component of the immediacy principle is designed by the ECtHR as an independent guarantee, closer to the English hearsay rule, that emphasises the requirement for cross-examination before trial.

To begin with, it is important to recall that 'article 6 § 3 (d) enshrines the principle that, before an accused can be convicted, all evidence against him must normally be produced in his presence at a public hearing with a view to adversarial argument'.[61] As a result, the ECtHR is regularly enquired about a potential offense to fair trial when a witness is absent from court and thus cannot be examined.

Two rulings are key to understand the Court's perspective on this matter: Al-Khawaja and Tahery v. the United Kingdom and Schatschaschwili v. Germany.[62] These decisions set out the principles to be considered in order to determine whether the possibility of examining that witness was essential to ensure the fairness of the proceedings. Hence, the three steps of compatibility with article 6(1) and 3(d) of the ECHR to bear in mind are:[63]

(i) whether there was a good reason for the non-attendance of the witness and, consequently, for the admission of the absent witness's untested statements as evidence;
(ii) whether the evidence of the absent witness was the sole or decisive basis for the defendant's conviction; and
(iii) whether there were sufficient counterbalancing factors, including strong procedural safeguards, to compensate for the handicaps caused to the defence as a result of the admission of the untested evidence and to ensure that the trial, judged as a whole, was fair.

As further noted by the ECtHR,[64] step *i)* is to be considered a preliminary one, which means that 'the requirement that there be a good reason for admitting the evidence of an absent witness (...) had to be examined before any consideration was given as to whether that evidence was sole or decisive'. However, the lack of a good reason to

---

[61] Al-Khawaja and Tahery v. the United Kingdom, § 118.

[62] Schatschaschwili v. Germany, no. 9154/10, 12 December 2012, *hudoc.echr.coe.int.*

[63] Al-Khawaja and Tahery v. the United Kingdom, §§ 119–125; §§ 126–147; Schatschaschwili v. Germany, § 107.

[64] Schatschaschwili v. Germany, § 111, § 113.

justify the absence of a witness does not imply, necessarily, that a violation of free trial took place. It remains, though, an important factor to be analysed when assessing the overall fairness of proceedings. In light of this, the Court was required to explain each one of these principles, which it did in the same decision.

First of all, it stated that 'good reason for the absence of a witness must exist from the trial court's perspective, that is, the court must have had good factual or legal grounds not to secure the witness's attendance at the trial. If there was a good reason for the witness's non-attendance in that sense, it follows that there was a good reason, or justification, for the trial court to admit the untested statements of the absent witness as evidence'. Such good reasons according to this criterion would be, for instance, absence owing to death or fear (Al-Khawaja and Tahery, §§ 120-125), absence on health grounds (Bobeş v. Romania, no. 29752/05, § 39, 9 July 2013; Vronchenko v. Estonia, no. 59632/09, § 58, 18 July 2013) or the witness's unreachability.

Second, the Court reiterated that 'sole' evidence is to be understood as the only evidence against the accused (Al-Khawaja and Tahery, § 131), whereas 'decisive' evidence should be narrowly interpreted as indicating evidence of such significance or importance as is likely to be determinative of the outcome of the case. Where the untested evidence of a witness is supported by other corroborative evidence, the assessment of whether it is decisive will depend on the strength of the supporting evidence; the stronger the corroborative evidence, the less likely that the evidence of the absent witness will be treated as decisive'.[65]

Concerning the third step, the ECtHR briefly suggested that these counterbalancing factors must lead to a fair and proper assessment of the reliability of that evidence (see Al-Khawaja and Tahery, § 147). Among many others, the Court asserts that 'an additional safeguard in that context may be to show, at the trial hearing, a video-recording of the absent witness's questioning at the investigation stage in order to allow the court, prosecution and defence to observe the witness's demeanour under questioning and to form their own impression of his or her reliability (see A.G. v. Sweden, cited above; Chmura v. Poland, no. 18475/05, § 50, 3 April 2012; D.T. v. the Netherlands (dec.), no. 25307/10, § 50, 2 April 2013; Yevgeniy Ivanov, cited above, § 49; Rosin v. Estonia, no. 26540/08, § 62, 19 December 2013; and Gonzáles Nájera v. Spain (dec.), no. 61047/13, § 54, 11 February 2014)'.[66] Similarly—although regarding the topic of the presence at the appeal hearing—in Bivolaru v. Romania,[67] the ECtHR considered that questioning via video-link could be a measure ensuring effective participation in the proceedings.

This reasoning from the Court, as well as the need to suggest well-built and thorough criteria on the matter, represent a very relevant clue as to the importance of this topic. In general, the right to examine witnesses is considered to be an essential

[65] Schatschaschwili v. Germany, § 123.

[66] Schatschaschwili v. Germany, § 127.

[67] Bivolaru v. Romania, no. 66580/12, 2 October 2018, *hudoc.echr.coe.int.*

requirement of fair trial. That being so, the ECtHR case-law has developed on the topic of the exceptions to such principle. The result: finding the core of this procedural guarantee and the basics standards that have to be met.

6.3.3 Final Remarks

On the whole, the immediacy principle has been included in the ECHR as a component of the right to a fair trial. As argued, its relevance as a general principle has been recognised under article 6(1) of the ECHR, whereas its specific implications in the proceedings have been provided in article 6(3)(d). In this case, inspiration in the English hearsay rule is undeniable.

From our perspective, it is interesting to observe that the ECHR clearly received multiple heritages, and still fights to find the proper balance between them. In this context, the main issues brought to the Court under the immediacy rule concern the changes to the composition of the trial and the right to examine witnesses.

In order to settle the conflicts, the ECtHR has been developing a multitude of criteria to be applied carefully, demanding a proper analysis of the case in dispute. Towards its own judicial activity, the Court has been able to shape the minimum content of the immediacy principle and the basic requirements of the right to examine witnesses.

Cited Case-Law

ECtHR

hudoc.echr.coe.int

Lucà v. Italy, no. 33354/96, 27 February 2001
Solakov v. the former Yugoslav Republic of Macedonia, no. 47023/99, 31 October 2001
P.K. v. Finland, no. 37442/97, 9 July 2002
Graviano v. Italy, no. 10075/02, 10 February 2005
Thomas v. The United Kingdom, no. 19354/02, 10 May 2005
Al-Khawaja and Tahery v. the United Kingdom [GC], nos. 26766/05, 22228/06, 15 December 2011
Hümmer v. Germany, no. 26171/07, 19 July 2012
Schatschaschwili v. Germany, no. 9154/10, 12 December 2012
Beraru v. Romania, no. 40107/04, 18 March 2014
Cutean v. Romania, no. 53150/12, 2 December 2014
Škaro v. Croatia, no. 6962/13, 6 December 2016
Cerovšek and Božičnik v. Slovenia, nos. 68939/12 68949/12, 7 June 2017

Bivolaru v. Romania, no. 66580/12, 2 October 2018
Svanidze V. Georgia, no. 37809/08, 25 July 2019
Chernika v. Ukraine, no. 53791/11, 12 March 2020
Iancu v. Romania, no. 62915/17, 23 February 2021

ICCass

Joint sections, 15 January 1999, no. 212395, Iannasso
Joint sections, 30 May 2019, no. 41736, Bajrami

FCCouncil

Decision no. 2019-778 DC, 21 March 2019
Decision no. 2019-802 QPC, 20 September 2019
Decision no. 2020-836 QPC, 30 April 2020
Order from the French State Council (*Conseil d'État)*, 27 November 2020

Portuguese SCJ

Decision to Standardize Case Law no. 11/2008, case no. 4822/07-3, 11 December 2008

References

Albuquerque P (2011) Comentário do Código de Processo Penal à luz da Constituição da República e da Convenção Europeia dos Direitos do Homem, 4th edn. Universidade Católica Editora, Lisbon

Barrenengoa A (2019) El uso de la videoconferencia en el proceso penal: utilidades, requisitos y limitaciones. Revista de Derecho, Empresa y Sociedad 13:27–41

Bossan J (2011) La visioconférence dans le procès pénal: un outil à maîtriser. Revue de science criminelle et de droit pénal comparé 4:801–816

Chmiel A (2016) Immediacy principle in the Roman Criminal Procedure. Krytyka Prawa. Niezależne Studia Nad Prawem, Krytyka Prawa. Niezależne studia nad prawem 8(2):2–16

Dumitrescu A (2014) Das Inmittelbarkeisprinzip im deutschen und schwezerischen Strafprozessrecht. Zeitschrift für die gesamte Strarechtswissenschaft 126(1):106–155

Hélie F (1866–7) Traité de l'instruction criminelle, ou Théorie du Code d'instruction criminelle. De l'instruction écrite, 2nd edn. Henri Plon, Paris

Holtzendorff F (1879) Handbuch des Deutschen Strafprozessrechts. Carl Habel, Berlin

Jiménez M (2015) El principio de inmediación penal y la prueba por videoconferencia (relación entre los arts. 229 LOPJ y 731 bis LECrim.). La Ley. https://noticias.juridicas.com/conocimiento/articulos-doctrinales/10122-el-principio-de-inmediacion-penal-y-la-prueba-por-videoconferencia-relacion-entre-los-arts-229-lopj-y-731-bis-lecrim-/

Leblois-Happe J (2014) Das Unmittelbarkeitsprinzip im französcischen Straverfahrensrecht. Zeitschrift für die gesamte Strarechtswissenschaft 126(1):185–193

Leborne J (2021) La vidéojustice: la justice pénale à l'ère de la vidéo. Cahiers Droit, Sciences & Technologies 13:93–109

Maas (1907) Der Grundsatz der Unmittelbarkeit in der Reichsstrafprozessordnung. Breslau

Manfrini G, Sartori D (2021) Il Principio Di Immediatezza nel Processo Penale, tra Ordinamento Interno e CEDU. Diritto di Difesa 4. https://dirittodidifesa.eu/wp-content/uploads/2021/08/MANFREDINI-SARTORI-IL-PRINCIPIO-DI-IMMEDIATEZZA-NEL-PROCESSO-PENALE-TRA-ORDINAMENTO-INTERNO-E-CEDU.pdf

Martyn G, Sontag R (2021) Can criminal procedure ever be 'modern'? A historical comparative perspective (Editorial of the Dossier 'History of Criminal Procedure in Modernity'). Revista Brasileira de Direito Processual Penal 7(2):697–748

Mesquita P (2015) Alguns sinais sobre tendências actuais do processo penal português – *convergências* metodológicas sobre o contraditório, a prova, a imediação e a confiança nos juízes. Julgar 25:109–144

Miletti M (2021) Le facce d'un diamante. Apunti per una storia dell'*immediatezza* nella procedura penale italiana'. Revista Brasileira de Direito Processual Penal 7(2):827–882

Mittermaier C (1845) Die Mündlichkeit, das Anklageprinzip, die Öffentlichkeit und das Geschworenengericht in ihrer Durchführung in den verschiedenen Gesetzgebungen dargestellt und nach den Forderungen des Rechts und der Zweckmäßigkeit mit Rücksicht auf die Erfahrung der verschiedenen Länder. Cotta, Stuttgart and Tübingen

Pérez F (2020) La inmediación y el proceso penal. Justicia 1:255–284

Selçuk H (2012) The actual role of the principle of immediacy in the Dutch criminal procedure. Master Thesis

Summers S (2007) Fair trials – The European Criminal Procedural Tradition and the European Court of Human Rights. Hart Publishing, Oxford/Portland

Vogler R (2014) The principle of immediacy in English criminal procedural law. Zeitschrift für die gesamte Strafrechtswissenschaft 126(1):239–247

Winter L (2019) Principio de inmediácion y *confrontation*: paralelismos, diferencias y tendencias en la prueba testifical'. In: Ambos K, Malarino E (eds) Fundamentos de Derecho Probatorio en Materia Penal. Tirant LoBlanch, Valencia, pp 279–332

Zamora M (2015) La suspension de los juicios orales: especial atención a sus causas y tratamiento procesal. J. M. Bosch, Barcelona

Chapter 7
Audio-Visual Recordings as Evidence in Criminal Procedure

António Brito Neves

7.1 Introduction

In this chapter, we will consider a particular kind of video and tape recordings. When one thinks of recordings as evidence, usually what pops up to mind is a direct demonstration of guilt: a video showing someone beating up another person or taking an object from the shelf of a store without paying; a tape that lets us hear someone confessing a crime. But we are more interested in another kind of recordings: the ones in which someone is shown or heard speaking about a crime she witnessed.[1]

Video and tape recordings are frequently presented as direct evidence, that is to say, evidence that straightforwardly establishes the truth or falsity of an utterance. For instance, a video showing the defendant leaving the victim's building can demonstrate that the statement 'the defendant left the house of the victim at 9 pm' is true.[2] Confessions or eyewitness testimonies also qualify as direct evidence,

[1] We will refer to defendants and judges as masculine and to witnesses as feminine.

[2] In cases such as Lamatic v. Romania, no. 55859/15, 1 December 2020, §§ 56 et seq., *hudoc.echr.coe.int*, the ECtHR seems to assume that so called objective evidence, like footage or documents, may play a corroborating role in a way that makes those elements function as an ultimate test of the truth, as though we could say courts should mistrust witnesses and trust recordings. This also seems to be the assumption present in decisions such as the one in Ignat v. Romania, no. 17325/16, 9 November 2021, *hudoc.echr.coe.int*, in which corroborating evidence like video recordings and transcripts of the phone conversations were the basis for the decision of the court of appeal to reverse the acquital of the applicant by the trial court and convict him without rehearing oral evidence from the witnesses. The court of appeal did not disregard the witnesses' statements, but 'reassessed their value and their significance to the proceedings when corroborated by the other

A. B. Neves (✉)
University of Lisbon School of Law, Research Centre for Criminal Law and Criminal Sciences (CIDPCC), Lisbon, Portugal
e-mail: antonioneves@fd.ulisboa.pt

H. Morão, R. Tavares da Silva (eds.), *Fairness in Criminal Appeal*,
https://doi.org/10.1007/978-3-031-13001-4_7

whereas indirect evidence covers both circumstantial and hearsay evidence. If a witness speaks about something she did not actually perceive with her own senses, that is hearsay testimony. But if the recordings only show or let us hear someone talking, they only prove that that person has said something, not that what she said is true (at least not directly). If the recorded person is shown or heard talking about something she directly perceived, we cannot really say that is direct evidence of the alleged fact either, since (it is a common rule that) she needs to say it in court under oath. Now, the need to summon the recorded person and demand that she repeats or explains what she was heard saying in the recording only comes into play when we want to determine the truth of her statement.[3] Being that the case, if she takes the stand and contradicts the recorded statement, or if she just refuses to take the stand, we are left with a very peculiar kind of evidence.[4] More important than classification concerns, though, are the consequences to the assessment of the evidence.

These are the main problems that shall occupy us. As we see it, the best way to approach these issues is by paying attention to the closest set of problems we find: the ones raised by hearsay evidence. We may use examples taken from some countries (like Portugal or Germany), but we hope our reasoning will not really depend as much on the configuration of any national legislation as on some rules and principles commonly found in several countries and invoked by the ECtHR.

7.2 Hearsay and Recordings

Let us picture a regular case of hearsay testimony: A claims in court that she heard B saying in a private conversation that C killed the victim. According to Article 129 (1) and (2), of PCPP, B must be called to take the stand, and this also applies to the reading of a document written by someone other than the present witness. Now suppose there is no witness A claiming B said such and such, neither a document with B's signature. Instead, we have a video or a tape recording of B proffering statements relevant to the matter in discussion.[5] Article 129 does not say anything

evidence' (§ 51). The assumption we mentioned is then made clear: 'the aspect which the appeal court was called on to assess in deciding on the applicant's conviction was whether the testimonial evidence, which supported the applicant's defence, reconciled with the other evidence, which was of a more objective nature, as it consisted of video footage and phone transcripts which provided more nuanced information about the factors that were relevant to the case' (§ 54).

[3]If the recording is brought forth to serve other purposes, such as to show the speaker is deranged, the summoning may be unnecessary. This may happen when the speaker is shown or heard saying something like 'nobody knows it, but I am actually Blackbeard the pirate in disguise' (assuming he is not really Blackbeard, of course).

[4]Admitting the recording is acceptable as such, a question with which we will deal up ahead.

[5]We may assume, for simplification, there is no problem of legality involved in the making of the video.

about this situation: does that mean a different rule applies? To answer that, we shall consider the main reasons behind the mentioned regime.[6]

First, we must look attentively at the right to confrontation. As stated in Article 6 § 3 (d) of the ECHR, 'everyone charged with a criminal offence' has the right to 'examine or have examined witnesses against him', so an accused must be given the opportunity to put questions to adverse witnesses. This is not exclusive to civil law. The Sixth Amendment to the United States Constitution provides that 'in all criminal prosecutions, the accused shall enjoy the right (...) to be confronted with the witnesses against him'.[7,8] It is understood that for the defendant in a criminal trial to have an effective opportunity to challenge the evidence against him, the (preferably physical) presence of the witness is a basic condition that must be fulfilled.[9] And to prevent the right to confrontation from being undermined (by allowing

---

[6] As we will see (2.2.), the rule we are considering does not necessarily depend on there being legal criteria like the Article 129 we cited. We are just using this Article as a starting point.

[7] In Crawford v. Washington 541 US 36 (2004), *supreme.justia.com*, the Supreme Court of the United States ruled that the confrontation clause applied to all evidence testimonial in nature and the Sixth Amendment offered no basis for admitting evidence only by virtue of its reliability. Regarding testimonial statements, their reliability should be determined exclusively by allowing confrontation. In consequence, testimonial evidence was considered inadmissible unless the witness took the stand or, if the witness was unavailable, the defendant had a prior opportunity for cross-examination.

[8] The questioning of witnesses differs in both systems. In common law systems, one expects the lawyers to make the witness say what the lawyers deem beneficial for their own case. In civil law systems, the witness is not usually limited to the questions raised, the public prosecutor has a nonpartisan role and shall lead an impartial investigation of the facts, and the judge, even when he tends to be more a spectator than an inquisitor, may question the witness himself, which should lead to a more thorough and objective probing of the facts: Bachmaier (2019), pp. 857 et seq. On the other hand, 'questioning by a neutral interrogator, such as the judge presiding over the trial, may have considerable benefit. But the judge is unlikely to have the incentive to prepare and press searching lines of examination. No alternative procedure is likely to reveal flaws in the testimony as thoroughly as is cross-examination, and no alternative procedure is likely to assure the accused that the testimony has been thoroughly tested': Friedman (2019), p. 869. See also Jackon and Summers (2012), pp. 334 et seq.

[9] This is far from obvious: one can picture, for instance, a system relying on affidavits (written testimonies confirmed by oath) instead of oral testimonies. Regarding what the defendant must be able to do in order to satisfy the principle of confrontation, '[a] closer look into the case law of the [ECtHR] reveals that the defendant, firstly, must be informed about the identity of any prosecution witness; secondly, the personal appearance of the witness for examination in the trial must be secured; thirdly, the defendant must be enabled to follow the examination of the witness acoustically and visually; and finally, he needs to obtain the opportunity to question the witness and to challenge his or her testimony': Arslan (2018), p. 219. It is also doubtful whether it really makes a difference if the examination of the witness is made in person or through technology like live-links: see Ellison and Munro (2014), discussing the findings of a study in which volunteers observed one trial reconstruction and were asked to deliberate as a group towards a verdict, in order to investigate the influence upon mock jurors of special measures made available to witnesses in England and Wales, including live-links and video-recorded evidence-in-chief followed by live-link cross-examination. The conclusion was that there was no clear or consistent impact as a result of these divergent presentation modes. Note, however, that the volunteers played the role of jurors, not that of judges.

someone to avoid examination by talking outside the court to another person and relying on that other person to pass her statement on to the court), the rule against hearsay is propounded.[10]

In the second place, there is the principle that evidence is to be produced in a public hearing. For the fact-finder to have a better assessment of the evidence, he shall be given direct contact with its sources. The rendering of the testimony at the trial helps him to better estimate the reliability of the witness. Only thus can the mechanisms intended to ensure that the evidence is truthful and accurate be put into practice: the witness's oath, cross-examination by the defendant, and observance of the demeanour of the witness (and maybe questioning) by the judge. So, when A reports what B has told him, summoning B is the only way not just to clarify what B's testimony really is, but also to determine if what B says is true.[11] Therefore, the immediacy principle, which requires judges to hear the parties, witnesses and experts in person, also plays a decisive role.[12,13]

Finally, because in most systems the witness is either required to take an oath or warned that she may be punished if she does not tell the truth, we have good reason to expect her to understand both the solemnity of the occasion and the consequences of her conduct. Both the confrontation with the accused (and with the court) and the threat of perjury charges encourage truthfulness.[14]

These arguments are all equally valid in the case of the recordings we alluded to, on which the judge sees or hears perhaps only a fraction of what the person has said, or maybe he lacks the context that would clarify the recorded statements as having a totally different meaning. There is also, of course, the adversarial argument: even assuming that the recording is one hundred per cent trustworthy, there will still be need of questioning B and subjecting her to cross-examination (so one may understand how did she gain knowledge of what she says, so one may find out if she has got some bias against the accused, etc.). One could argue that other reasons invoked now and then to make the summoning of the first-hand witness mandatory do not apply here, such as the risk of error in transmission (maybe the witness A has

[10] Friedman (2019), pp. 866–867.

[11] Spencer (2008), p. 9.

[12] This is true even if "the 'immediacy principle' itself means very little to English or American lawyers": Vogler (2014), p. 240. This is due to the fact that the immediacy principle emerged as a response to problems the Anglo-Americans fight against by adopting other measures (*ibid.*). The concerns, however, are essentially the same. See also Summers (2017), pp. 47 et seq.

[13] There is no (direct) logic connection between the immediacy principle and the public hearing requirement: Summers (2017), p. 44. If the judge hears the witness before the trial, far away from the eyes and ears of the public, one could argue the immediacy principle was complied with. But we believe that the public nature of the trial, as well as the formalities the judge and the parties must observe there, are crucial elements to achieve the purposes of the immediacy principle, as they help to ensure that the judge never deviates from what objectivity he is able to maintain in assessing the evidence and adjucating.

[14] Friedman (2019), pp. 865 et seq.

misunderstood what non-witness B said),[15] but we should not discard the possibility of the recording having been manipulated.

We may infer that the rule against hearsay still applies when we are dealing with recordings of statements instead of oral testimonies or documents. Therefore, the recorded witness shall be called to take the stand. But we must not conclude that the rule forbids hearsay evidence completely.

7.3 Admission of Hearsay Evidence

7.3.1 Some Context

Let us imagine the first-hand witness B refuses to give testimony (making use of a right to do so, being the suspect's wife, for instance[16]). Shall the hearsay testimony simply be excluded, or can it be admitted as evidence?

We must start by noticing that the rules pertinent to the immediacy principle and the right to confrontation are far from being uniform in European countries. When it comes to the exclusion of out-of-court pretrial statements, we see that in Germany, section 250 of StPO stipulates the principle of examination in person, according to which the hearing of the witness 'may not be substituted by reading out the record of a previous examination or reading out a statement'.[17] In Switzerland, as stated in Article 350 (2) of SStPO, the court may 'take account of the evidence taken in the preliminary proceedings', which may include statements from witnesses (not necessarily made before a judge). So, even when the witness is available, the court may dispense with her live testimony if the reading of her statement taken during the pretrial stage is deemed sufficient.[18] In Spain, in spite of Article 120 (2) of the Spanish Constitution stating that 'proceedings shall be predominantly oral, especially in criminal cases', and notwithstanding the general rule that pretrial statements do not count as evidence, there are several exceptions to it. According to Article 714 of LECrim, for instance, if, during the trial, a witness contradicts what she said before the trial, her previous statement may be read and the judge may ask her to explain the contradiction.[19] The scene is somewhat similar in France.[20]

---

[15] Spencer (2008), pp. 9–10.

[16] The right to refuse testimony in cases such as this is very common: see, for instance, Articles 134 (1) b) of PCPP and 168 (1) a) of the Swiss Criminal Procedure Code (SStPO) and Section 52 1 (1) of StPO.

[17] On this corollary of the immediacy principle and its exceptions in German law, see Roxin and Schünemann (2017), pp. 403 et seq.

[18] Riklin (2014), pp. 176–177.

[19] Winter (2014), pp. 198 et seq.

[20] Leblois-Happe (2014), pp. 187 et seq.

In spite of the apparently clear indication in Article 6 § 3 (d) of the ECHR, for which no exception is mentioned, the ECtHR has permitted on occasion the assessment of testimonies given by witnesses cross-examined before (but not during) the trial, even when the cross-examination had not occurred before a judge.[21] In recent years, the ECtHR has even come to accept that courts take into account testimonies given without the opportunity for the defence to cross-examine the witness either during or before the trial.

In early decisions, the ECtHR found that the admission of reports of what someone had said outside the court violated the ECHR whenever the hearsay statements had been the main basis for conviction and there had not been cross-examination of the declarants.[22] But as long as the statements (which could be taken from anonymous witnesses) were not used as sufficient evidence to found a conviction, they could be admitted.[23] At some point, the 'sole or decisive rule' (according to which, a conviction based solely or decisively on the statement of an absent witness was generally considered to be incompatible with the requirements of fairness under Article 6) came to be treated as absolute.[24]

In accordance with this, as hearsay statements had been the sole or decisive basis for the conviction of the defendants Al-Khawaja and Tahery, the ECtHR's Fourth Chamber, in the cases of Al-Khawaja and Tahery v. The United Kingdom, found that the ECHR had been violated.[25] Furthermore, the Fourth Chamber rejected the Government's argument that there was no absolute rule prohibiting the use of untested statements. Even though it acknowledged its past practice of considering whether the national court's use of hearsay evidence included procedures to help counterbalance difficulties caused to the defence, it 'doubt[ed] whether any counterbalancing factors would be sufficient to justify the introduction in evidence

---

[21] Asch v. Austria, no. 12398/86, 26 April 1991, §§ 27 et seq., *hudoc.echr.coe.int*; Lüdi v. Switzerland, no. 12433/86, 15 June 1992, §§ 47 et seq., *hudoc.echr.coe.int*; Krasniki v. The Czech Republic, no. 51277/99, 28 February 2006, § 75, *hudoc.echr.coe.int*; Gani v. Spain, no. 61800/08, 19 February 2013, §§ 38 et seq., *hudoc.echr.coe.int*. See also Arslan (2018), pp. 220 et seq. We will not pay attention here to the problem of determining what counts as 'witness statement' when dealing with Article 6 § 3. On this issue, see, for instance, Redmayne (2012), pp. 285–286.

[22] See, *e.g.*, Unterpertinger v. Austria, no. 9120/80, 24 November 1986, § 33, *hudoc.echr.coe.int*; Bricmont v. Belgium, no. 10857/84, 7 July 1989, §§ 78 et seq., *hudoc.echr.coe.int*; Kostovski v. Netherlands, no. 11454/85, 20 November 1989, §§ 41 et seq., *hudoc.echr.coe.int.*; Windisch v. Austria, no. 12489/86, 27 September 1990, §§ 26 et seq., *hudoc.echr.coe.int.*

[23] Doorson v. The Netherlands, no. 20524/92, 26 March 1996, § 76, *hudoc.echr.coe.int.*

[24] This happened especially after the decision in Luca v. Italy, no. 33354/96, 27 February 2001, *hudoc.echr.coe.int*: 'where a conviction is based solely or to a decisive degree on depositions that have been made by a person whom the accused has had no opportunity to examine or to have examined, whether during the investigation or at the trial, the rights of the defence are restricted to an extent that is incompatible with the guarantees provided by Article 6' (§ 40).

[25] Al-Khawaja and Tahery v. The United Kingdom, nos. 26766/05 and 22228/06, 20 January 2009, §§ 41–43 and 45–48, *hudoc.echr.coe.int.*

of an untested statement which was the sole or decisive basis for the conviction of an applicant'.[26]

Eleven months after this decision, the United Kingdom Supreme Court, in a rare departure from the Strasbourg jurisprudence, 'decline[d] to follow' it and did not apply the sole or decisive test in a case where a testimony not given at trial was used as decisive evidence.[27]

In 2011, the ECtHR's Grand Chamber decided the appeal from the Fourth Chamber's decision in Al-Khawaja & Tahery v. United Kingdom we just mentioned. Presenting the guarantees in Article 6 § 3 (d) as 'specific aspects of the right to a fair hearing', the ECtHR elected as its 'primary concern under Article 6 § 1 (...) to evaluate the overall fairness of the criminal proceedings', which involved looking at the proceedings 'as a whole'.[28] Dropping the sole or decisive rule, the ECtHR set forth three steps to determine whether decisive hearsay evidence of absent witnesses resulted in a breach of Article 6 § 1. The courts should consider 'whether it was necessary to admit the witness statements';[29] 'wheher their untested evidence was the sole or decisive basis for [the] conviction; and thirdly, whether there were sufficient counterbalancing factors (...) to ensure that each trial, judged as a whole, was fair'.[30] Although, just like the Fourth Chamber had noted, the hearsay statements in the cases *sub judice* had been the sole or decisive evidence used to condemn, the Grand Chamber pointed the existence of sufficient counterbalancing factors to conclude that the admission of the hearsay evidence to condemn Al-Khawaja did not result in a breach of the ECHR, though the contrary was said regarding Tahery.[31]

The Grand Chamber applied its (new) three-step analysis in 2015 to state that the lack of good reason for the absence of a witness 'cannot of itself be conclusive of the unfairness of a trial.' The decisive character of the evidence depended on the relative strength of the other (corroborative) evidence. The use of corroborative evidence

---

[26] Al-Khawaja and Tahery v. The United Kingdom (No. 1), §§ 37–38.

[27] R v. Horncastle and others [2009] United Kingdom Supreme Court 14, 11. and 108., https://www.supremecourt.uk/cases/.

[28] Al-Khawaja and Tahery v. The United Kingdom, nos. 26766/05 and 22228/06, 15 December 2011, § 118, *hudoc.echr.coe.int.*

[29] This required a good reason for the non-attendance of the witness at trial. A good reason for the non-attendance is usually provided by the death of the witness, or the fear by the witness attributable to threats or other actions of the defendant or someone acting on his behalf. But the demonstration that the trial court made all reasonable efforts within the existing legal framework to secure the attendance of a witness may suffice: Schatschaschwili v. Germany, §§ 132 et seq. Note that when the defence turned down a possibility to have questions put to witnesses, this may lead to the conclusion that there is no violation of the ECtHR: B. v. Finland, no. 17122/02, 24 April 2007, § 45, *hudoc.echr.coe.int.*

[30] Al-Khawaja and Tahery v. The United Kingdom (No. 2), § 152. A more detailed list of guidelines was offered in the case Batek and others v. The Chezch Republic, no. 54146/09, 12 January 2017, § 38, *hudoc.echr.coe.int.*

[31] Al-Khawaja and Tahery v. The United Kingdom (No. 2), §§ 156 et seq.

was equally taken as a counterbalancing factor to be considered in the third step.[32] This time, however, despite the fact that there were counterbalancing factors identical to the ones mentioned in the case of Al-Khawaja and Tahery (like the opportunity to cross-examine the corroborative witnesses, or the similarity between the crime and another one the defendant was also accused of), the ECtHR reached a different conclusion (that the defendant had been denied the right to a fair trial) by focusing mainly on the impossibility of cross-examine the main witnesses.[33] This could mean the ECtHR is taking a step back from its previous decision and focusing more on the right to confrontation,[34] but there is still no clear sign in that direction.[35]

7.3.2 Inferences

In this scenario, we may infer that in spite of the good reasons to exclude hearsay evidence, there is an open gate to exceptions whenever other factors sustain the conclusion that the defendant was fairly treated. Maybe the scope of the ECtHR is too broad,[36] but by focusing on the immediacy principle and the right to confrontation we may come to some plausible justification to accept as admissible evidence the recordings we were considering. We shall think of these requirements in association.[37]

---

[32] Schatschaschwili v. Germany, no. 9154/10, 15 December 2015, §§ 111–113, 123 and 128, *hudoc.echr.coe.int.*

[33] Schatschaschwili v. Germany, §§ 153 et seq.

[34] Paruch (2018), pp. 147–148.

[35] On the contrary: 'the statement of a witness does not always have to be made in court or in public if it is to be admitted as evidence': Smajgl v. Slovenia, no. 29187/10, 4 October 2016, § 63, *hudoc.echr.coe.int.*

[36] The ECtHR has embedded the right to examine prosecution witnesses into the more generic right to a fair trial. The method of examining if there is a violation of some specific right by considering factors relative to other rights or to more generic principles may result in a weaker protection of some important rights or principles: '[r]egrettably, the Court has held in a number of cases that although some of the minimum guarantees had not been complied with, an evaluation of the proceedings as a whole revealed that the trial had nevertheless been fair. Thus, in Asch the defendant had not had the opportunity to cross-examine the main witness – yet, the Court decided that taken as a whole, the trial could not be characterized as having been unfair'—Trechsel (2005), p. 87. See also the joint partly dissenting and partly concurring opinion of judges Sajó and Karakaş in Al-Khawaja and Tahery v. The United Kingdom (No. 2): 'the issue is to what extent the right to a fair trial, which is an institutional concern and a matter of striking a fair balance between the conflicting interests of the accused and the administration of justice, can absorb or undermine specific individual rights which are defined in the Convention in absolute and categorical terms' [and Thörnich (2017), p. 44].

[37] The immediacy principle demands that, as a rule, only oral testimony be admitted and that this be given in person. It does so in order to guarantee the maximum of proximity between the court and the (sources of) evidence, thus avoiding intermediation of any kind. One might say immediacy does not strictly require cross-examination, much less an adversarial model. We find, however, good

One might think the problem we are considering (can the hearsay testimony be admitted as evidence if the reported witness validly refuses to take the stand?) only appears before legal criteria like Article 129 of PCPP. Taking as an example the section 250 of StPO we cited, the principle of examination in person is usually interpreted by German authors and courts as impeding only the substitution of personal evidence (oral testimony) for material evidence (reading of documents), not the use of hearsay testimony *per se*. However, the immediacy principle, the right to confrontation and the obligation of the court (in more inquisitorial systems) to extend *ex officio* the taking of evidence to all means of proof which are relevant may be taken as sufficient reasons to impose the duty to summon the witness even where the law does not explicitly state so. Therefore, the same authors see it as mandatory for the judge to summon the first-hand witness in cases of hearsay.[38] As long as one accepts those reasons as good, one will not feel reluctant to acquiesce to this course of action.

7.3.3 *What to Do with Hearsay Evidence When the First-Hand Witness Contradicts It or Refuses to Speak*

When the first-hand witness is summoned and speaks, her testimony may contradict what she was reported to say. In this case, we see no reason to exclude the hearsay testimony. We may require that the judge explain why he believes one witness and not the other, and maybe corroboration, but nothing more. This means that the summoning of the first-hand witness is not imposed in order to take the only testimony admissible. It is imposed instead with a view to give her the opportunity to speak for herself, so that she can be subject to examination. This kind of reasoning, together with the treatment the right to confrontation is given by the ECtHR, suggest that none of these rules and principles are prescribed as absolute, or even as having a completely autonomous value. Instead, they are meaningful as ways to guarantee that a more accurate decision is reached and that the defendant receives fair treatment. If the judge must summon the first-hand witness in order to respect the immediacy principle and the defendant's right to confrontation, that is because this is the only way to give the defendant fair treatment, and the best one to ensure the judge is in a good enough position to decide.

---

reasons to associate them. We want the contact of the court with the evidence to be the most direct it can be because we presume that is the best way to make sure that the inferences based on what is seen or heard are consistent and true. But scrutiny and cross-examination are the most efficient means to guarantee that those inferences are solid. Partiality is not recommended as path to the truth, and only through those means we may rest thinking we did what we could to secure the court's impartiality. And only by complying with the immediacy requirement are we able to say that.

[38] Hellmann (2006), p. 230; Roxin and Schünemann (2017), pp. 414–415.

What happens when the first-hand witness validly refuses to take the stand? Of course, the defendant is left with no opportunity to confront her, but the court still gave him the fairest treatment possible in the circumstances.[39] The predicaments thus originated for the defendant shall not be disregarded by the court, and it seems advisable that measures be taken to counterbalance them. But we do not have to include the discharge of the hearsay testimony in those measures. On the other hand, the judge would surely be in a better position to decide if the first-hand witness had spoken, but this does not mean he cannot decide. He must do so, in fact, and the deficiencies related to the hearsay evidence shall be atoned by demanding corroborative evidence and a more detailed and elaborated justification of the final decision.[40]

7.4 Turning Back to Recordings

Does the same solution apply to video and tape recordings? If the recorded person validly refuses to give testimony, is the video to be taken as admissible evidence?

We may start again by asking what happens if the witness contradicts what she apparently says in the video. She may say she was not being serious when it was made, or that the lack of context makes it deceiving. It is not possible to cross-examine the video, it will never change its responses. But that should not be interpreted as meaning no inspection is available: the lawyers can still dispute its content either by having the recorded person denying her statements and explaining what drove her to issue them, or by alleging other relevant statements were made which do not appear in the video, for example. One should also not forget that recordings can be tampered with.

In a way, the case for admitting the recording as evidence in this scenario is stronger than in the hearsay witness one. If the court may choose to believe the hearsay testimony over what the first-hand witness says, it seems easier to accept the preferred evidence to be a recording, as it is a more direct demonstration of what the first-hand witness said. And the fact that the recorded witness validly chooses not to speak instead of contradicting the recording does not seem to bring about any relevant change to this assertion.[41]

---

[39] Let us also not forget that the adversarial requirements were complied with as far as the second-hand witness is concerned.

[40] We find several decisions from Portuguese courts stressing that judges may take into account the hearsay testimony when the quoted person validly refuses to testify, seeing that she was given the opportunity to speak for herself and the adversarial principle was observed as far as the second-hand witness is concerned: see, for instance, CCA, no. 27/05.6GDFND.C1, 26/11/2008, *dgsi.pt*; GCA, no. 376/10.1TAPTL.G1, 5/03/2012, *dgsi.pt*.

[41] We will not consider here the question of whether the exercise of the right to refuse to give testimony, for the sake of coherence, should also bar the admission of the recording.

This does not mean we should disregard important differences between both scenarios. There seems to be a peculiar contrast between recorded statements and recorded actions.

When dealing with videos showing someone doing something, there is not a natural impulse in the watcher to question the authenticity of the video. We tend to simply accept what it shows. Someone may raise up questions of veracity, but only then will the watcher face doubts about it. So, if a video of this kind is brought to court (supposing no exclusionary rule applies for reasons concerning how it came to existence), as a rule, it will simply be accepted as evidence. The situation is very different regarding the video or audiotape of someone saying something. In this instance and as we have seen, if the statements are deemed relevant, that person must be summoned to repeat and clarify them in court—and even when she simply repeats what she says in the video, the relevant evidence will normally be the testimony given before the court, not the recording.[42]

We may explain this in part by observing that while in the case of recorded actions the meaningful content is apprehended simply by watching and listening to the recording, in the case of registered declarations the interpreter needs to be given the opportunity to question and cross-examine the speaker, and also because one needs to hear them repeated under oath before a court. But we have already sustained that the judge may choose to believe the recording over what the witness says when she takes the stand. Can we say the immediacy requirement is satisfied in this scenario?

The summoning of the (recorded) witness allows us to give a positive answer, at least formally. If she denies the recorded statements and makes other ones, we can even say she was heard by the judge and cross-examined. But if the judge chooses to believe the recorded statements, it is not totally clear which kind of evidence we are talking about. Since they were made out of court and not under oath, those statements cannot be seen as testimony. But there is no room for much doubt about this video not being the same kind of evidence as the one that captures some person's actions instead of words. In any case, what really matters here is to determine whether the principles and rules we have been invoking force us to reject such recordings as evidence—not so much when the reported witness contradicts them (we already have an answer for that case) as when she does not talk at all.

If the recorded witness validly chooses not to speak, there is no one left for the defendant to confront, neither for the judge to question. For sure, the recording compensates for the absence of the second-hand witness in a way: instead of being quoted, the first-hand witness is shown or heard in her own (registered) voice making statements. But the judge shall be alert to the dangers of trusting the recording too much. He can never forget that those statements were not made under oath before a court, neither subject to cross-examination, and, depending on circumstances, that

[42]Note the contrast: one would be surprised if the individual caught on tape beating up someone was asked to re-enact the beating before the court. We are confident in saying this is not due exclusively to the obvious purpose of saving the victim from another beating.

they were not proffered during an inquest conducted by someone officially mandated to find the truth. He must also always remember that films and tapes capture nothing more than mere fragments of reality, so it is impossible to put aside the risk that one is not getting the whole picture by watching or listening to them. Finally, he cannot establish a dialogue with the recorded person relocating himself to the context in which the video was made.

These seem to be good enough reasons to also require corroborative evidence when dealing with recordings of statements, in addition to the same demands pertaining the justification of the final decision we mentioned above.[43] But that should not be enough: we have seen that some counterbalance measures must be taken to compensate for the absence of cross-examination and immediacy in cases of hearsay testimony.

We may face scenarios in which some of those measures are not available. In some cases, the ECtHR stresses that the reliability of witness evidence is afforded through the examination of the witness by the trial court, even if the defence has comparatively less opportunities to do so.[44] But if the witness is dead or validly refuses to speak, we are left with the recording and no examination of the recorded person. In these circumstances, one can hardly say that conditions were created that mirror the hearing of a witness in open court.[45]

Perhaps another advisable way of approaching the issue is by process of elimination. If, for instance, the recorded witness cannot be summoned because she died or simply can't be found, this may result in very little being known about her—maybe not even her identity is certain. In addition to the impossibility of cross-examination and to the deficiencies in immediacy, the defendant is thus left with no way of challenging the statements in question: he is not able to point the reasons the speaker could have for lying, or the ones that made it impossible for her to know what she was talking about.[46] In such a case of word against (registered) word, the recording must be excluded.

---

[43] Note that in view of these considerations, one shall always require good reason to even consider admitting as evidence the hearsay testimony or the recording when the witness does not take the stand, such as she being dead or being impossible to find: Ferrantelli and Santangelo v. Italy, no. 19874/92, 7 August 1996, §§ 51–53, *hudoc.echr.coe.int*. In the case of Portuguese law, as we have seen, there is no room for doubt about it.

[44] Al-Khawaja and Tahery v. The United Kingdom (No. 2) § 142. Note that the extent of the counterbalancing factors seen as necessary so that a trial may be considered fair is cause for notorious divide between the judges of the ECtHR: in Schatschaschwili v. Germany, nine judges took the factors as insufficient to ensure a fair trial, while eight thought that they were sufficient for this purpose.

[45] So the conditions portrayed in the video shall also be considered as regards to that approximation: '[a]n additional safeguard (. . .) may be to show, at the trial hearing, a video-recording of the absent witness's questioning at the investigation stage in order to allow the court, prosecution and defence to observe the witness's demeanour under questioning and to form their own impression of his or her reliability': Schatschaschwili v. Germany, § 127.

[46] On the importance of being granted an opportunity to undermine the credibility of the witness through cross-examination, see, for instance, Pichugin v. Russia, no. 38623/03, 23 October 2012, § 207, *hudoc.echr.coe.int*.

Short of this extreme scenario, one must insist on the caution the judge shall adopt when approaching the untested evidence. The ECtHR recognizes this prudence as a measure worthy of note, but it must be perceivable.[47] In the first place, the judge shall explain why he found the evidence reliable despite the impossibility of having the statements confirmed by their author in court.[48] Additionally, at least as a rule, the corroborative evidence shall be direct evidence, not circumstantial or hearsay. So, an eyewitness testimony may be used in this sense, but not a hearsay one. Of course, this means recordings such as the ones we are considering end up having a secondary role.[49] We must accept that as an unavoidable consequence of respecting the rights and principles we mentioned.[50] One can only argue for something different when the recording is adduced by the defence, as reasonable doubt shall suffice to acquit the defendant in criminal procedures.

All this caution may appear as excessive if the recorded pretrial statements were made in answer to questions put by the authorities. One shall differentiate.

If the questioner was the same judge who is now assessing the evidence in order to decide the case,[51] one could argue that the immediacy principle is observed, seeing that the judge had direct contact with the witness and was able to question her. But if the defendant was not given the opportunity to cross-examine the witness, counterbalance measures are still in order. Note that not only the defendant sees his rights diminished in such circumstances; the immediacy principle itself is not fully complied with, as the judge is expected to examine the witness not merely by observing her demeanour when answering his questions but also by considering the way she responds to those raised by the defence. In light of these considerations, we may dispense with the need for the corroborative evidence to be direct evidence, but nothing else should be different from what we said before.

47 'The fact that the domestic courts approached the untested evidence of an absent witness with caution has been considered by the Court to be an important safeguard. The courts must have shown that they were aware that the statements of the absent witness carried less weight (. . .). The Court has taken into account (. . .) whether the domestic courts provided detailed reasoning as to why they considered that evidence to be reliable, while having regard also to the other evidence available': Schatschaschwili v. Germany, § 126.

48 Note that this explanation adds up to the normal (and common) duty to state the reasons of the decision.

49 The ECtHR never expressed the requirement of having direct evidence as corroboration, but nevertheless, it still ascribes great importance to the weight of the absent witness evidence: 'the greater the importance of the evidence, the greater the potential unfairness to the defendant in allowing the witness to remain anonymous or to be absent from the trial and the greater the need for safeguards to ensure that the evidence is demonstrably reliable or that its reliability can properly be tested and assessed': Al-Khawaja and Tahery v. The United Kingdom (No. 2), § 139.

50 Regarding normal cases of hearsay, some authors, not surprisingly, argue against this kind of remedies, campaigning instead (at least *de lege ferenda*) for a simple exclusion of the hearsay evidence: Fezer (2007), p. 725; Roxin and Schünemann (2017), p. 415.

51 As a rule, any cross-examination shall take place before the judge deciding the case, but the ECtHR has allowed exceptions: Kashlev v. Estonia, no. 22574/08, 26 April 2016, § 47, *hudoc.echr.coe.int.*

If the questioner is any other person than the judge, then all requirements apply, regardless of him being a policeman, a prosecutor, a lawyer or a layperson. He may even be another judge. This is due to the fact that immediacy does not merely provide the decider with the best position to take the evidence, as if he were a mere spectator, but also with the opportunity to direct his own line of interrogation and to search for the truth by his own initiative. It is not, therefore, merely a question of direct observance of the witness, but also of entering in dialogue with her, and everything that is involved in that. Maybe this judge thinks that some of the questions put to the witness by the other judge are irrelevant, or maybe he feels other issues needed more clarification. Perhaps the way the questioning was conducted keeps him from some wonderings and doubts that would have led him in another direction had he been the questioner. We should not underestimate the possibilities. This means that all the precautions we mentioned keep their rationale in such a scenario, regardless of it eventually being easier for the judge to explain why he believes the recorded witness when her answers were given before another judge, instead of in a far-from-the-court context.

7.5 What About Appeals?

What inferences are we to draw from all this regarding appeals?

In the first place, in a recordings appeal immediacy system and in the light of the immediacy principle, as a rule if not always, the recording of the trial should be audio-visual, not merely audio, as that is the best way to leave the court of appeal judge in the closest position possible to the trial judge.[52]

On the other hand, one should never make the mistake of thinking the trial court and the court of appeal are in the same position to adjudicate. At least when it comes to examining witnesses, listening with the help of a tape to the answers given during the trial, or watching the witness giving them in a video, are never the same as conducting the interrogation.[53]

Bearing this in mind, perhaps one finds an argument to say that if the court of appeal judge does not find himself in the same position as the trial judge, that may be due to the fact that the decisions they are required to make are not of the same kind. We expect the trial judge to establish the facts, based on the evidence offered at the

[52] However, Article 364 (1) of PCPP admits both variants (audio and audio-visual) without conferring preference to neither.

[53] By way of illustration (also of the reasons given above), let us suppose it was demonstrated that A was guilty of speeding when he ran over B. The court of appeal judge thinks it would be relevant to know if the running over would still have taken place had A been driving observing the speed limit. However, the trial judge never asked that to the expert witness, for he thought that demonstration was sufficient to establish causality and no further inquiry was necessary.

trial, and to apply the law accordingly. Maybe the court of appeal judge has a different task: besides looking for breaches of law, he shall examine the evidence (namely, the recording of the trial) with a view to verify whether the final decision of the trial judge appears as coherent in the light of what happened during the trial.[54]

This line of reasoning might prove important to determine the margin of appreciation of the court of appeal. If that assumption is correct, then, when facing two alternative versions of the facts, the court of appeal judge will not be able to choose one instead of the alternative just because he finds one witness more reliable than the other. He must limit himself to verify if the trial judge has chosen in coherence with what happened during the trial. And if the witness the trial judge believes is not the one the court of appeal judge would have preferred, that is not a good enough reason to overturn the decision.[55]

There is, however, another way of looking at the position of the court of appeal judge. There is no doubt it is not the same position as that of the trial judge, as he is not able to put questions to witnesses, but this does not mean he is necessarily at a worst position to decide. He may even be in a better one.

Being more distant, this judge's perspective gains in objectivity. Like the birds seeing the city from afar in the famous shot from Alfred Hitchcock's *The Birds* (a bird's-eye view over Bodega Bay), in a way, he can see everything. Once the birds start descending, they become true players again, loosing that distance. The same happens to the judge if, for instance, he summons the witness to clear up some point. If, on the contrary, he does not do that and just sees or listens to the trial recordings and reads the trial documents, he is able to see more and even to detect possible blind spots: he can stop the recording, rewind and repeat. He may also notice details, inflections or little gestures and manifestations that the trial judge, being too immersed (especially when doing the examination himself), did not apprehend.

This can mean that the immediacy principle serves different purposes in both stages (trial and appeal). The appeal will come out as the moment in which both perspectives merge: the more subjective one (of the trial judge) and the more distant one (of the court of appeal judge). And this seems to us a very solid reason to infer that the court of appeal judge shall make a new assessment of the evidence. So, based on recordings of the trial, if he finds witness A more convincing than witness B, he may overturn the decision whenever the testimony given by B was decisive to the final decision of the trial court.

[54] We believe this is the line of reasoning followed in decisions such as the ECtHR's in the case Lamatic v. Romania, §§ 59 et seq.: it was not important that the court of appeal would hear the witness, but to see if what she had said during the trial, together with the rest of the evidence, explained the trial court's decision.

[55] The Portuguese Supreme Court of Justice has decided in accordance with this view: SCJ, no. 07P4822, 29/10/2008, *dgsi.pt*.

7.6 Conclusions

In cases of hearsay, the immediacy principle, the right to confrontation and the obligation of the court to extend *ex officio* the taking of evidence to all means of proof it finds relevant (when such obligation exists) serve as sufficient reasons to make it necessary to call the first-hand witness to take the stand.

The rule against hearsay testimony applies equally to video or tape recordings of statements. Therefore, the recorded witness shall be called to take the stand whenever her declarations are deemed relevant.

However, despite the valid motives to exclude hearsay evidence as a rule, the conclusion that the defendant was fairly treated may serve as reason enough to allow for exceptions.

In principle, as long as the immediacy requirement and the right to confrontation are sufficiently accounted for, both hearsay testimonies and recordings of statements can be admitted as evidence.

Some precautions are to be taken regarding the assessment of the evidence in these situations. In more extreme cases, there may be reason to simply exclude it. In any case, special requirements on the stating of the reasons for the judicial decision will always be in order.

In recordings appeal immediacy models, at least as a rule, the recording of the trial should be audio-visual, as that is the most effective way to get the court of appeal judge as near as possible to the position of the trial judge. This does not mean that both judges share the same function, seeing that only the trial judge is able to conduct the interrogation of witnesses.

Assuming the immediacy principle serves different aims across the procedure, and that the court of appeal judge has a more distant and objective position than the trial judge, we may infer that his margin of appreciation will be larger.

Cited Case-Law

ECtHR

hudoc.echr.coe.int

Unterpertinger v. Austria, no. 9120/80, 24 November 1986
Bricmont v. Belgium, no. 10857/84, 7 July 1989
Kostovski v. Netherlands, no. 11454/85, 20 November 1989
Windisch v. Austria, no. 12489/86, 27 September 1990
Asch v. Austria, no. 12398/86, 26 April 1991
Lüdi v. Switzerland, no. 12433/86, 15 June 1992
Doorson v. The Netherlands, no. 20524/92, 26 March 1996
Ferrantelli and Santangelo v. Italy, no. 19874/92, 7 August 1996
Luca v. Italy, no. 33354/96, 27 February 2001

Krasniki v. The Czech Republic, no. 51277/99, 28 February 2006
B. v. Finland, no. 17122/02, 24 April 2007
Al-Khawaja and Tahery v. The United Kingdom, nos. 26766/05 and 22228/06, 20 January 2009
Al-Khawaja and Tahery v. The United Kingdom, nos. 26766/05 and 22228/06, 15 December 2011
Pichugin v. Russia, no. 38623/03, 23 October 2012
Gani v. Spain, no. 61800/08, 19 February 2013
Schatschaschwili v. Germany, no. 9154/10, 15 December 2015
Kashlev v. Estonia, no. 22574/08, 26 April 2016
Smajgl v. Slovenia, no. 29187/10, 4 October 2016
Batek and others v. The Chezch Republic, no. 54146/09, 12 January 2017
Lamatic v. Romania, no. 55859/15, 1 December 2020
Ignat v. Romania, no. 17325/16, 9 November 2021

Coimbra Court of Appeal

dgsi.pt

CCA, no. 27/05.6GDFND.C1, 26/11/2008

Guimarães Court of Appeal

dgsi.pt

GCA, no. 376/10.1TAPTL.G1, 5/03/2012

Portuguese Supreme Court of Justice

dgsi.pt

SCJ, no. 07P4822, 29/10/2008

Supreme Court of the United States

supreme.justia.com

Crawford v. Washington 541 US 36 (2004)

United Kingdom Supreme Court

https://www.supremecourt.uk/cases/

R v. Horncastle and others [2009] United Kingdom Supreme Court 14

References

Arslan M (2018) The right to examination of prosecution witnesses. Zeitschrift für Internationale Strafrechtswissenschaft 13(6):218–228

Bachmaier L (2019) Rights and methods to challenge evidence and witnesses in civil law jurisdictions. In: Brown DK, Turner JI, Weisser B (eds) The Oxford handbook of criminal process. Oxford University Press, New York, pp 841–864

Ellison L, Munro VE (2014) A 'special' delivery? Exploring the impact of screens, live-links and video-recorded evidence on mock juror deliberation in rape trials. Soc Leg Stud 23(1):3–29

Fezer G (2007) Die Rechtsprechung des Bundesgerichtshofs zum Strafverfahrensrecht seit 1995 – Teil 2. Juristenzeitung 62(14):723–729

Friedman R (2019) The confrontation right. In: Brown DK, Turner JI, Weisser B (eds) The Oxford handbook of criminal process. Oxford University Press, New York, pp 865–886

Hellmann U (2006) Strafprozessrecht, 2nd edn. Springer, Berlin/Heidelberg/New York

Jackon JD, Summers SJ (2012) The internationalisation of criminal evidence – beyond the common law and civil law traditions. Cambridge University Press, Cambridge

Leblois-Happe J (2014) Das Unmittelbarkeitsprinzip im französischen Strafverfahrensrecht. Zeitschrift für die gesamte Strafrechtswissenschaft 126(1):185–193

Paruch D (2018) Testimonial statements, reliability, and the sole or decisive evidence rule: a comparative look at the right of confrontation in the United States, Canada, and Europe. Cathol Univ Law Rev 67(1):105–163

Redmayne M (2012) Confronting confrontation. In: Roberts P, Hunter J (eds) Criminal evidence and human rights reimagining common law procedural traditions. Hart Publishing, Oxford/Portland, pp 283–307

Riklin F (2014) Das Unmittelbarkeitsprinzip im schweizerischen Strafverfahrensrecht. Zeitschrift für die gesamte Strafrechtswissenschaft 126(1):173–184

Roxin C, Schünemann B (2017) Strafverfahrensrecht, 29th edn. C. H. Beck, München

Spencer JR (2008) Hearsay evidence in criminal proceedings. Hart Publishing, Oxford/Portland

Summers SJ (2017) Fair trials – the European criminal procedural tradition and the European Court of Human Rights. Hart Publishing, Oxford/Portland

Thörnich D (2017) Art. 6 Abs. 3 lit. d EMRK und der unerreichbare (Auslands-)Zeuge: Appell zur Stärkung des Konfrontationsrechts bei präjudizierender Zeugenvernehmung im Ermittlungsverfahren. Zugleich Besprechung von EGMR, Urt. v. 15.12.2015 – 9154/10 (Schatschaschwili v. Deutschland). Zeitschrift für Internationale Strafrechtswissenschaft 12(1):39–55

Trechsel S (2005) Human rights in criminal proceedings. Oxford University Press, Oxford

Vogler R (2014) The principle of immediacy in English criminal procedural law. Zeitschrift für die gesamte Strafrechtswissenschaft 126(1):239–247

Winter LB (2014) Das Unmittelbarkeitsprinzip im spanischen Strafverfahren. Zeitschrift für die gesamte Strafrechtswissenschaft 126(1):194–213

Chapter 8
Neuroscience of Memory and Philosophy of Knowledge Challenges to Immediacy

Ricardo Tavares da Silva

8.1 The Epistemic Problem Regarding Immediacy in Criminal Appeal

The problem I wish to address is whether there are special reasons, concerning epistemic reliability, supporting the demand, advocated by the ECtHR following the Court's interpretation of the fair trial guarantee contained in paragraph 1 of article 6 of the ECtHR, that personal evidence be produced again before the court of appeal, who then will have to hear the witnesses and the accused directly, or if, on the contrary, such a requirement proves to be epistemically harmful. Namely, I will assess whether there are epistemic considerations that lead to preferring direct contact with witnesses to accessing visual and audio recordings of their intervention in 1st instance.

This is an epistemic (that is, knowledge-related) problem, which does not belong exclusively to one field of knowledge. Its study is transversal to Philosophy of Knowledge, Cognitive Science, Psychology and Neuroscience strictly speaking.

Going back to the fundamental problem that is at the root of the presented one: the judge, in order to decide according to the Law, must possess all the factual information necessary to back that decision and, in order to acquire that information, the judge has to rely on sources of information, namely, reliable sources of information, the so-called 'means of proof'; now, one must identify these reliable sources of information, and if one wishes to go beyond what the Law says, one has to resort to research carried out in the Neurosciences and Philosophy of Knowledge (Epistemology). Therefore, it is necessary to discuss whether the so-called 'testimonial

R. Tavares da Silva (✉)
University of Lisbon School of Law, Research Centre for Criminal Law and Criminal Sciences (CIDPCC), Lisbon, Portugal
e-mail: ricardosilva@fd.ulisboa.pt

H. Morão, R. Tavares da Silva (eds.), *Fairness in Criminal Appeal*,
https://doi.org/10.1007/978-3-031-13001-4_8

evidence', largely based on the faculty of memory, fulfills the requirements of a reliable source of information, especially when produced on criminal appeal.

It becomes clear that the underlying epistemic problem is the problem of the possibility of knowledge, which already presupposes choices regarding the problem of the source of knowledge. It is the way we acquire information from reality that is at stake.

8.2 Sources of Information vs Reliable Sources of Information

I have mentioned two concepts, the concept of 'source of information' and the concept of 'reliable source of information'. That wasn't by chance since that distinction is usually made in Epistemology (although not by all). But how do they differ from each other?

Source of information (I mean cognitive information, information in the brain[1]) is anything capable of making information appear in us. In a non-technical fashion, one may say that *x* is a source of information if and only if at least sometimes we acquire information through *x*, even if not always and even if only a few times. One might be more demanding and require not to be improbable that information is generated by *x*. This is 'source of information' in a psychological sense.

In this sense of 'source of information', tradition identifies four different sources: *i)* perception; *ii)* reason; *iii)* memory; *iv)* testimony.

Memory[2] may be or may be not a psychological source of information depending on whether information is required to be absolutely or relatively new. In fact, one may always say that, with memory, one is not acquiring previously non existing information in the cognitive system, but only reproducing previously acquired information. Hence, the stored information had to be acquired by one of the three genuine sources of information. But one may also say that this reproduction of information is, in a certain sense, acquisition of information, as retrieval of stored information (which was "still", without being "used").

---

[1]It makes sense to say that information already exists outside living organisms (namely, those with a nervous system). Light carries information, air carries information, devices such as televisions, radios and smartphones carry information, etc.; ultimately, things themselves can be known only because they carry information (and thus reveal themselves). However, I'm only speaking of information as the content of neurological processes, and for that we have a name, 'knowledge'. So, the sources of information I'm speaking about are the traditional sources of knowledge in Epistemology. For a theory of knowledge as information flowing in the brain see Dretske (1981, 1985).

[2]Not in the sense of the capacity to store the acquired information, nor in the sense of the very act of storing the information—memorizing—, nor, still, in the sense of the stored information itself, but in the sense of reproducing stored information—remembering, reminding.

In Epistemology, when one speaks of 'source of information' pointing out those four, one is really thinking of acquisition in the latter sense, which means the same as information becoming "consciousness" by an experience (becoming "running information", information being "used").

Within these four, some are sources of information in a strictly epistemic sense: from the initial domain of psychological sources of information, there are those which are reliable. Under the most demanding requirements, reliable sources of information must be infallible sources: they must guarantee information, under any circumstances. The key word here is 'warrant' (or 'certainty', 'safety', 'sufficiency', etc.). If we are less demanding, it is required the generation of information only with a high degree of probability.

It is at the level of reliability that the greatest epistemic discussions take place, and it is at the level of reliability that the sources of information are especially significant to Criminal Procedural Law. Here are some of reliability problems that have been pointed out to each source of information:

a) perception: from the outset, there are wrong perceptions, hallucinations; furthermore, what is perceived depends on several factors that may corrupt information, such as the subject's mere "angle of vision", his emotional state, the degree of involvement in the experienced fact, the degree of attention, the degree of attention to detail, the degree of understanding, as well as biological factors such as age, sex, species, etc. (not to mention the putative influence of alcohol or drugs)
b) reason: this is the source of inferences; similarly to the first criticism regarding the reliability of perception, there are incorrect inferences, logically invalid reasoning; moreover, they only work if one starts from true prior information, which is not always the case (and is dependent on other sources, which may not be reliable); finally, it is only useful to acquire propositional information, not information about objects[3]
c) testimony: again, there are false testimonies, communication of false information (I mean, no communication of information whatsoever); and, from here, one is left with two hypotheses: *i)* the witness may simply be lying; *ii)* or maybe she is being honest but she herself has the wrong information; one may wonder how is this last hypotheses even possible (if the witness had sensory experience of the object/fact); first, due to the reliability problems already pointed out to perception; second, due to memory reliability problems, which I will talk about later and is one of the central points of this work.

But these sources are natural sources. To those one must add all the sources of information deriving from technology (I shall call them 'artificial sources').

[3]It doesn't make sense, for instance, to infer a breathing person from a living person: both premises and conclusion must express propositions (ideally, refer facts). The meaningful inference will be something like 'John is alive, therefore John is breathing'. However, our knowledge extends far beyond propositional knowledge.

Following the theory of the extended mind presented by Clark and Chalmers in the paper *The Extended Mind*, from 1998, I think they are extensions of natural sources: a simple compass, a GPS, a watch, a calculating machine, a thermometer, a smartphone (which has it all), a scale, a tape measure, etc.[4] Most of them are extensions of perception but it docsn't have to be that way. The calculating machine, for example, is an extension of reason. A smartphone, on the other hand, constitutes (among other things) an extension of memory insofar as we store acquired information there, which can be "used" at any time.

I include visual and audio recordings in this category. From the outset, I would not include them in the testimony category, as some authors do, although they may contain information about testimonies (which is different). They are extensions of perception, since images and sounds are captured by machines that operate as extensions of our sensory organs (and of memory, through the recording function itself). If they are recordings of testimonies, then yes, in addition, they will also be extensions of the testimonial source, insofar as they extend the range of the testimony.

8.3 Reliability in Court

Close to but not coincident with the distinction between psychological sources of information and reliable sources of information is the distinction between the context of discovery and the context of justification (which I prefer to call 'context of validation').

The context in which the means of proof are relevant in court is a context of validation: there are certain statements "floating in the air", hypotheses of truth (propositions[5]) brought to court, which need to be confirmed; it is necessary to check whether or not they correspond to facts. More specifically: the procedural subjects present to the judge certain information, which they acquired in a certain way (context of discovery), albeit from reliable sources, and it is necessary to validate this information, making use, now necessarily, of reliable sources (context of validation). Only in the latter case do reliable sources of information count as 'means of proof', even if they coincide with those of the context of discovery. It is all about testing, verifying, or demonstrating the truth of the propositions "represented" in court. I am using the terms 'confirmation', 'verification', 'validation', 'demonstration', 'proof', 'test', etc. as synonyms.

[4]The strong extended mind thesis consists of the conjunction of the following propositions: *i)* if it functions like the mind, it is a mind (functionalism); *ii)* if it functions like the mind and we use it to replace/complement our mind, it is our mind. The weak version theorist will argue that if it functions analogously/similarly to the mind and if we use it to replace/complement our mind, then we use it as we use our mind. For the purposes of this essay, no version is preferred. For a foundational work on functionalism, see Putnam (1967).

[5]For an objective account of propositions (and of truth), see Bolzano (1837).

As I said before, this information may have already reached the procedural subjects through a reliable source of information. But it also might not have been the case. This is irrelevant because, at this stage, all criminally pertinent information must be validated in court in order to participate of the institutional weight of a judicial decision. And one must necessarily resort to a reliable source of information. The process is the reverse of that of a discovery: one already has information from the start and goes back to its source. It is like a simulation of the information acquisition by a reliable source (in an *ex ante* analysis: a judgment of posthumous prognosis is being made).

Nevertheless, I think that such distinction (between context of discovery and context of validation) has more of an institutional rather than an epistemic value. Information, if acquired through a reliable source of information in the privacy of the personal investigation, would already by definition be certainly true. The point is that, in that case, it would not share the solemnity or institutional weight associated with judicial activity. This is exactly what happens in science: it is necessary to demonstrate the truth of the proposed theory to peers, publishing in specialist journals, even if repeating the steps used in field research. Validation is, after all, validation before peers: one must convince them. In court, it is necessary to convince the judge.

However, the sources of information that are strictly relevant in court are necessarily reliable sources of information (which, remembering, are those that guarantee the truth of the propositions brought to trial), meeting the procedural and constitutional guarantees enjoyed by the defendants.

There is also another important distinction, between reliability and admissibility, resulting from the distinction between means of proof and means of obtaining proof (in Portuguese law, articles 128 and following vs. articles 171 and following of the Criminal Procedure Code). Since testimony is considered a means of proof (articles 128 *et seq*), coercion to obtain a testimony, for example, is a means (inadmissible, article 126/1) of obtaining proof. Since an audio recording is a means of proof (article 167), the telephone tapping by which that recording was obtained will be a means of obtaining proof (admissible under certain conditions, article 187).

8.4 On the Reliability of Testimony: The Unreliability of Memory

Are there epistemic reasons that justify requiring the court of appeal to directly assess personal evidence, namely, to hear the witnesses again? This is the main question of this chapter: one must evaluate, from an epistemic point of view, the orientation of the ECtHR according to which, in the case of first convictions in appeal, and as a guarantee of fair trial imposed by the article 6 of the ECHR, the court of appeal must personally hear the witnesses again, repeating the evidence, in opposition to the idea that consulting the testimonies recordings is sufficient to respect the principle of immediacy (in conjunction with the principle of orality regarding testimonial evidence).[6]

Earlier, I mentioned some of the obstacles usually pointed out to the reliability of testimony. The first one is that there are false testimonies. One can imagine an ideal world in which people do not lie but false testimonies subsist (even with an unproblematic original acquisition of information, which is improbable[7]). Why? Because investigation carried out in the last decades showed us that memory, on which the testimonial evidence depends, is itself fallible.[8] At least, that's what the interference theory tells us.

It should be noted that interference theory only concerns new information added to previously stored information in memory, and not the natural degradation of that same information. Regarding this last aspect, Ebbinghaus, in a well-known empirical study conducted in the nineteenth century,[9] had already detected that about half of the total stored information disappears after one hour. Factors such as age accentuate this "forgetting curve".

Later, Hebb[10] and Bliss and Lomo[11] showed how this process of memory degradation takes place in neurophysiological terms.

Interference theory also does not focus on those disturbances in the act of remembering that are common to perception, such as the way the subject "looks again" at that experience, his current emotional state, the degree of involvement in the remembered fact, the possibility of being under the influence of alcohol or drugs, etc.

Interference theory is restricted to those cases of stored information corruption. And this corruption can take place *a priori*—the so-called 'proactive interference'—, when previous information interferes with the most recently stored information (corrupting the latter), or it can take place *a posteriori*—the so-called 'retroactive interference'—when the most recently stored information interferes with previous information (corrupting the latter). New information is corrupted by old information and old information is corrupted by new information.

More specifically, the theory developed through studies focusing on retroactive interference, experiments in which false information is added to the range of

[6] I am repeating, to a large extent, Helena Morão's exposition of this jurisprudential orientation in Chap. 1 and in 2020, pp. 179 *et seq.*

[7] For an exploration of this particular deficiency of testimony, see Greer (1971).

[8] Testimony in itself does not depend on memory: it is possible to communicate information at the same time it is being acquired for the first time (in sync with experience). However, I'm thinking about testimony produced in court.

[9] Ebbinghaus (1885).

[10] Hebb (1949).

[11] Bliss and Lomo (1973).

information available to subjects, such as the experiments conducted by Elizabeth Loftus.[12]

In one of them, some individuals were placed to watch movies of road disasters and then they were asked some questions about what they saw. It was found that the way the questions were asked already induced individuals to a certain "memory". For example, if asked how fast they thought the cars were going when they hit each other, they would answer *x*, but if asked how fast they were going when they smashed, they would answer a much higher speed. A week later, those who had been asked the question using the word 'smashed' were asked if glass had been broken, and answered yes, when that was not the case.

In another pioneering study (carried out and reported in the 1990s), false information was induced in a 14-year-old boy named Chris. First, based on information from the mother and brother, three (allegedly) true descriptions of Chris' childhood were made available. Along with these, a made-up description was introduced, according to which Chris got lost in a shopping mall (which the family often went to) when he was 5 years old. Chris was asked for the first five days to write down all additional information he could add to those descriptions, and if he couldn't, write down that he didn't remember. Chris was "remembering" more and more details related to the fake episode, such as the appearance of the person who found him and helped him to look for the family, as he was very nice. He also said that he remembered that he had been very afraid of not seeing his family again and that his mother had scolded him. A few weeks later, Chris was asked to rate, on a scale from 0 to 11, how clear he was of the four memories described. He gave 1, 10 and 5 to true, 8 to false. And he "remembered" even more details: that he got lost in a toy store, that the gentleman who helped him had glasses, was old, had a flannel sweater, and so on.

Rebecca Helm[13] also tells us about anomalies related to facial recognition: people are very easily able to recognize similar facial patterns, namely, when they are familiar to them, without, afterwards, being able to recognize details; thus, they think they are identifying the aggressor when they are simply reacting to a familiar facial pattern. This phenomenon, called 'ghost memory' and identified by Fuzzy-Trace Theory, has led to several wrongful convictions, as noted by Joyce Lacy and Craig Stark:[14] in the USA, about 75% of convictions later overturned based on DNA testing had been based on facial recognition.

Neuroscience in the strict sense has also addressed the issue of memory manipulation. In *Memory Manipulation During Sleep: Fundamental Advances and Possibilities for Application*, Lucia Talamini surveys recent studies involving memory manipulation during sleep. The starting point is that sleep is essential for the consolidation of memory: as she states, "the importance of sleep for mental function

[12] Loftus and Palmer (1974), Loftus (1975), Loftus and Pickrell (1995), Loftus et al. (1996) and Loftus and Davis (2006).

[13] Helm (2021).

[14] Lacy and Stark (2013).

is not merely due to a general restorative effect of sleep", since, "rather, it seems to be related to brain-specific processes, whereby information acquired during the day is reprocessed and reorganized".[15] Now, interfering with this mechanism, it becomes possible to manipulate the information to be sedimented: "pivotal contributions to our understanding of these processes, especially regarding the memory function of sleep, have come from studies using manipulations to directly influence these sleep-related processes".[16]

Talamini analyses some of these memory manipulation techniques: "some such manipulations have been aimed at neuronal activity, imposing artificial memories during sleep, some act on oscillatory population dynamics, boosting or interrupting particular EEG patterns, while still others have targeted the system at the sensory level, through presentation of memory cues during sleep". Finally, "a recent development in this field concerns the use of closed-loop stimulation techniques, to precisely target stimuli at particular neural activity patterns".[17]

Another study (Vetere et al. 2019), carried out in mice, managed to create false memories by combining a normal conditioning technique with optogenetic stimulation, a technique that allows acting on neurons with light emission, as the stereotyped anatomical and molecular organization of the olfactory system of mice makes it possible to genetically target specific olfactory sensory neurons. More specifically, researchers acted directly on the olfactory sensory neurons that express the same gene activated by acetophenone, while a footshock was administered. The result was the same as subjection to the odor of acetophenone in conjunction with footshock, that of aversion to that odor.

In 2013, the pioneering experience in the use of this same technique was reported in the article *Creating a False Memory in the Hippocampus*.[18] A mouse was placed in a box, allowing it to form a (real) memory of the environment. Then, the same mouse was placed in another box, and the memory of the environment of the first box was activated with a laser while the mouse was footshocked. The mouse was placed back in the first box, in which it froze in fear, "remembering" the footshock.

In another experience,[19] scientists concluded that "RNA extracted from the central nervous system of *Aplysia* given long-term sensitization (LTS) training induced sensitization when injected into untrained animals".[20]

The problem gets worse since it's possible to "inject" false memories directly into the brain. Amílcar Santos, in *The Hypothesis of Connecting Two Spinal Cords as a Way of Sharing Information between Two Brains and Nervous Systems*,[21] tells us about three situations through which it's possible to artificially introduce information into the brain: *i)* direct communication between different nervous systems (through

---

[15] Talamini (2017), p. 313.

[16] *Idem.*

[17] *Idem*, pp. 313–314.

[18] Ramirez et al. (2013).

[19] Bédécarrats et al. (2018).

[20] Bédécarrats et al. (2018), p. 1.

[21] Santos (2017).

Brain-to-Brain-Interfaces and brained); *ii)* closed loops systems between the brain and the spinal cord from the same individual; *iii)* connection between different nervous systems through the spinal cord (the hypothesis that he introduced).

The conclusion is as expected: memory is fallible. And, since testimonial evidence depends on memory, obviously it will be as fallible as the latter. There is no guarantee that the information the witness provides in good faith actually corresponds to facts, as this same information will most likely be corrupted, to a greater or lesser extent.

One could argue that these problems affect all testimonial evidence, not just the one made in Criminal Appeal. That's true. In fact, strategies have been devised in order to, at least, reduce the handicaps of testimonial evidence in general, recognizing the existence of those same handicaps. However, it affects testimonial evidence made in the context of appeal even more. First of all, because of the principle of (natural) degradation of information: the more time passes, the less information remains. Second, because, in the meantime, new information was acquired, which potentiates (retro-active) corruption of the relevant information for the process. Finally, because the new recall will already be made "on top" of the recall operated in the 1st instance (in fact, of the entire experience of the trial), again potentiating the reproduction of information with interferences.

8.5 On the Reliability of Perception: The Reliability of Recordings

If the judge could see what happened, he would: this seems to me to be indisputable. Perception—direct contact with the object—must still be considered a reliable source of information, perhaps the most reliable (or even the only) one. It is true that natural perception has, as already pointed out, its reliability problems. However, to fill this gap, extensions are available—which are an enhancement to the natural source—, such as visual and audio recordings.

Likewise, the judge's direct access to testimonial evidence—the principle of subjective immediacy—seems epistemically preferable to the alternative, indirect testimony (referred to in article 129 of the Portuguese Criminal Procedure Code). The principle of immediacy already reflects, from an epistemic perspective, the preference of perception (of testimony) over testimony (of testimony). And the impossibility of the appeal court naturally accessing the testimony made in the 1st instance may perfectly be overcome through the recordings of that testimony, as artificial extensions of natural perception. The appeal court still maintains direct experience of testimony evidence.

I venture to say that access to testimonial evidence produced in first instance through visual and audio recordings avoids the mentioned problems regarding its renewal in criminal appeal (that is, diminishes degradation and corruption of the information reproduced with testimony) while respecting the principle of immediacy. That's a principle of immediacy itself extended, which implies certain specificities (such as the impossibility of asking questions and getting answers).[22] But it is still immediacy.

The main disadvantage of renewing testimonial evidence in criminal appeal arises, therefore, from adding the reliability problems inherent to memory to the reliability problems inherent to testimony. If it is true that testimony, in general, as a means of proof, must be viewed with skepticism, it is still preferable to resort to it avoiding as much as possible corruption of the reproduced information.

I said that visual and audio recordings are available to suppress natural perception's reliability problems. However, most of them do not even concern its intrinsic reliability. There is a difference between intrinsic reliability—regarding that particular way of acquiring information, distinctive from the others—and extrinsic reliability—regarding those factors that may surround that way of acquiring information, as part of its "environment".

Information acquisition disturbing factors such as the subject's emotional state, involvement in the experienced event, lack of attention, lack of understanding, biological factors such as age, sexual gender, animal species, the influence of substances such as alcohol or drugs, etc., are extrinsic to perception (they do not characterize it) and, hence, are (controllable) variables. They do not affect perception's intrinsic reliability.

Even the possibility of hallucination as an obstacle to natural perception's reliability must be relativized. In some way, sensorial information is always about something (real); otherwise, it wouldn't be information.[23] In fact, this is one of the strongest reasons for treating knowledge as information: the intentionality of any cognitive entity is the "aboutness" of information.[24] So, although not the entire hallucination, at least its parts are bits of information, which refer to something (real).

So, those bits of information do refer but to something that is no longer present to the subject: they are maladjusted to that epistemic context. They were formed in

---

[22] It is usually pointed out the gain of objectivity in relation to face-to-face interaction as big advantage. I believe that this is a disadvantage, since the so-called "subjectivity" of face-to-face interaction is what makes it a genuine perceptual experience. On the other hand, the possibility of manipulating information controlling how testimony is recorded (shots and angles of the footage, sound volume, etc.) is pointed out as a disadvantage. But this is the equivalent of all those reliability obstacles about the subject's perception mentioned at the beginning.

[23] The same says Dreske:

> No structure can carry the information that *s* is *F* unless, in fact, *s* is *F*. False information, misinformation, and (grimace!) disinformation are not varieties of information – any more than a decoy duck is a kind of duck. A glance at the dictionary reveals that information is related to intelligence, news, instruction, and knowledge – things that have an important connection to *truth*. And so it should be with any theoretical approximation to this notion, Dretske (1985), p. 57

[24] For now two classic accounts of the nature and role of intentionality, see Brentano (1874) and Searle (1983).

another context (where the source of information, the object of knowledge, was present) but used outside that context (just like dreams[25]). What we call 'hallucination' in one context is, at least partially, veridical perception in another context (in which that information was generated). Only the assemble of those bits of information is not veridical.

Thus, perception, as a source of information, may be accused of scarcity (it doesn't capture everything, neither in a single stroke), not of excess.

8.6 Testimony: Believing Without Seeing

The epistemic inadequacy of testimony is such that I do not even consider it a source of information. Testimony may be capable of generating belief in the interlocutor, but it is not able to produce judgments: that it's exactly what happens in religious contexts, belief (psychological conviction) without judgment (cognitive information). Crucial is the distinction between judgment (mental support of informative/ cognitive content) and belief (mental attitude of conviction towards truth): sources of information are those able to produce judgments, not beliefs. Note that, in general, it is also possible to produce judgment without belief: just imagine being in disbelief before an real experience (for instance, seeing a UFO land in front of you and small ETs come out of it).

The definition of 'source of information' I am giving is inspired by the so-called 'causal theories of knowledge', such as Goldman's theory presented in *A causal Theory of Knowing*.[26] However, those are theories about the definition of 'knowledge', to which to know that *p* is to have the belief that *p* properly caused by the fact that *p*. On the contrary, I am just arguing that knowledge only exists if the possessed information has been caused by the object of knowledge itself (directly or indirectly); I'm not saying what it is to know. And I'm not talking about beliefs but information (judgments). Because of that, I can argue (contrary to causal theories of knowledge), for example, that *S* does not know that he has a house in front of him (the only one, because next to it there are only facades) even when the view of the facade of the house, together with other operations (namely, inferences), generated his belief that he has a house in front of him: the only information available from the house he has in front of him is that of the facade (that's all he sees); the belief that a house is there is already an extrapolation from the possessed information (strictly speaking, not even the belief was caused by the existence of the house).

The Gettier-type cases also get an explanation according to this account.[27] Let us imagine that *A* burned himself on the hand with sulfuric acid and that some cream on

[25]Continuing a respectful tradition that goes back to Aristotle and Descartes, Macpherson (2013) thinks that dreams count as hallucinations in the philosophical sense.

[26]"We can now formulate the analysis of knowing as follows: *S knows that* p if and only if *the fact p is causally connected in a "appropriate" way with S's believing that p.* ", Goldman (1967), p. 369.

[27]For the original Gettier cases, see Gettier (1963).

the burnt surface concealed the burn, to the point that his friend *B* assumed that nothing had happened and even inferred that, fortunately, *A* didn't put his hand on a fire that was close to him. Traditionally, *B* is said to know that *A* has not put his hand in the fire because he believes this truth in a justified manner (that is, with good reasons to believe). However, it was only by chance that he got it right, because the premise of his inference (*A* doesn't have his hand burned) was false. That is why, despite the traditional reading, he doesn't have knowledge.[28] In my opinion, this fact (*A* not putting his hand in the fire) did not cause any information in *S* about what happened, directly (veridical perception) or indirectly (valid reasoning with true premises), so *B*'s belief is not accompanied by knowledge.[29]

Therefore, in short, testimony is not even a source of information (knowledge) as it does not allow, directly or indirectly, causation of information, in the subject, by the known object itself. There is a "causal gap" between the possession of information in the sender and the putative possession of the same information in the receiver: the cognitive reference to reality (intentionality) is not communicable.

However, that does not necessarily stain testimonial evidence: it may be the case that the purpose of Criminal Procedure is to produce beliefs in the judge (although grounded on objectively acceptable reasons) and not information about the facts. Perhaps the epistemic guarantees sought by Criminal Procedure are not purely epistemic guarantees: perhaps a judicial decision based on verification of the information brought to court, on a pure epistemic validation (characterizing an epistemic-deontological model of Criminal Procedure), is not required, and any path, even if extrinsic, that leads to a good decision based upon the facts is acceptable

[28] For a glimpse of the traditional view, see Chisholm (1977).

[29] Similarly, Dretske:

> Furthermore, this account of knowledge neatly avoids some of the puzzles that intrigue philosophers (and bore everyone else to death). For example, Gettier-like difficulties (Gettier 1963) arise for any account of knowledge that makes knowledge a product of some justificatory relationship (having good evidence, excellent reasons, etc.) that *could* relate one to something false. For on all these accounts (unless special ad hoc devices are introduced to prevent it), one can be justified (in a way appropriate to knowledge) in believing something that is, in fact, false (hence, not know it); also know that *Q* (which happens to be true) is a logical consequence of what one believes, and come to believe *Q* as a result. On some perfectly natural assumptions, then, one is justified (in a way appropriate to knowledge) in believing the truth (*Q*). But one obviously doesn't *know Q* is true. This is a problem for justificational accounts. The problem is evaded in the information-theoretic model, because one can get into an appropriate justificational relationship to some-thing false, but one cannot get into an appropriate informational relationship to something false, Dretske (1985), p. 59

However, instead of differentiating judgment from belief, Dretske distinguishes between an extensional (getting information: seeing a duck, for instance) and an intensional (processing that information: recognizing it as a duck) way of describing perceptions. The latter is responsible for generating believes, which will be false if not generated in the adequate way. I don't get it: seeing a duck without recognizing it as a duck is not having information that that thing is a duck; therefore, one may even believe it is a duck but one does not know that it is a duck.

(characterizing an epistemic-consequentialist model of Criminal Procedure). Perhaps the judge isn't required to know: he just has to decide well. Of course, as we move from judgment confirmation to belief justification, testimonial evidence starts to be grounded, not on the reliability of the testimony, but on the reliability of the witness: reasons for believing will be based on personal credibility.

Bibliography

Axmacher N, Rasch B (eds) (2017) Cognitive neuroscience of memory consolidation. Springer, Gewerbestrasse

Bédécarrats A, Chen S, Pearce K, Cai D, Glanzman D (2018) RNA from trained *Aplysia* can induce an epigenetic engram for long-term sensitization in untrained *Aplysia*. eNeuro 5(3):1–11

Bliss T, Lomo T (1973) Long-lasting potentiation of synaptic transmission in the dentate area of the anesthetized rabbit following stimulation of the perforant path. J Physiol 232(2):331–356

Bolzano B (1837) Theory of science. Translated from the German by Terrell B (1973). D. Reidel Publishing Company, Dordrecht

Brentano F (1874) Psychology from an empirical standpoint. Translated by Rancurello A, Terrell DB, McAlister L (1973). Routledge, New York

Capitan WH, Merrill DD (eds) (1967) Art, mind, and religion. Pittsburgh University Press, Pittsburgh

Chisholm R (1977) Theory of knowledge. Prentice Hall, Englewood Cliffs

Clark A, Chalmers D (1998) The extended mind. Analysis 58(1):7–19

Dretske F (1981) Knowledge and the flow of information. MIT Press, Cambridge

Dretske F (1985) Precis of knowledge and the flow of information. In: Kornblith H (ed) Naturalizing epistemology. MIT Press, Cambridge, pp 169–187

Ebbinghaus H (1885) Memory: a contribution to experimental psychology. Translated by Ruger HA, Bussenius CE (1913). Teachers College Press (Columbia University), New York

Gettier E (1963) Is justified true belief knowledge? Analysis 23(6):121–123

Goldman A (1967) A causal theory of knowing. J Philos 64(12):357–372

Greer D (1971) Anything but the truth? The reliability of testimony in criminal trials. Br J Criminol 11(2):131–154

Hebb D (1949) The organization of behavior: a neuropsychological theory. Wiley, New York

Helm R (2021) Evaluating witness testimony: juror knowledge, false memory, and the utility of evidence-based directions. Int J Evid Proof 25(4):264–285

Kornblith H (ed) (1981) Naturalizing epistemology. MIT Press, Cambridge

Lacy J, Stark C (2013) The neuroscience of memory: implications for the courtroom. Nat Rev Neurosci 14(9):649–658

Loftus E (1975) Leading questions and the eyewitness report. Cogn Psychol 7:560–572

Loftus E, Davis D (2006) Recovered memories. Annu Rev Clin Psychol 2(1):469–498

Loftus E, Palmer J (1974) Reconstruction of automobile destruction: an example of the interaction between language and memory. J Verbal Learn Verbal Behav 13:585–589

Loftus E, Pickrell J (1995) The formation of false memories. Psychiatr Ann 25(12):720–725

Loftus E, Coan J, Pickrell J (1996) Manufacturing false memories using bits of reality. In: Reder L (ed) Implicit memory and metacognition. Psychology Press, New York, pp 195–220

Macpherson F (2013) The philosophy and psychology of hallucination: an introduction. In: Macpherson F, Platchias D (eds) Hallucination. Philosophy and psychology. MIT Press, Cambridge, pp 1–38

Macpherson F, Platchias D (eds) (2013) Hallucination. Philosophy and psychology. MIT Press, Cambridge

Morão H (2020) Pela Renovação da Renovação da Prova. Anatomia do Crime 12:171–198

Putnam H (1967) The nature of mental states. In: Capitan WH, Merrill DD (eds) Art, mind, and religion. Pittsburgh University Press, Pittsburgh, pp 37–48

Ramirez S, Liu X, Lin PA, Suh J, Pignatelli M, Redondo R, Ryan T, Tonegawa S (2013) Creating a false memory in the hippocampus. Science 341(6144):387–391

Reder L (ed) (1996) Implicit memory and metacognition. Psychology Press, New York

Santos A (2017) The hypothesis of connecting two spinal cords as a way of sharing information between two brains and nervous systems. Front Psychol 8:1–5

Searle J (1983) Intentionality: an essay in the philosophy of mind. Cambridge University Press, Cambridge

Talamini L (2017) Memory manipulation during sleep: fundamental advances and possibilities for application. In: Axmacher N, Rasch B (eds) Cognitive neuroscience of memory consolidation. Springer, Gewerbestrasse, pp 313–334

Vetere G, Tran L, Moberg S, Steadman P, Restivo L, Morrison F, Ressler K, Josselyn S, Frankland P (2019) Memory formation in the absence of experience. Nat Neurosci 22:933–940

Chapter 9
AI Assistance in the Courtroom and Immediacy

Catarina Abegão Alves

9.1 Conceptual Definitions and Differentiations

The European Commission for the Efficiency of Justice (CEPEJ) refers to AI as 'a set of scientific methods, theories, and techniques whose aim is to reproduce, by a machine, the cognitive abilities of human beings. Current developments seek to have machines perform complex tasks previously carried out by humans'.[1] The purported benefits of AI have already led many to test its application in the judicial system. AI systems may be used as a tool in the trial phase, to predict and prepare judicial decisions, functioning as input data of legislative criteria, the facts of the case and legal reasoning, and output data of formal judgements.[2] Nevertheless, our focus in this chapter will not be the use of AI system as a predictive system of judicial outcomes or as a predictive system of recidivism, but only as an instrumental tool, to assist judges in the process of testimonial evidence analysis, perhaps to ensure and improve the application of ECtHR's criteria, set out in the case of Gómez Olmeda v. Spain, no. 61112/12.

This AI assistant must be distinguished from other digital systems already used in courts, normally known as 'traditional' digital technologies, which may include a wide range of applications, used for case management, e-filing, integrated justice chains, e-justice platforms, video technologies, legal databases, human resources, and accounting systems.[3] And this assistant must also be distinguished from the use of AI to produce evidence in criminal law, through electronic devices, not only to

[1] CEPEJ (2019), p. 69.
[2] Ulenaers (2020), p. 5.
[3] Contini (2020), p. 5.

C. A. Alves (✉)
University of Lisbon School of Law, Research Centre for Criminal Law and Criminal Sciences (CIDPCC), Lisbon, Portugal
e-mail: caa@fd.ulisboa.pt

H. Morão, R. Tavares da Silva (eds.), *Fairness in Criminal Appeal*,
https://doi.org/10.1007/978-3-031-13001-4_9

gather evidence, such as body and car-cameras, but also to process it, such as voice and image recognition and fraud detection systems.[4]

The AI assistant will use automated data processing techniques, like an algorithm, to prepare human decisions,[5] namely the judge's decision on the evidence. AI assistant may function as an input data base which congregates the hearings produced during the trial phase, as well as the facts of the case, and then may help the judge during the appeal phase to select which testimony is truly relevant or not to prove certain facts and which is credible or not, to avoid the repetition of the hearings that may be indicated by the appellants in the appeal.

Therefore, this kind of system will not replace a human judge, but will only improve their work and efficiency, as a complement of the judge's work, helping them to filter irrelevant from relevant data.[6] Concerning the evidence data, this system may suggest to the judge a decision regarding testimonial evidence, providing an algorithmic analysis of the relevance of each testimony, sustaining their credibility to prove the facts. Whereas the human judge may focus on the legal reasoning and justification of the decision, since normally these tasks fall outside the scope of the abilities of AI,[7] the AI assistant may help the judge on a previous analysis of the evidence, leading to more objectivity.

This will only be possible because AI systems will have the possibility to congregate big data, i.e., they will receive a large amount of data, analyse it, and utilize these massive flows of information, verifying trends within the data, overcoming the traditional human analysis.[8] These techniques of data processing are done through an algorithm to select the relevant information in a large amount of data, so it 'need not be software: in the broadest sense, they are encoded procedures for transforming input data into a desired output, based on specified calculations'.[9] The collection of a large amount of data will improve the accuracy of the output results, but this data needs to also have a quality baseline to achieve useful predictions.[10]

In our hypothesis the big data will be the transcriptions and the audio and video recordings of the selected hearings mentioned in the appeal, the allegedly 'relevant' and 'determinant' testimonies which were produced during the trial phase and whose hearings should be renewed during the appeal phase in order to ensure the principle of immediacy, according to ECtHR.

---

[4]Seng and Mason (2021), pp. 243, 258 ff. About machine learning evidence, Nutter (2019), *passim*.

[5]Council of Europe (2018), p. 3.

[6]Sourdin (2018), p. 1130 and Sourdin and Cornes (2018), p. 94 (referring to it as 'co-bots'). With the same opinion regarding the attorney, Surden (2014), p. 101.

[7]Ulenaers (2020), p. 11.

[8]Lim (2021), pp. 285–286.

[9]Gillespie (2014), p. 167.

[10]Nutter (2019), pp. 935–936.

Algorithm decision making is a combination of automation, data analysis and adaptability.[11] These characteristics are the major difference between 'traditional' digital technologies and AI technologies, which are interactive, autonomous, and self-learning, contrary to traditional digital technologies which congregate software codes that are designed to remain stable.[12] Therefore, in AI systems with machine learning technology the systems may take autonomous decisions, since they will be able to autonomously extract patterns from input data, learning and improve their performance.[13] This type of AI assistant may perform different tasks. First of all, the assistant may resort to speech-to-text software (transcription), in order to transform the speech of each testimony in a written text and to classification (using image or facial recognition). Thereafter AI assistant may resort to machine translation (e.g., translating from one natural language to another) and structured output (e.g., image recognition in which the machine can describe the image in grammatical sentences). Then, it may perform regression, predicting a numerical value given certain conditions. After that, it may resort to anomaly detection (to detect fraudulent and not credible testimonies) and to imputation of missing values (predicting certain data points given other data points), and denoising (matching an inputted 'corrupted' exampled with a 'clean' example). Finally, the AI assistant may perform synthesis and sampling (generating new examples similar to the examples it has learned).[14]

If this AI system works with machine learning technology, it will only be able to perform these above-mentioned tasks when the machine learns from examples. To achieve that, data must be transformed into numbers and then the programmer needs to have access to data whose properties are already known ('training data') and must teach the machine about the rules and associations that will be useful when the machine later analyses new data with data that is not already known ('supervised learning').[15]

Nevertheless, the use of algorithms error rates related with test set error rate concerning training data and with the capturing of the algorithms' performance 'when it is unleashed upon real-world examples with unknown properties' is also inherent to systems of machine learning. Specifically in the transposition of a spoken testimony to a text (speech recognition algorithms), the errors may occur since it is known that these technologies may vary their accuracy according to different accents from different regions. In addition, the accuracy of the technology also varies with race, gender or age, having problems with black and mixed-races speakers.[16]

As an example, the Italian judicial system already uses AI technology during the testimonies—speech-to-text—an algorithm which converts a spoken act into a

[11]Council of Europe (2018), pp. 5–7.

[12]Contini (2020), p. 9.

[13]Bampasika (2020). '[m]achine learning involves computer algorithms that have the ability to "learn" or improve in performance over time on some task', Surden (2014), p. 88.

[14]About these different tasks, Nutter (2019), p. 929.

[15]Nutter (2019), p. 930.

[16]Nutter (2019), pp. 933–935.

written text, to obtain swift and accurate court hearing records, mainly during civil proceedings and often for documents drafting. This technology implies the inscription of the full set of equivalences between phonemes and written terms, and of the rules regulating oral and written communications, transforming analogical acoustic waves through digital reconstruction, making them accessible to machines. Afterwards, digital flow is fragmented in short signals that, in the end, are associated with phonemes and words, with resource to techniques of deep learning and neural network. This system may be helpful not only to transform speech into a written text, but to improve the accuracy of the transcripts made by courts, since it may be used to increase transparency and efficiency when adopting the double screen system in court hearings. And this technology does not create any problems concerning due process or accountability, since the judge must be in power, controlling the equivalence between inputs and outputs.[17]

This AI system that we imagined works not only with acoustic waves of audio records of the testimonies, but also with video records,[18] which may also allow access to the behaviour and gestures of the testimony during the hearing, converting it into algorithms.

Although it was not still possible to discover an AI system with the goals referred to above, there already exists some commercial forensic IT to electronically discover processes, such as EnCase Forensic and Nuix, that are already used in the process not only of proof obtention and proof treatment, but eventually to judicial presentation of proof.[19]

The use of these kinds of systems also summons reflections about transhumanism and enhancement of human capacities. In the future, the integration of computer circuits and programs in judges' human bodies, or the modification of their biological characteristics, physically or genetically, to enhance their intelligence and memory capacities, increasing their abilities to process and manage information and to reduce fatigue symptoms as well may be discussed.[20]

The technologies can be supportive, can replace functions and activities previously carried out by humans or can promote disruptive justice. So, first, these AI systems may inform, support and advise the judge in their task of evidence analysis, as a supportive technology, or can even replace functions that were previously carried out by humans. Furthermore, this technology may also imply a change in the way that judges work, changing the process of proof analysis, providing a different form of justice (disruptive technology), promoting therefore a change in

[17] Contini (2020), pp. 11–12. In double screen system the judge has a screen. The case parties have other. Therefore, they can control in real-time the hearing report made by the programme and can ask for amendments, Contini (2020), pp. 11–12. As to the problem of due process, according to the Fifth Amendment to the American Constitution, there is a proposal that machine learning output will be a form of expert testimony, so the defendant may have the opportunity to cross-examine an expert on the machine's capabilities and process, Nutter (2019), pp. 945–948.

[18] Ash (2018), pp. 1–2.

[19] Mendes (2020), p. 60.

[20] Sourdin (2018), p. 1131.

the adjudicative process.[21] AI assistance will not just expedite the judicial proceedings but may in fact influence the judicial decision in the form of advice and legal analysis (legal analytics).[22] Therefore, it may be more than a mere functional approach, leading to institutional consequences, since it may influence the rights and principles that encompass the criminal proceedings, such as independence, impartiality, fairness, and accountability.[23]

Throughout this chapter we will try to perceive if this may occur. We will try to understand if the use of this kind of AI assistants in the appeal phase, mainly during the process of testimonial proof analysis, will accomplish the criteria set out by ECtHR, without compromising the rights mentioned above. But to understand if AI assistants may be a convenient tool for the judge in the analysis of evidence, the focus must not be on the algorithm, but on how decision-making processes around algorithms may affect the human rights involved. We can only know that if we know how human decision-making functions.[24] And to achieve this comparison it will be necessary to analyse the methods of evidence analysis traditionally used by the judge.

9.2 Free Appreciation of Evidence, Legal and Human Reasoning and AI

In criminal procedures like the Portuguese, the rule of the free appreciation of proof, according to the rules of common experience, anticipates two characteristics of the modern spirit: the openness to the experience and the autonomy of the observer (the judge),[25] since the proof will be analysed according to their free conviction. The rules of experience generate simple judicial presumptions, natural, from people, from fact or from experience. Thus, these rules are not set down by the law, but are grounded on life experience. If the conclusions to be drawn from the rules of experience are truly simple presumptions or presumptions of fact, they are submitted to free appreciation by the judge.[26] The use of maxims of experience must be based on rational criteria: there must be a broad consensus in the average culture of the place and of the moment of the decision, so they can be acceptable as inference criteria; on the other hand, the inference has to take into consideration the specific nature of the maxim, to avoid for instance the use of no general maxims to carry out inferences of 'certainty'.[27]

---

[21] Sourdin and Cornes (2018), pp. 91–92.

[22] Contini (2020), p. 6.

[23] Contini (2020), p. 6.

[24] Council of Europe (2018), pp. 8–9.

[25] Mendes (2010), p. 1000.

[26] Mendes (2010), p. 1011.

[27] Taruffo (2005), pp. 424–425.

The use of rules of experience by the judge does not lead necessary to subjectivity. The judge does not use previously set down legal criteria (as in the system of legal proof), but they still must follow their legal duty to prosecute the material truth of criminal procedure. Nevertheless, the appreciation must be releasable to objective criteria, and therefore subject to motivation and control. Even the 'intimate' conviction of the judge could not be purely subjective, emotional and without reasons. The judge's conviction must be a personal conviction, then not only cognitive activity may play a relevant role, but also some elements not completely rationally explainable and even emotional elements can be involved. At the end of the day, it must be an objectifiable and reasoned conviction.[28] So, in the system of free appreciation of evidence one may talk of a 'liberty for objectivity' and not a free will of the judge or arbitrariness. The need of objectivity is a legal principle and the evidentiary conviction will only be valid if it is reasoned. Then it should be reasoned and controlled by the appeal court.[29]

The judge's life experience can influence the establishment of these rules of life experience, according to their common experience. The implications of the evidence are a result of the interaction between the 'evidence', in a formal sense, and belief structures of the fact finder. Hence, decisions on facts cannot be known *ax ante* since they are a result of the decision-making process. The evidence process is a creative one, instead of a static one given that the implications of evidence cannot be known *a priori*.[30]

In some aspects of judicial analysis, it is inevitable that the judge may be confronted with non-rational motives which may drive the litigants coming before them. So, the judge needs to have the ability to comprehend and to deal with and respond to them, requiring the application of emotional intelligence,[31] also in the analysis of testimonial proof.

But the utilisation of AI assistance does not eliminate the possibility to resort to rules of experience, since the output extracted from the assistant must be overseen by

---

[28] Dias (2004), pp. 202–205. This idea was also visible in the thought of M C Ferreira, according to whom the judge, instead of being linked to pre-fixed and abstract norms on the assessment of evidence, must be subordinate to the principles of evidentiary law and to norms of experience, logic, and incontestable rules of scientific nature, Ferreira (1986), pp. 211–212. In this regard, Melim (2013), pp. 152–153.

[29] Neves (1968), pp. 50–51. Also, excepting the system of free proof as a kind of arbitrariness, based on the ideas that free proof is scientific proof and judge's intime conviction was reinforced by a new requirement of reasoning decisions, Mendes (2010), pp. 1000–1001. Also, Matta (2004), pp. 254–256.

[30] Allen (2001), p. 103. 'Every decision maker will have an idiosyncratic belief set precisely because no two humans have lived the same lives', Allen (2001), p. 103. '[t]he trial judge may exclude evidence that bears no logical relationship to the cause of action and thus the only effects of which can be to waste resources and generate erroneous conclusions. Under modern law these decisions are truly given to the discretion of the trial judge. Some precedents do arise that constrain that discretion somewhat, but not much. Thus, this form of regulation of the proof process depends crucially on the judgment of a human actor', Allen (2001), p. 107.

[31] Sourdin and Cornes (2018), p. 88.

the judge. So, we cannot understand the output of AI assistance as a kind of legal proof. The intervention of human judgment, in the interpretation of the output's result, will then enable discretionary and social considerations, according to life experience, and to personal life, that are beyond the capacity of the AI assistant.[32] Even the algorithms cannot replicate judicial discretion without the use of some randomness and arbitrariness.[33]

In criminal procedures of common law systems, the process of evidence analysis is related to the rules of evidence, i.e., to the legal rules that compose the judicial reasoning to the proof of facts. Then, one may question how the use of AI assistance may be compatible with the standards of proof. The judge must observe the facts and, in relation with the evidence, must consider each fact 'proved' or not 'proved', according to the standards of proof required in each case, namely the standard of beyond reasonable doubt in criminal cases. This standard of proof implies a qualitative judgment of legal reasoning made by the judge, then it may be impossible to express it in mathematical and quantitative terms.[34]

Another problem that we may face is whether we may accomplish the process of legal reasoning with AI systems. The reasoning of legal sentences must contain the following criteria: (i) list of evidence carried for the process; (ii) critical and rational analysis of the reasons that led to give relevance to certain evidence and not to other evidence; (iii) rational and logical concatenation of relevant evidence and investigated facts; (iv) assessment of the facts considered established under the current law.[35] Later on in this chapter we will return to this issue.

In addition, we may face a question regarding proof analysis vis-à-vis the vulnerability of outliers (i.e. data that are drastically different from others) and corner case's weakness of AI, that resort even in more advanced technology, such as machine learning. These techniques are bound by the data that they are trained with, or solely exogenous observations. Differently, judicial decisions take into consideration not only the understanding of specific laws and facts but also the appreciation of exogenous contexts in which laws are made and the cases are

[32] Sourdin (2018), pp. 1130–1131; Sourdin and Cornes (2018), pp. 95, 100, 105, 111; Ulenaers (2020), pp. 11, 18. '[t]he default availability of a responsive human judge permitted to review all aspects of the AI input, and able to call on a complex array of communication and social skills, remains desirable to support understanding and compliance with the law', Sourdin and Cornes (2018), p. 100.

[33] Lim (2021), p. 305. 'To achieve the same effect with AI, one would either have to use different training sets of data to achieve different predictive formulae, which would be the equivalent to knowingly citing only some relevant case law but not all of it, or to add a random factor into the equation, which would be anathema to the concept of fair and transparent judicial decision-making', Lim (2021), p. 305.

[34] Lim (2021), pp. 294–295, 302. '[t]he experience of the English courts shows that it is one thing to accept probabilistic reasoning in the evaluation of one aspect of the evidence, and another to use probabilistic reasoning in an overall assessment of the evidence', Lim (2021), p. 296.

[35] Matta (2004), p. 265.

decided, so the decisions imply discretion by the judges to determine how to characterise the present case's inputs.[36]

Furthermore, AI is also incapable of taking cognisance of material or information that is not contained within the data input that the system receives[37] and, mainly in machine learning systems, AI is incapable of analysing new information that is not similar to the information previously analysed.[38]

Besides that, the argument is also added that AI is still incapable of comprehending the meaning of human language.[39] According to Searle, one must recognize the difference between syntax and semantics, since computer programs possess syntax, based on formal symbols because of the operation of the computer, but do not possess semantics, i.e. the ability to understand the meaning behind these operations.[40] Therefore, this could reflect some difficulty in assessing the credibility of the testimony by the AI system. Even though there already exist some models that recognise hidden emotions, such as the Hidden Markov model-based speech emotion recognition,[41] that will be essential to analyse the importance of emotions expressed not only in the speech, but also in the behaviour of the testimony.

Finally, the influence of psychoanalytic analysis may lead to the conclusion that the way forward must not be the replacement of the judge, since 'a "a judge" is not a single data processing unit to be adequately represented in code. Judges are intimately and psychically linked to the wider social system within which they operate'.[42]

Therefore, the way forward must be, according to a precautionary principle, that AI should not replace human judgment with regard to the evidence, but should only help the judge, to enhance, augment their assessment, seeing that inevitably there are some final judgments that must be made by humans: (a) the ones to which probabilistic analysis is either not possible or not helpful, (b) those a human must exercise

[36] Lim (2021), pp. 302–303.

[37] Lim (2021), p. 303.

[38] Sourdin (2018), p. 1125; Surden (2014), p. 105.

[39] Lim (2021), p. 303.

[40] Searle (1984), p. 28 ff. Recovering this distinction, Sourdin and Cornes (2018), p. 102.

[41] With the proposal of 'affective computing', 'computing that relates to, arises from, or influences emotions', suggesting models for affect recognition, Picard (1995), pp. 1–2, 7–8, 14. 'The input would be a set of observations, the output a set of probabilities for each possible emotional state', Picard (1995), p. 7. About Hidden Markov Models for speech emotion recognition, among others, Mao et al. (2019), p. 6715 ff.

[42] Sourdin and Cornes (2018), p. 112. Adding: 'For any Judge AI project the problem thus arises: how to code to allow for the influence of a similar range of varying *personal, human, and societal* inputs in addition to reflecting legal rules and principles? The problem is especially difficult because such personal inputs, emanating from human judges', and society's unconscious, are by definition not consciously knowable and therefore not translatable into code. (. . .) While, therefore, many aspects of the judicial task may ultimately be captured in code, the human heart of the judicial process, being a combination of conscious and currently unknowable unconscious thought, remains quite literally beyond the comprehension of the most talented programmer', Sourdin and Cornes (2018), p. 112.

in order to develop the capacity to judge and, finally, (c) those the law or other first principles require to be exercised by humans.[43]

It should be noted that with this collaboration between the judge and the AI system, and not with the total replacement of the human judge, we may safeguard the requirements of the rule of law and the right to a fair trial, improving predictability and consistency in evidence analysis. On the other hand, this collaboration may perhaps speed up the legal processes and enhance the efficiency of judiciary, by increasing timesaving and the accessibility of justice, which is also a requirement of the rule of law,[44] for instance avoiding the necessary renewing in the appeal phase of the hearing of relevant testimonies selected in the appeal, according to the criteria of the ECtHR.

9.3 Fairer and More Efficient Justice System?

One may question if the use of AI assistants, even only as a tool for judicial analysis regarding proof, may promote a fairer and more efficient justice system, thereby shaping fairness standards in criminal trials, since AI could avoid human bias during the analysis of witness credibility.

The decision of AI is based on an algorithmic decision-making process. At first glance one may suppose that this may lead to more objective and fairer decisions, in comparison with decisions by human judges, for whom it may be difficult to cross over and not be influenced by their prejudice that result from extreme bias in the evaluation process.[45] Contributing to this objectivity is also the fact that algorithms are grounded in data representative of the community where the decisions will be applied.[46]

In a decision of the US Court of Appeals for the Second Circuit - 138 F.2d 650 (2d Cir. 1943), from 8 November 1943, Judge Jerome Frank said: 'In addition to those acquired social value judgments, every judge, however, unavoidably has many idiosyncratic "learnings of the mind", uniquely personal prejudices, which may interfere with his fairness at a trial. He may be stimulated by unconscious sympathies for, or antipathies to, some of the witnesses, lawyers or parties in a case before him. (...) The conscientious judge will, as far as possible, make himself aware of his biases of this character, and, by that very self-knowledge, nullify their effect'.[47]

[43] Spaulding (2020), pp. 396–401.

[44] Ulenaers (2020), pp. 11–12, 15, 18.

[45] Lepri et al. (2018), pp. 611, 622; Bampasika (2020). Also, about unconscious judge bias, Sourdin and Cornes (2018), pp. 95–96.

[46] Lepri et al. (2018), p. 622.

[47] In Re JP Linaham (1943) 138 F.2d 650 (2d Cir), Justia, 652, https://law.justia.com/cases/federal/appellate-courts/F2/138/650/1481751/.

For instance, when we think of the perspectives of criminal sociology, like in the labelling approach, even knowing that these perspectives are created to explain criminal behaviour,[48] it may be suggested that when judges assess witness trustworthiness, they also resort to a previous process of labelling, according to the gender, race, and social appearance of the victim. So, the assessment of the trustworthiness of the testimony does not lie only on the analysis of credibility but has also something to do with the process of interaction between the judge and the witness.

In fact, besides their biases, there are many factors that may influence judicial decisions, such as personal values, unconscious assumptions,[49] reliance on intuition, the attractiveness of the individuals involved, emotion and, even when and what that person has eaten.[50]

Using an algorithm on the analysis of the testimony, AI assistants may help the judge to achieve more objectivity. At the end of the day, this kind of systems may be useful to reduce errors in judicial decisions and in the correction of judges' individual biases, even more so if we add the argument that many times judges are unaware of the extraneous factors that affect their decisions so that they cannot include them in their reasoning process. The process can be more transparent and verifiable.[51]

Nevertheless, the decision made according to algorithms may also include some bias and discrimination, lack of transparency, accountability and information asymmetry,[52] and opacity, unpredictability and inexplicability as well,[53] which is related to the problem of the 'black box' of the algorithm. In the last instance, these AI systems may jeopardize the right to a fair trial.[54] By way of example, a study was published about COMPAS Recidivism Algorithm (an algorithm used to inform criminal sentencing decisions by predicting recidivism software), that sustains that these algorithms also resort to some labels, since the algorithm is more favourable to recidivism of black people than of white people.[55] So that one may suppose that with AI assistance we may also find bias.

---

[48] Becker (1966), p. 8 ff.

[49] About the role of unconscious in legal reasoning and on the 'legal self', on 'a psychoanalytical understanding of the judicial mind', Sourdin and Cornes (2018), pp. 104, 110–111.

[50] Sourdin and Cornes (2018), pp. 95–96.

[51] Ash (2018), pp. 3, 6.

[52] Lepri et al. (2018), pp. 612–614, 622, 624. About biases of algorithms, since they are trained on biased data, and also about their complexity and obscurity, Ash (2018), p. 4. This last author proposes a solution: to make the code open source, but the evidence weights used by the algorithm private. Then, the public will be able to verify whether the parameters were learned fairly, without knowing the particular action or evidence used by the algorithm, Ash (2018), p. 5.

[53] Council of Europe (2018), p. 10. Bampasika (2020). About this problem of 'black box', Spaulding (2020), p. 389 and Ulenaers (2020), pp. 11–12, 16.

[54] '[t]here is a danger that support systems based on artificial intelligence are inappropriately used by judges to "delegate" decisions to technological systems that were not developed for that purpose and are perceived as being more "objective" even when this is not the case. Great care should therefore be taken to assess what such systems can deliver and under what conditions that may be used in order not to jeopardise the right to a fair trial', Council of Europe (2018), p. 12.

[55] Angwin et al. (2016).

This concern has led to many proposals to overcome this problem, namely the lack of transparency and discrimination. The focus is to create machine learning models featuring transparency, accountability, and fairness (in the sense of lack of bias and discrimination), for instance, precluding the use of sensitive attributes.[56] The European Ethical Charter on the use of Artificial Intelligence in judicial systems and their environment also foresees principles such as the principle of equality and security, the principle of transparency, impartiality, and fairness and, finally, the principle of 'under user control'. So, it will be necessary to construct cybernetics rules, to ensure the principles of transparency, fairness and neutrality, and avoid bias.[57]

Furthermore, it is also proposed that in cases where computers can read emotions, such as in the above-mentioned Hidden Markov model-based speech emotion recognition, the system should show us what it is reading. The emotional state must be observable, so the models should indicate which emotional state was recognized by the computer,[58] to avoid the problem of opacity.

But the problem of the 'black box' evokes also a problem related to the duty of the judges to give reasons, to ensure their freedom from actual or apparent bias. In every judicial decision the judge must proceed to a detailed evidence analysis, discussing which testimony was and was not credible in order to prove a certain fact. Thus, we may question whether we can also find a minimum degree of explanation with regard to the decision-making process in AI systems to avoid pure arbitrariness.[59] We may design programs that cannot only produce conclusions and reasons, but also detail each step of this process, by creating rationalized decisions.[60] Notwithstanding, the problem cannot be overcome if we are still confronted with opacity. Nevertheless, if the equivalence between input and output could be checked or, if the procedure that transforms the input to output does not remain obscure even when this check cannot be performed, we do not have a problem of opacity.[61] To avoid the problem of the 'black box' of the AI, a human judge must always be involved in this procedure, in 'semi-automated' decision-making.[62]

However, if neither the judge nor the experts can surpass the problem of the 'black box' because the result of the AI system is incomprehensible, the judge cannot give reasons for their decision. So, one may question how can the parties

---

[56]Lepri et al. (2018), pp. 615, 622 and Lim (2021), pp. 289–290. But of course, this may also be utopic: 'There is the possibility that our own human intelligence is also incompletely explainable, and it would therefore be futile to expect humans to be able to build a completely explicable artificial intelligence', Lim (2021), p. 288, n. 41.

[57]CEPEJ (2019), pp. 60–61.

[58]Picard (1995), p. 9.

[59]Lim (2021), p. 289.

[60]Greco (2020), pp. 34–35.

[61]This is possible in Italy in the already mentioned system of speech-to-text, Contini (2020), p. 12.

[62]Ulenaers (2020), p. 16.

contest the assessment of testimonies that was made with the help of an AI system.[63] This problem is related to the legitimacy of judicial power. If the decision regarding testimonial evidence is only made by the AI system, how can the parties and all society accept the decision, since it is impossible for the AI to interact with people, with compassion, emotion, or agile or intuitive responsiveness[64]?

The answer can be achieved by two paths. One may be by training the judges on the complexity of the algorithms. Just when the judge understands the output of the system, he may understand the decision and give reasons for the analysis of the proof. But one cannot demand that the judge should be an expert in AI. Therefore, we prefer the other path: to treat the output of the system as expert evidence, so when the judge does not understand the algorithmic analysis he may resort to the help of an expert to produce an expert report, since the outcome of the AI analysis will be analogous to expert proof, based on specific knowledge to support the judicial decision.[65]

9.4 Principle of Immediacy and the Right to a Fair Trial

After these considerations, we may finally ask if the use of an AI assistant may be a way to promote the principle of immediacy and the right to a fair trial, enshrined in article 6, § 1 of the ECHR. According to the criteria set out by ECtHR in the case of Gómez Olmeda v. Spain, no. 61112/12, in the appeal phase the judge will have to hear the relevant and decisive testimonies, and the video or audio recordings are not sufficient to accomplish the principle of public hearing. Although the appellants have already defined the object of the appeal, according to facts, evidence and questions, and then may have already selected the relevant testimonies, this AI system may function as a second filter of this relevance, as an aid to the judge in the appeal phase. With the help of this AI system, even if the judge has access to all the evidence, he will have access to an algorithm analysis of the relevant and decisive proof. AI assistant may congregate all the hearings produced during the trial phase, helping the judge during the appeal phase, to select which testimony is relevant or not to prove certain facts and is credible or not, to avoid the repetition in the appeal phase of each hearing indicated in the appeal, allegedly the 'relevant' testimonies.

Despite the strictest criterion of the ECtHR, even with video and audio recordings, one may question if it will be necessary to have this kind of AI assistants, when

[63] On the perspective of the right of confrontation of the defendant, Bampasika (2020).

[64] Sourdin and Cornes (2018), p. 99.

[65] About expert systems, Mendes (2020), pp. 53–54. Supporting that 'machine learning evidence will likely only be admissible in the form of expert testimony', Nutter (2019), p. 931 ff. Nevertheless, the outputs of the AI system will not be a machine learning substantive evidence in itself. They are only a toll to analyse the testimonial evidence.

we have already the recordings of the hearings, that could be analysed during the appeal phase, without the need to repeat the hearings.[66] Nevertheless, this AI system will not be limited to just receiving the data (i.e. video and audio recordings). It will set up various correlations between each hearing and the facts, set down mathematical judgements, according to algorithms, to supply the judge in the appeal phase with an output of selection of relevant and credible testimonies to prove the relevant facts.

The use of AI assistance may avoid the repetition of the hearing of 'relevant' testimonies previously selected in the appeal. Thereby, after being provided with the analysis of the AI system in the appeal phase the judge need only request the hearing of the testimonies which are relevant and determinant, according to the ECtHR criteria, if they have any doubts about the outputs given by the AI assistant. If doubts persist, they may request the hearing of some additional relevant testimonies, or when in doubt regarding the interpretation of AI results they may request the hearing of the expert. Actually, judges may use the evidentiary inference made by algorithms to help them decide the case, but they may always request the direct hearing of the relevant testimonies and may ask questions. In this case they will combine the AI systems analysis with the inferences that result from the direct hearing of the testimony, to improve their assessment.

It is also important to emphasise that the judges can always distance themselves from the AI assistant's output, they therefore must have access to the analysis of the algorithm and need to have the ability to understand it. And the reasoning for this divergence does not have to be so demanding as the reasoning for removal of expert proof, like in article 163, no. 2 of PCPP. The last word about evidence assessment must belong to the judge, according to the free appreciation of proof.

Since the human judge will always have direct contact with the proof, this AI system will only allow for an extension of the judge's cognitive capacities. Therefore, this AI system will not jeopardize the immediacy given that even though the system has direct contact with the proof the presupposition of immediacy remains untouched as a relationship between the judge and the proof and not a relationship between the AI system and the proof. The judge continues to have direct access to all the evidence and controls the proof. Preferably the judge must not accept without objections the result of the AI system, despite the problem that some scholars identify related to the acritical acceptance of the algorithm results.[67] In the interpretation of the algorithm analysis, the judge must carry out a reasoning similar to that of the free appreciation of proof.

The question must be whether this system interferes in the relationship between the judge and the proof. That is, it is important to question whether the relationship between the judge and the evidence is necessarily mediated by the AI system. One

[66] Defending that the existence of these video files may change the role of the appeal trial, eventually allowing for an adequate evaluation of demeanour evidence, Lederer (2000), pp. 260, 266 and Lederer (2021), pp. 314–315.

[67] Greco (2020), p. 63.

may question, at the end, if AI system will interfere in the judge's evidence assessment according to the rules of experience. In our opinion, this interference, if it exists, insofar as it can assist the judge in the analysis of the evidence, will be beneficial if can avoid biased reasoning, prejudice and discrimination. Ultimately, as the judge will always be present during the proceedings and they will make the final analysis, there will be no changes in the decision-making process on evidence, according to the rules of experience, typical and inherent to human reasoning. Nevertheless, returning to a question already raised in this chapter, this technology may not only be supportive, but also disruptive. In the end, it will not have impact in the structural nature of the process of proof analysis, but it will ultimately influence judicial analysis, changing the adjudicative process, since it may avoid eventual bias and discrimination.

When the AI system is based on a comprehensible algorithm, we may apply the 'extended mind' concept. Once the system functions as an auxiliary to the work of the judge, it is as if the judge's brain was linked to an external entity (the AI system), in a two-way interaction that results in a cognitive system—a coupled system, in an active externalism since not only the judge's mind but also the AI system plays a causal role in the cognitive process.[68] The AI system will promote the extension of the cognitive capacities of the judge. One can raise the hypothesis that this system is a part of the judge's mind, but we may also question whether this cognitive process might be accepted as an individual experience between the judge and the proof, since it is mediated by this AI system. Nevertheless, we may move forward and, in a restrictive perspective, defend that only when we have an embryony relationship between natural and artificial agents, in this case the judge and the AI system, do we have a kind of hybrid system, a unit.[69] Then, the relationship between the judge and the proof will not be in fact mediated and filtered by the AI system, it will be immediate, since judge and AI system compose a unit. But this will only be possible when the judge can not only have access to algorithms and to all the process of algorithms analysis, but also can understand this analysis.

The resource to an AI system by the judge, as a tool, can bring benefits above all in the assessment of the credibility of the testimony. We know that an expert can also pronounce on the greater or lesser probability of evidentiary inferences but the help of the AI system's analysis may guarantee greater objectivity and avoid the inclusion of prejudices when compared to using an expert, especially if the AI system can be programmed to avoid the reproduction of biases, except in machine learning systems.

In addition, when the algorithm is comprehensible by the judge the problem of the 'black box' will be surpassed and the judicial duty to given reasons may be fulfilled.

---

[68] Clark and Chalmers (1998), pp. 8–9.

[69] About the concept of hybrid agents, a computational hybrid, 'joint-agent systems', that work on a joint performance developed by the human component and the machine component, so they share the epistemic credit for the purposes of responsibility ascription, Matthias (2016), p. 145 ff.

Moreover, the use of these AI systems does not compromise the right of the defendant to confrontation and to the cross-examination of the witness, even if the defendant does not have access to the algorithm used by the system to assess the testimonies, when the algorithm's analysis may be explained by an expert.[70] When this is not be possible, not only the right to confrontation and to immediacy would be at stake, but also the right to a fair trial, to equality of arms, to presumption of innocence,[71] and to appeal.

But the use of an AI system will compromise the principle of immediacy when one resorts to algorithms which cannot be apprehensible to judges and do not have stable software codes. Therefore, the AI system's result could not be controlled. In this case, the judge cannot have direct access to the proof. When the system does not allow for a control process by the user, more often in machine learning systems, deep learning and neural networks, we may also face a problem of accountability,[72] because the programmer cannot be responsible for autonomous and self-learning nature of the decisions made by the system.[73] When the programmer cannot apprehend the output's results, they cannot draw up an expert report for the judge. Therefore, if the judge cannot understand the meaning behind the output, they cannot give reasons for their decision. When the judge does not have epistemic access to the global context in which the AI develops algorithms related to the proof, it becomes impossible to assess responsibility for the effects of the decision.[74] In this case, we surely will have a kind of artificial mind interfering in the relationship between the judge and the proof. Subsequently, we face an inevitable problem of immediacy, given that AI will present an output result which expresses an evidentiary reasoning that the judge cannot apprehend, since such judge does not know the process by way of which it was obtained. Finally, the use of this AI system will jeopardize the right to a fair trial.

[70] 'Moreover, machine learning output would likely be introduced in the form of expert testimony, meaning the defendant would have the opportunity to cross-examine an expert on the machine's capabilities and processes', Nutter (2019), p. 947.

[71] Bampasika (2020). Adding that 'The party concerned should have access to and be able to challenge the scientific validity of an algorithm, the weighting given to its various elements and any erroneous conclusions it comes to whenever a judge suggests that he/she might use it before making his/her decision', defending that this would be easier in European countries, because of General Data Protection Regulation, while in the United States private interests (particularly the protection of intellectual property) prevail over the rights of defence, CEPEJ (2019), p. 55.

[72] Contini (2020), p. 15.

[73] Bampasika (2020).

[74] 'Responsibility for the effects of an action requires not only control over the process of decision, but also adequate epistemic access to the world context in which the decision takes place', Matthias (2016), p. 150.

9.5 Conclusions

The use of an AI assistant in the appeal phase of the criminal proceedings may only be a tool, an instrument, to help the judge in their analysis of the proof, although the appellants have already defined the object of the appeal, according to facts, evidence and questions, and then may have already made a selection of the relevant testimonies, the AI system may function as a second filter. With the aid of this AI system, even if the judge has access to all the evidence, they will have access to an algorithm analysis of the relevant and decisive proof, helping the judge during the appeal phase to select which testimony is truly 'relevant' and 'determinant' or not to prove certain facts and is credible or not, to avoid the repetition in the appeal phase of each hearing that may be indicated in the appeal, allegedly the 'relevant' testimonies. So, the judge may only hear these truly relevant testimonies, according to the analysis made by the AI assistant if they have any doubts about the outputs given by the AI assistant. If doubts persist, they may request the hearing of some additional relevant testimonies, or when in doubt regarding the interpretation of AI results they may request the hearing of the expert. Judges can always distance themselves from the output of the AI assistance, therefore they may have access to the analysis of the algorithm.

In fact, the AI assistant will be a filter in the selection of relevant and determinant testimonies. Judges may use the evidentiary inference made by algorithms to help them to decide the case, but can always request the direct hearing of the relevant testimonies and may ask questions. In this case they will combine the AI systems analysis with the inferences that result from the direct hearing of the testimony to improve their assessment. In these cases, the AI system will be a kind of 'extended mind' of the judge, and even more restrictively may have an embryony relationship between the judge and the AI system, a kind of hybrid system. Therefore, the judge will continue to have direct access to the proof and since the relation between the judge and the proof will not be mediated by the AI system it will not compromise the principle of immediacy.

The utilisation of AI assistance does not eliminate the possibility to resort to rules of experience, since the output extracted from the assistance must be overseen by the judge, who will include in their analysis discretionary and social considerations, according to life experience and their personal life that are beyond the capacity of the AI assistant.

Problematic will be when one resorts to algorithms which could not be apprehensible to judges or even to the experts, and do not have stable software codes, mainly in systems of machine learning. In these cases, we will face a problem of accountability and the judges cannot give reasons for their decisions, because when the programmers cannot apprehend the output, they cannot not draw up an expert report. This will inevitably jeopardize the principle of immediacy and the right to a fair trial.

Cited Case-Law

ECtHR, Gómez Olmeda v. Spain, no. 61112/12, 29 March 2016, hudoc.echr.coe.int

US Court of Appeals for the Second Circuit - 138 F.2d 650 (2d Cir. 1943), from 8 November 1943, In Re JP Linaham (1943) 138 F.2d 650 (2d Cir), Justia, 652, available in https://law.justia.com/cases/federal/appellate-courts/F2/138/650/1481751/. Accessed 24 April 2022

References

Allen RJ (2001) Artificial intelligence and the evidentiary process: the challenges of formalism and computation. Artif Intell Law 9:99–114

Angwin J, Larson J, Mattu S, Kirchner L (2016) Machine bias. ProPublica, https://www.propublica.org/article/machine-bias-risk-assessments-in-criminal-sentencing. Accessed 6 Apr 2022

Ash E (2018) Judge, jury, and execute file: the brave new world of legal automation. Social Market Foundation, http://www.smf.co.uk/publications/judge-jury-and-execute-file-paper/, 1–10. Accessed 20 Apr 2022

Bampasika E, Artificial intelligence as evidence in criminal trial. Paper presented at SETN 2020: 11th Hellenic Conference on Artificial Intelligence, Athens, Greece, 2–4 September 2020., https://pure.mpg.de/rest/items/item_3325158_2/component/file_3325159/content. Accessed 14 Apr 2022

Becker HS (1966) Outsiders – studies in the sociology of deviance. Free Press, New York

CEPEJ (2019) European Ethical Charter on the use of artificial intelligence in judicial systems and their environment. Council of Europe, https://rm.coe.int/ethical-charter-en-for-publication-4-december-2018/16808f699c. Accessed 7 Apr 2022

Clark A, Chalmers D (1998) The extended mind. Analysis 58(1):7–19

Contini F (2020) Artificial intelligence and the transformation of humans, law and technology interactions in judicial proceedings. Law Technol Hum 2(1):4–18

Council of Europe (2018) Algorithms and human rights: study on the human rights dimensions of automated data processing techniques and possible regulatory implications. Prepared by the Committee of Experts on Internet Intermediaries (MSI-NET), Council of Europe study DGI (2017) 12, Strasbourg, https://rm.coe.int/algorithms-and-human-rights-en-rev/16807956b5. Accessed 7 Apr 2022

Dias JF (2004) Direito Processual Penal, reprint of 1st ed. from 1974. Coimbra Editora, Coimbra

Ferreira MC (1986) Curso de Processo Penal, I. Danúbio, Lisboa

Gillespie T (2014) The relevance of algorithms. In: Gillespie T, Boczkowski PJ, Foot KA (eds) Media technologies: essays on communication, materiality, and society. MIT Press, Cambridge, pp 167–194

Greco L (2020) Poder de julgar sem responsabilidade de julgador: a impossibilidade jurídica do juiz-robô. Marcial Pons, São Paulo

Lederer FI (2000) The effect of courtroom technologies on and in appellate proceedings and courtrooms. J App Pract Process 2(2):251–274

Lederer FI (2021) The evolving technology-augmented courtroom before, during, and after the pandemic. Vanderbilt J Entertain Technol Law 23(2):301–339

Lepri B, Oliver N, Letouzé E, Pentland A, Vinck P (2018) Fair, transparent, and accountable algorithmic decision-making processes – the premise, the proposed solutions, and the open challenges. Philos Technol 31:611–627

Lim S (2021) Judicial decision-making and explainable artificial intelligence – a reckoning from first principles? Singap Acad Law – Special Issue on Law and Technology 33:280–314
Mao S, Tao D, Zhang G, Ching PC, Lee T (2019) Revisiting Hidden Markov models for speech emotion recognition. ICASSP 2019 - 2019 IEEE International Conference on Acoustics, Speech and Signal Processing (ICASSP), pp 6715–6719
Matta PS (2004) A livre apreciação da prova e o dever de fundamentação da sentença. In: Palma MF (scientific coordination) Jornadas de Direito Processual Penal e Direitos Fundamentais. Almedina, Coimbra, pp 221–279
Matthias A (2016) The extended mind and the computational basis of responsibility ascription. Anatomia do Crime 3:129–153
Melim MM (2013) *Standards* de prova e grau de convicção do julgador. Revista de Concorrência e Regulação – C&R 4(16):143–193
Mendes PS (2010) A prova penal e as regras da experiência. In: Andrade MC, Antunes MJ, Sousa SA (org) Estudos em Homenagem ao Prof. Doutor Figueiredo Dias, vol III. Coimbra Editora, Coimbra, pp 997–1011
Mendes PS (2020) A representação do conhecimento jurídico, inteligência artificial e os sistemas de apoio à decisão jurídica. In: Rocha ML, Pereira RS (coord), Trigo AC (colab) Inteligência Artificial § Direito, reprint. Almedina, Coimbra, pp 51–63
Neves AC (1968) Sumários de Processo Criminal (1967-1968). Typed, Coimbra
Nutter P (2019) Machine learning evidence: admissibility and weight. J Constit Law 21(3):919–958
Picard RW (1995) Affective computing. M.I.T Media Laboratory Perceptual Computing Section Technical Report, 321, pp 1–16
Searle J (1984) Can computers think? In: Searle J (ed) Minds, brains and science. Harvard University Press, Cambridge, pp 28–41
Seng D, Mason S (2021) Artificial intelligence and evidence. Singap Acad Law – Special Issue on Law and Technology 33:241–279
Sourdin T (2018) Judge v robot? Artificial intelligence and judicial decision-making. UNSW Law J 41(4):1114–1133
Sourdin T, Cornes R (2018) Do judges need to be human? The implications of technology for responsive judging. In: Sourdin T, Zariski A (eds) The responsive judge – international perspectives. Springer, Singapore, pp 87–119
Spaulding NW (2020) Is human judgment necessary?: Artificial intelligence, algorithmic governance, and the law. In: Dubber MD, Pasquale F, Das S (eds) The Oxford handbook of ethics of AI. Oxford University Press, New York, pp 375–402
Surden H (2014) Machine learning and law. Wash Law Rev 89(1):87–115
Taruffo M (2005) La prueba de los hechos, 2nd ed. (trad. Beltrán JF). Trotta, Madrid
Ulenaers J (2020) The impact of artificial intelligence on the right to a fair trial: towards a robot judge? Asian J Law Econ 11(2):1–38

Part IV
Concluding Thoughts

Chapter 10
On the Legitimacy of the ECtHR's Criminal Appeal Immediacy Requirement

Helena Morão

10.1 A Comparative View on Criminal Appeal Immediacy Models

This final chapter brings into view the net results of the preceding chapters, outlining the merits and limitations of the European Court of Human Rights' immediacy requirement as a fair trial standard in criminal appeal, in light of the European Convention on Human Rights' Article 6.

Part I critically engaged the ECtHR's case-law on fair criminal appeal immediacy with the law revisions it has lately inspired in European countries, as well as with the critiques and difficulties that it continues to raise, noticeably in contexts of first instance acquittals overturning and of sentences increasing on appeal.

The Italian appeal system on factual questions was selected by its recent close adoption of the European Court's criteria sketched in Chap. 1. As seen in Chap. 2 and unlike the German 'second first instance' model,[1] in Italy appeals are designed as critical re-examinations of the lower courts' decisions by higher tribunals, led by the issues submitted by the appellants. Notwithstanding, after the 2017 *Legge Orlando* came into force—the breaches of the ECHR's Article 6 found in the cases Lorefice v. Italy, Tondo v. Italy and Maestri and others v. Italy relate to the former law[2]—, each time the public prosecution appeals against an acquittal based upon the declarative evidence assessment, the appellate court is bound to an

[1] Roxin and Schünemann (2017), p. 465; Bohlander (2021), pp. 226 et seq.

[2] Lorefice v. Italy, no. 63446/13, 29 June 2017; Tondo v. Italy, no. 75037/14, 22 October 2020; Maestri and others v. Italy, no. 20903/15, 8 July 2021, *hudoc.echr.coe.int*.

H. Morão (✉)
University of Lisbon School of Law, Research Centre for Criminal Law and Criminal Sciences (CIDPCC), Lisbon, Portugal
e-mail: helenamorao@fd.ulisboa.pt

H. Morão, R. Tavares da Silva (eds.), *Fairness in Criminal Appeal*,
https://doi.org/10.1007/978-3-031-13001-4_10

'evidence renewal'. Although before the renewal of evidence could already exceptionally take place, in this type of cases the court of appeal must now rule on a possible acquittal reversal by directly (re)hearing the relevant oral evidence,[3] not by (indirectly) assessing the probably available audio or audio-visual records of the evidence produced in the first instance trial or their transcripts,[4] as the Strasbourg Court deems imperative.

As Massimo Ceresa-Gastaldo made clear in Chap. 2, the Italian system stands out, however, by the asymmetry between the (wider) powers legally attributed on *appelo* to the public prosecution to challenge acquittals and the (comparatively narrower) powers legally attributed to the defence to question convictions.[5] Yet, even though a substantial part of the ECtHR's case-law does refer to overturning acquittals, its appeal immediacy requisite is not restricted to first-time convictions on the appellate level, broadly concerning situations of full assessment of the accused's guilt or innocence, as observed in Chap. 1. In cases such as, among others, Strzałkowski v. Poland, where the defendant had appealed a first instance conviction, or as Cooke v. Austria, where both the accused and the public prosecution had contested in their appeals the penalty imposed by the lower instance, the European Court applied the exact same fair appeal immediacy requirement.[6] I suspect that the Italian legislator has, thus, made an incomplete transplant of the ECtHR's case-law criteria, apparently due to a misapprehension of its appeal fairness standard, to the detriment of equality between appeal proceedings and, therefore, of the principle of equality of arms in the Italian appeal procedure globally considered.

Still, we should bear in mind that a certain inequality of arms between accusation and defence in appeal matters is, after all, favoured by the European Convention on Human Rights, though in a different way. Unlike the International Covenant on Civil and Political Rights,[7] the ECHR does not set forth a right to a criminal appeal among the accused's defence guarantees. On the other hand, Protocol no. 7, to which not all States of the Council of Europe are States parties, allows the domestic legislators, in

[3] See Article 603 § 3-bis ICPP.

[4] See Article 139 § 6 and Article 590 ICPP.

[5] See also Ceresa-Gastaldo (2017), pp. 167–168: '(. . .) the defendant acquitted at first instance has the right to a fair appeal process, while the convicted defendant, who also criticizes the sentence for reasons relating to the assessment of the evidence, can be satisfied with a second inquisitorial degree? (. . .) *the prosecution will have an effective tool available to reverse the result*; an instrument *that the accused*, instead, *will not be able to invoke* to remove the error of the conviction. It is difficult to deny that, like this, hypotheses that are substantially identical are unreasonably treated in a (very) different way.'

[6] Strzałkowski v. Poland, no. 31509/02, 9 June 2009; Michael Edward Cooke v. Austria, no. 25878/94, 8 February 2000, *hudoc.echr.coe.int*.

[7] See its Article 14 (5): 'Everyone convicted of a crime shall have the right to his conviction and sentence being reviewed by a higher tribunal according to law.'; Human Rights Committee (2007), no. 47: 'Article 14, paragraph 5 is violated not only if the decision by the court of first instance is final, but also where a conviction imposed by an appeal court or a court of final instance, following acquittal by a lower court, according to domestic law, cannot be reviewed by a higher court.'; and Schabas (2016), p. 930: 'International human rights law recognizes the right to an appeal as a fundamental component of due process in criminal proceedings.'

its Article 2 (2), to exception from the objective scope of the defendant's right of appeal convictions following appeals against acquittals.[8] Hence, the ECHR and Protocol no. 7 do not preclude the public prosecution to appeal against an acquittal by a lower tribunal, but, simultaneously, do not guarantee the right of the accused firstly convicted by an appellate court to rebut his or her conviction in a higher instance, namely in a court of final instance with powers to review elements of fact. Consequently, national laws are permitted to structure their appeal systems by providing more chances of appeal to the accusation to obtain a conviction than to the defence to attain an acquittal, unfairly deviating from the equality of arms principle in the same criminal process, as well as from the presumption of innocence.

In turn, the Spanish appeal system on issues of fact (*apelación*) was chosen by its alternative solution—also proposed in the Strasbourg Court case-law[9]—to the repetition of personal evidence in appeal. As explained in Chap. 3, in Spain, instead of a double instance model, the appeal court, if it confirms a mistake in the evidence evaluation, is forbidden to convict a defendant acquitted at first instance or to increase his or her sentence. The same court of appeal may, nonetheless, annul the appealed acquittal or penalty and order a retrial (with full immediacy).[10] For this to happen, however, the accusation must demonstrate at least one of three errors: the insufficiency or lack of rationality of the factual reasoning; a manifest departure from a maxim of experience; or the omission of all reasoning regarding evidence that might be relevant or whose nullity has been wrongly declared.[11] This legislative amendment dates back to 2015, even before the ECtHR's Gómez Olmeda v. Spain ruling,[12] after the *Sentencia* 120/2009 of the Spanish Constitutional Court excluded the use of the first instance trial audio-visual recordings as an adequate immediacy source to take a divergent position on the decisive facts and convict the previously acquitted defendant or to aggravate his or her punishment.[13]

As Antonio Mª Lara López points out in Chap. 3, since, in the Spanish criminal procedure, these appeals against the accused are limited to topics unconnected with a re-examination of the lower court's factual version, they are decided without a hearing by an appellate tribunal that does not directly assess the evidence. The accused has, thus, no opportunity, at second instance, to oppose the quash of his

[8] 'This right may be subject to exceptions (...) in cases in which the person concerned (...) was convicted following an appeal against acquittal.' See also Council of Europe (1984), no. 20; and Kashlev v. Estonia, no. 22574/08, 26 April 2016, §§ 52–53; Styrmir þór Bragason v. Iceland, no. 36292/14, 16 July 2019, § 88; *hudoc.echr.coe.int*.

[9] See Júlíus Þór Sigurþórsson v. Iceland, no. 38797/17, 16 July 2019, §§ 38 and 42, *hudoc.echr.coe.int*.

[10] Article 792 § 2 LECrim.

[11] Article 790 § 2 (3) LECrim.

[12] Gómez Olmeda v. Spain, no. 61112/12, 29 March 2016, *hudoc.echr.coe.int*.

[13] Decision no. 120/2009, *hj.tribunalconstitucional.es*.

or her acquittal or imposed penalty, and avoid a new trial, on immediacy related grounds. I would emphasize as well that precisely because the prosecutorial appeal is this reduced, in the Spanish system, contrary to what occurs in Italy, the accusation is given much less powers to achieve a first-time conviction at the appellate stage than the convicted defendant has to reach an acquittal at the same level. The defendant, when alleging a mistake in the evidence evaluation in his or her appeal, is not constrained by article 790 § 2 (3) and in these appeals it can otherwise be requested, in certain cases, new evidence production at the appeal hearing or, more extensively, the reproduction of the audio-visual recordings of the statements given at the first instance trial.[14] Yet, such imbalance stands against a central role played by the public prosecution on appeal in several Continental European countries that distance themselves from the Anglo-American tradition of double jeopardy.[15] This disparity is even more accentuated in the new LECrim Preliminary Draft, which plainly narrows to matters of law all accusation appeals aimed at acquittals reversal and sentences increasing.[16] The Preliminary Draft also authorizes, at the defendant's appeals that request the hearing of additional evidence, the viewing of the first instance trial's recorded evidence or the mere reading of its transcripts, in alternative to evidence repetition at second instance.[17]

Lastly, the Portuguese appeal system against findings of fact was picked by its use of the first instance hearings' audio-recordings as a basis for case reviewing, a technology-based model implemented in 1998, long before the ECtHR's Gómez Olmeda v. Spain jurisprudence made objections to the akin Spanish system. As noted in Chap. 4 and 5, similarly to what happens in the Italian criminal procedure, in Portugal appeals are devised as critical re-evaluations of the lower tribunals' decisions by higher courts, driven by the points aroused by the appellant, not as second trials. Dissimilarly to what occurs in part in Italy though, here appellate courts are allowed to rule on factual matters of guilt or innocence as well as of sentencing—including on the overturning of acquittals and on the increasing of penalties—by assessing the audio records of the evidence produced in the first instance trial, rather than (re)hearing the relevant oral evidence in person.

[14] Articles 790 § 3 and 791 LECrim.

[15] For instance, in Italy, the 2006 *Legge Pecorella*, which ruled out the *appello* of the *Pubblico Ministero* against acquittals, unless it was founded in new and decisive evidence, was deemed unconstitutional by the Italian Constitutional Court, as an unjustified inequality of arms between accusation and defence and, in consequence, an infringement of the constitutional fair trial principle inscribed in Article 111 § 2 of the Italian Constitution (*Sentenza* no. 26/2007, *www.cortecostituzionale.it*). Notwithstanding, the 2018 legislative reform, that curtailed the *Pubblico Ministero*'s *appello* against sentencing to specific cases (see the latest alteration of Article 593 § 1 of the ICPP), was not considered constitutionally illegitimate (*Sentenza* no. 34/2020, *www.cortecostituzionale.it*).

[16] Articles 728, 730 § 2 and 732 of the new LECrim Preliminary Draft.

[17] Articles 736 § 3 and 737 § 3 of the new LECrim Preliminary Draft.

As Rita do Rosário highlighted in Chap. 4, an overview of the Portuguese courts of appeal (*Relações*) case law shows a certain unwillingness to change the lower courts' account of facts, except for cases of more obvious errors in the evidence examination, in spite of the access to trials audio records, on grounds of appeal courts having less immediacy and orality than the first instance tribunals. Furthermore, this tendency to maintain the appealed decisions—which Tiago Geraldo and Nuno Igreja Matos ironically called *in dubio pro trial court* principle—appears to comprise both acquittals and convictions, which might, in the latter case, collide with the presumption of innocence principle. I would say that it is unclear, nevertheless, if this line of jurisprudence derives from a remaining practice of only reading written transcripts of the trials records and not hearing them, from the lack of a visual element in the trials audio-recordings, from the absence of a hearing at second instance, or simply from a judicial resistance to modifying rulings already made by other courts.

As Tiago Geraldo and Nuno Igreja Matos added in Chap. 5, the European Court's case-law on fair appeal immediacy is usually not taken into account by the Portuguese appellate tribunals when interpreting the Portuguese Criminal Procedure Code (PCPP). As a result, appeal hearings rarely take place and defendants, when convicted for the first time on the appellate level, are so without an appeal defence hearing, the same occurring when they see their sentences aggravated at this stage. Although, as in the Italian CPP, an 'evidence renewal' at appeal is also established in the PCPP, it only covers scarce situations and is almost never used; still, occasionally the appealed sentence is annulled, and a retrial takes place.[18] Expectedly, the ECtHR has by now held that there has been a violation of Article 6 of the ECHR by Portuguese courts of appeal in three distinct cases: Moreira Ferreira, for denying the accused an appeal hearing;[19] Pereira Cruz and others, for declining fresh evidence adduced by the defendant at appeal;[20] and Paixão Moreira Sá Fernandes, for reversing an acquittal on appeal without directly hearing the witnesses and the accused.[21] I would underline that, contrasting with what transpired in the Gómez Olmeda v. Spain case, however, none of these judgements implied a censure of the Portuguese audio-recordings immediacy appeal model. In fact, in the case of Paixão Moreira Sá Fernandes, the overturning acquittal had been exclusively founded on the analysis of the first instance sentence, and not on the hearing of the trial audio records by the appeal tribunal.[22]

Nonetheless, the first instance trial evidence records system, by comparison with the Italian and Spanish immediacy appeal models, enables the Portuguese appeal procedure to ensure full equality of arms between accusation and defence at appeal,

[18] Articles 430 and 426 PCPP.

[19] Moreira Ferreira v. Portugal, no. 19808/08, 5 July 2011, §§ 32–35, *hudoc.echr.coe.int*.

[20] Pereira Cruz and others v. Portugal, no. 56396/12, 26 June 2018, §§ 220–232, *hudoc.echr.coe.int*.

[21] Paixão Moreira Sá Fernandes v. Portugal, no. 78108/14, 25 February 2020, §§ 61–66, *hudoc.echr.coe.int*.

[22] Morão (2020), pp. 173 et seq.

offering parallel powers to the prosecution (as well as to the victims/'assistants') to dispute acquittals and to the defendant to defy convictions: both can make use of the first instance trial audio-recordings to sustain any mistake in the evidence assessment before the court of appeal. Therefore, it keeps the prosecutorial function of the public prosecution on appeal untouched, while also granting the accused firstly convicted at the appellate level a right to appeal to the Supreme Court,[23] even though this right does not encompass most factual grounds and does not extend to all cases of penalties increasing at appellate stage.

Averting the typical downsides of double trials (procedural inefficiency, risks for the search for truth and for the *ne bis in idem* principle[24]), the recordings immediacy appeal model further displays two other advantages that should not be devalued. On the one hand, by its time-saving effect compared with a total or partial hearings repetition, it facilitates the review at second instance of long and complex trial cases.[25] On the other hand, it prevents an unnecessary secondary victimization that can come out of personal evidence re-hearing, and the consequent likely disincentive of appeals by vulnerable victims.[26]

Perhaps, then, the problem might not lie in the recordings immediacy appeal model itself, but in the way it has been implemented—in the Portuguese system, written transcripts do not guarantee the actual listening of trial audio recordings, the visual component of statements made at the first instance trial is not recorded, and appeal hearings are infrequent—and how it could be improved. Even so, not giving up on a recordings appeal model—given its upsides from the standpoint of equality of arms, procedural efficiency (including in lengthy and complicated cases), protection of truth-seeking, of the *ne bis in idem* principle, and of vulnerable victims—presupposes admitting that audio-visual recordings provide a suitable source of immediacy, oppositely to what the ECtHR suggested in the Gómez Olmeda case, and that is what we tried to find out in Part II.

[23] Article 400 § 1 (e) PCPP.

[24] See Chap. 1.

[25] It is certainly not a coincidence that the German *Berufung*, a second instance retrial system, does not comprehend the most serious criminal cases and that Germany, despite having signed Protocol no. 7 to the ECHR and restricted the application of its Article 2 (1) to errors of law, has not, to date, ratified it (*www.coe.int*).

[26] See Díaz-Roncero (2019), pp. 98 et seq.

10.2 An Interdisciplinary Approach to Criminal Appeal Immediacy

Thus, Part II interweaved insight from criminal procedure theory with new discoveries in the field of cognitive sciences (neuroscience of memory, philosophy of knowledge, AI), shedding an interdisciplinary light on the (in)adequacy and limits of the Strasbourg Court's jurisprudence on fair appeal immediacy.

Chapter 6 depicted the procedural principle of (subjective) immediacy at the first instance trial as a demand of direct contact between the judge and the evidence, so that the former may apprehend by him or herself the decisive facts. In this way, the immediacy principle is intrinsically linked with the trial hearing, where all evidence should be presented, witnesses orally questioned, and in which the defendant takes part. Immediacy, as a legal tool, intends, then, to secure that the criminal court gradually arrives through its own perception at the factual elements necessary to decide, hence supplying a solid foundation for the conviction or acquittal of the accused.

Remaining a pillar in most European criminal procedures, the immediacy principle has evolved towards the use of modern technologies: reflecting a general social trend, audio and video recordings have been increasingly employed in the courtroom as an appropriate method of establishing an immediate connection between the judge and the evidence, for example in the context of a change in the composition of the trial court. In the opinion of Mafalda Moura Melim, this development should be discerned more as a technological adaptation of the essential idea of immediacy than as a set of technological exemptions to the principle, as its main purpose has not been abandoned, it is the means of attaining it that has become more flexible. Besides, nowadays the immediacy principle is considered a procedural right of both the defendant and the victim, guaranteeing a direct access by the key participants in the criminal trial to every evidence examined at the hearing, either testimonies, documents, or recordings, as a condition of fair trial, including in the ECtHR case-law.

I would argue that the current state of the art of the principle of immediacy does not, therefore, reveal any inherent incompatibility with the use of the first instance trial audio or audio-visual recordings on appeal. If, among other situations, the listening or viewing of these records can already replace, in the first instance, the repetition of statements made in person, there is no valid reason why they cannot form the basis for the review of the case at the appellate level. If, on the one hand, with the mere reproduction of sound and image the judge may miss meaningful information about a witness—primarily non-verbal aspects of communication—; on the other hand, he or she may as well perceive additional details that might have gone unnoticed had the testimony been heard directly before the court.

Rightly implemented, a recordings appeal system can then be understood as one of the technological modellings of the immediacy principle, and as an alternative way to obtain immediacy at appeal stage, given the acknowledged drawbacks of second trials. Yet, as immediacy also implies that the judge can ask questions to resolve doubts and deal with contradictions, the trial recordings reproduction may not entirely do without an evidentiary appeal hearing every time the high instance court believes there is the need to further question the deponents.

Chapter 7 addressed the differences between examining a recorded statement and hearing a witness in person at trial, seeing that, aside from other important dissimilarities, a recording cannot be cross-examined, which calls for distinct modalities of corroboration and contradiction of that evidence. If fairly adjusted to those differences, a criminal trial mostly or completely dependent on audio or visual recordings is, nevertheless, still able to meet the minimum immediacy requirements.

António Brito Neves claims that, as part of the same dissimilarities persist when it comes to first instance trial recorded depositions, this conclusion, when combined with the notion unfolded by some scholars that immediacy serves a distinct goal at appellate level—not so much to assure the oral discussion of the evidence, but to check the coherence between the trial and the decision—, has repercussions as well in appeal matters. So, as an illustration, the appeal court may legitimately opt between two plausible versions of facts in conflict if it finds the recorded testimony of a witness more convincing than that of another. This assertion is substantiated on the viewpoint that the court of appeal assumes a more distant and objective position towards the evidence and has, thus, a more comprehensive perspective, by comparison with the trial court position (closer and more involved).

This outlook seems, in the end, to have implicit two concepts of immediacy: the traditional concept of the first instance trial; and one specific of appeals, sculpted by the recordings appeal model. In this second sense, the contact between the judge and the declarative evidence is established, as a rule, through audio or video recorded statements, with a degree of immediacy identical to what the trial judge has with non-personal evidence (documents, expert reports, and so on).[27] While in the first conception we are looking at a judge-actor, in the second we are facing a judge-spectator.[28] This diverse meaning of immediacy in appeal appears to fit particularly well with procedural systems where appeals are conceived as critical re-evaluations of the lower courts' rulings by higher tribunals rather than as second trials.

Chapter 8 looked into the question of whether testimonial evidence on criminal appeal can be regarded as reliable or more reliable than other competing evidence, such as audio and video recordings, contextualizing it as an epistemic problem. Working in the criminal process with the epistemological differentiations between psychological sources of information and epistemic sources of information, on the one hand, as well as between discovery context and justification context, on the other hand, Ricardo Tavares da Silva frames audio and audio-visual records as extensions of perception and memory, following an extended mind thesis.

In what concerns testimony reliability, the interference theory—which beholds memory as a fallible means of storing and retrieving information due to retroactive and ultra-active interference effects—was approached, together with (psychological

[27] Brito (2013), p. 61.

[28] Brito (2013), p. 62.

and neurophysiological) empirical studies that support it. Based on these data, Ricardo Tavares da Silva asserts that the probability of information corruption in a deposition repetition at second instance increases in relation to that of the testimony given by the same witness at the first instance trial. In addition to a process of natural information deterioration, this happens because the witness has meanwhile acquired new information that heightens the (retroactive) corruption of the information previously kept; and because the recollection operates on top of the memories of the statements already made at the trial, intensifying the corruption of the remembered information.

Distinguishing between intrinsic and extrinsic credibility, Ricardo Tavares da Silva further holds that, although there are no obstacles to the intrinsic trustworthiness of perception (including that arising from audio and video recordings)—since perception can be short, but not excessive—, there is a lack of trustworthiness intrinsic to testimony. Even if there are reasons to believe what a witness says, in the light of a causal theory of knowledge we will not be watching an information transmission, that is, a knowledge caused in the interlocutor by the object of knowledge itself. Testimonies are thus able to arouse beliefs (psychological convictions), but not judgments (cognitive information). Testimonial evidence trial immediacy does not provide the judge with information to cognitively sustain a decision (criminal procedure epistemic-deontological model), but a conviction of truth to legitimize a decision (criminal procedure epistemic-consequentialist model).

Hence, it seems contemporary philosophy of knowledge does not back up the allegation that the listening or viewing of first instance trial audio or audio-visual records, as perception and memory extensions (extended immediacy), constitutes a less credible epistemic information source than the direct hearing of a witness. At the same time, neuroscience of memory points to yet another major benefit of a recordings appeal system: first instance trial audio or video recorded witness statements reflect a less neuronally modified testimonial memory of the procedurally relevant events than testimonies reheard at appellate stage.[29]

Chapter 9 was concerned with how AI may validly be used in the future as an assistant tool of the appeal court, namely through algorithms that select the relevant and irrelevant information in the first instance trial testimonies, or the credible and non-credible first instance trial testimonies, aiding the judge of appeal in the reassessment of the evidence and avoiding hearings repetition. Catarina Abegão Alves thought of this technology as a supportive technology, intended to improve the appellate judge's work and objectivity, but which would not replace his or her decision-making role on the evidence, which appears to be, at least for now, beyond the capacity of AI, due to the limitations of data input and of human language understanding.

Catarina Abegão Alves contends that, despite its supportive character, this conjectural technology, unlike the mere listening or viewing of the first instance trial audio or video depositions records, would also be a disruptive technology, insofar as

[29] Morão (2020), pp. 188–189, n. 39.

it filters and sets up mathematical correlations between the witnesses' statements to supply an output of decisive and trustworthy information, therefore altering the evidence analysis and the adjudication process. Employing an appeal judge's cobot would, however, become problematic for fair trial rights wherever the appellate court (or the key participants in the criminal process) could not scrutinize, even with the help of an expert, the links between inputs and outputs or, consequently, control algorithmic biases and discrimination or figure out unpredictable and inexplicable results, owing to the black box paradox of machine learning systems and programs.

While AI assistance is of particular interest for appeals relating to long and intricate trial cases as well as to avert the judges' own prejudices, it is debatable how it will affect the idea of immediacy and whether it will enhance or diminish the contact between the judge of appeal and the evidence. In cases of explainable machine learning, where the output corresponds to a selection of data comparable to that made by appellants when they choose facts and evidence in their appeals to be evaluated by the court of appeal, or to a collection of reliable and non-reliable witnesses similar to the technical analysis made by experts when appraising evidentiary inferences, it seems that the cobot's output, as the audio and audio-visual recordings, can still integrate the judge's extended mind notion. In contrast, in black box models, an autonomous and opaque artificial mind appears to intervene between the judge and the evidence. But perhaps even the output of these non-interpretable models may be acceptable from a fairness viewpoint, presuming its greater impartiality and accuracy, as long as more favourable to the accused.[30]

10.3 Criminal Appeal Immediacy Beyond the ECtHR Case-Law: Fairness Guidelines for Criminal Appeal Law Interpretation and Reform

The key findings of the research undertaken in this book enables us now to comprehensively reappraise the European Court's jurisprudence on immediacy in criminal appeal, as well as to recommend appellate fair trial criteria to be taken into account by the Contracting States to the ECHR either in the interpretation of the existing domestic criminal appeal laws or in criminal appeal lawmaking.

As we learned in the preceding chapters, the immediacy appeal system that we named recordings appeal model is able to avoid the disadvantages of a double trial (procedural inefficiency, hazards to the truth discovery and for the *ne bis in idem* principle), while also offering the advantages of expediting the review of lengthy and complex cases, as well as of preventing revictimization and consequently protecting rights to appeal of vulnerable victims. Additionally, it confers the bonuses of permitting to retain the legal power of the public prosecution to appeal in matters

[30] On this line of reasoning, see Levy (2016), p. 179.

of fact against the defendant—that is characteristic of Continental inquisitorial systems[31]—, without at the same time undermining the guarantee of equality of arms between accusation and defence at appeal. Another trump card of a recordings immediacy appeal system, brought by memory neuroscience and strengthening the discovery of the truth argument, is that a first instance trial audio or video recorded deposition of a witness discloses a presumably less (retroactive and ultra-active) corrupted testimonial memory of the procedurally decisive facts than a statement repetition by the same witness at second instance.

Associating the points of view of criminal procedure theory and epistemology, this book also reveals that audio and audio-visual trial recordings, as extensions of perception and memory, are, to a certain extent, immediacy technological tools, i.e., ways of presenting the oral evidence produced in the first instance trial—and in the closest way to that in which it was presented to the trial court[32]—to the judge who will decide the case on appeal. Considering that the listening or viewing of first instance trial audio or video records does not constitute a less credible epistemic source of information than the hearing of a testimony in person, a recordings appeal model can be understood as a technological modelling of the procedural immediacy principle and an alternative method to acquire immediacy at the appellate level (a technologically extended immediacy). On the other hand, criminal procedure immediacy theory debated in this book further unveils that the appeal stage does not necessarily require a direct and uncritical transposition of the traditional first instance trial immediacy concept, especially in appeal systems where courts of appeal do not approach the case *de novo*, as a second trial, but, indirectly, through identifiable errors in the lower tribunal's prior ruling on the same case. In a recordings appeal model one can eventually conceive of a specific notion of appeal immediacy, in which immediacy with personal evidence is established, as a rule, identically as with non-personal evidence, even though it does not coincide with the maximum degree of immediacy.[33]

I would argue that, for lack of scientific grounds, we should not then read the ECtHR's criminal appeal immediacy requisite that motivated this book's inquiry, including the Gómez Olmeda doctrine, in the sense that any appeal decisions on factual findings made solely on the basis of the first instance trial recorded evidence should be deemed inconsistent with the right to a fair trial. Not by chance, the Strasbourg Court itself has stressed that its own case-law on this subject is not an

---

[31] Or hierarchical model of authority—typical of civil law systems—, by opposition to the coordinate model—typical of common law systems—, in Damaska's less trial-centric—and more inclusive of appeals—alternative dichotomy to the classic duality inquisitorial/adversarial models. See Damaska (1975), pp. 481 et seq.; Marshall (2011), pp. 14–16; Langer (2014), pp. 901 et seq.; Thaman (2019), pp. 939–940.

[32] Capus (2018), p. 206: '(. . .) audio or video recordings are the best way of authentically preserving what has been said (. . .)'.

[33] See Ceresa-Gastaldo (2017), p. 164.

automatic rule.[34] National legislators may, therefore, institute recordings appeal systems as a substitute to evidence repetition, as long as they improve its immediacy source, by preferring audio-visual to purely audio records for broader access to non-verbal communicative aspects, and by ceasing written transcripts in order to ensure that the case review is effectively based on the viewing of the trial hearing recordings. Besides, if they choose to develop and adopt evidence assessment AI assistants, it looks like fairness favours, for the time being, explainable machine learning models, which the human appellate judge can fully oversee and, for that reason, know solidly whether to adhere to or disagree with the appeal cobot's output.

Nonetheless, as immediacy means as well—as this collective study has also marked—the possibility for the court to pose questions to clarify doubts and handle contradictions, the mere first instance trial recordings reproduction will not be sufficient and an evidentiary appeal hearing will be required, whenever the high instance judge concludes that it is relevant to further question the witnesses, the accused, or other deponents. An appeal hearing for evidence production is likewise and obviously unavoidable whenever the defendant wishes to introduce new evidence at this level, when admissible—albeit with some restrictions—, as in the Italian[35] and Spanish[36] appeal systems, or as, according to Pereira Cruz and others v. Portugal, it must be accepted as well in the Portuguese appeal system as a fair trial condition and even if not expressly stated in the PCPP.[37] An evidence renewal at the appellate level will also be needed when the appeal court, having convicted the accused for the first time, has to decide on sentence founded on personal traits of the defendant that the trial instance may not have ascertained precisely because it acquitted, i.e., without benefiting from a prior assessment by the lower tribunal made with reference to trial recorded evidence.[38] In all these three situations (among others possible) or when a recordings immediacy appeal model is not adopted, an immediacy appeal system such as the Italian (that we called evidence renewal

[34] See Chiper v. Romania, no. 22036/10, 27 June 2017, § 63, *hudoc.echr.coe.int*: '(. . .) although it is necessary for the court convicting an accused for the first time to directly assess the evidence on which it bases its decision, this is not an automatic rule which would render a trial unfair for the only reason that the court in question did not hear all the witnesses mentioned in its judgment and whose credibility it had to assess.'; and Di Martino and Molinari v. Italy, no. 15931/15 and 16459/15, 25 March 2021, § 29, *hudoc.echr.coe.int*.

[35] Article 603 § 1 and 2 ICPP.

[36] Article 790 § 3 LECrim. See also Articles 733 § 2 and 736 § 2 of the new LECrim Preliminary Draft.

[37] Pereira Cruz and others v. Portugal, §§ 229–232. Following this ECtHR's ruling, the Portuguese Constitutional Court has already issued a decision whose underlying rationale seems to allow, on criminal appeal, supervening evidence capable of influencing the conviction or sentence in favour of the accused (see *Acórdão* no. 289/2020, *www.tribunalconstitucional.pt*).

[38] See Botten v. Norway, no. 6206/90, 19 February 1996, § 50: 'In view of the nature of the offence, sentencing was, whatever the considerations relied on by the Supreme Court, capable of raising issues going to such matters as the applicant's personality and character (. . .). However, in deciding on sentence, the Supreme Court did not even have the benefit of having a prior assessment of the question by the lower court which had heard the applicant directly.'; and Júlíus Þór Sigurþórsson v. Iceland, no. 38797/17, 16 July 2019, § 43; *hudoc.echr.coe.int*.

model), in which the appeal hearing is limited to the crucial evidence, appears procedurally more efficient than the Spanish system (that we titled retrial model), bearing in mind that the latter will generate a new first instance ruling potentially appealable again to a higher court.

Even if not necessary to repeat evidence or to produce additional evidence, a defence appeal hearing may still have to take place and involve the reproduction and debate of recorded evidence, as a matter of appeal fairness, whenever the defendant wants to personally address the court of appeal to exercise his or her adversarial rights. Indeed, we should agree with the ECtHR on the point that the appellate court must, *ex officio*, give the accused the opportunity of being heard in a public hearing (though he or she has not requested it[39] and may waive it), as a complete second chance to influence the evidentiary inferences of the appeal judge who will determine the facts relating to his or her guilt or innocence.[40] First of all, because within the framework of an expressive theory of punishment, i.e., of the communicative function of public censure ingrained in the conviction,[41] the probability of a first-time conviction or of a sentence aggravation on appeal signifies that the appeal has to be acknowledged as an extension of the trial.[42] Second, because the procedural right to immediacy—as a demand of immediate connection between the judge and the evidence that overlaps with the orality principle—and the right to be heard—as an opportunity to adduce arguments that the court's decision must engage with—embody autonomous dimensions that flow from the larger fair criminal trial guarantee, and, for that reason, one can be infringed without infringing the other. From this perspective, it looks like the *Sentencia* 142/2011 of the Spanish Constitutional Court is correct when it sustains that even a modification of the lower instance's factual assessment strictly grounded on non-personal evidence, but that reverses an acquittal on appeal, has to be preceded by the hearing of the defendant, since even though the immediacy principle is not in question, the right of defence is.[43]

[39] Botten v. Norway, § 53, for instance.

[40] This hearing can be held through videoconferencing: Bivolaru v. Romania (no. 2), no. 66580/12, 2 October 2018, §§ 138–139.

[41] See Chap. 1.

[42] A theory of trial presupposes a theory of punishment: see Dubber (2004), p. 85: 'Whatever else it might be, a theory of the trial is also part of a theory of the practice of punishment as a whole. By the theory of a practice I mean (also) an attempt to legitimise it, ie, to develop – or at least to identify – relevant legitimising principles and to match the practice against these principles.' See also Damaska (1975), p. 491: 'Where judicial decisions are normally subject to reconsideration, (...) the appellate process becomes a continuation of trial adjudication.'; Marshall (2011), p. 15: 'Because reconsideration of first instance decisions is standard, appeals in hierarchical systems are regarded as a continuation of the trial process.'; and Spano and Bårdsen (2020), p. 587: 'Article 6 comes into play even in (...) appeal proceedings, as an extension of the trial process (...)'.

[43] Decision no. 142/2011, *hj.tribunalconstitucional.es*. Accordingly, Article 737 § 1 (3) of the new LECrim Preliminary Draft clearly states: 'In no case may the court of appeal modify or annul the contested decision to the detriment of the accused without having summoned him/her to be heard personally at a hearing.'

Finally, regardless of the position of the ECHR and its Protocol no. 7 on the subject, I would claim that a fair appeal theory cannot be detached from the right to appeal. As discussed earlier in this chapter, the ECHR and Protocol no. 7 allow domestic laws to unequally structure their appeal systems by legally providing more chances of appeal to the accusation to obtain a conviction than to the defence to attain an acquittal in the same criminal process, unfairly departing from both the equality of arms and the presumption of innocence guarantees. Full appeal fairness, however, demands more. Thus, whenever national appeal laws do not grant the accused a subsequent right of appeal to a higher tribunal against an overturning acquittal or a penalty increasing on appeal, or whenever such higher instance does not possess analogous factual review powers,[44] the retrial model, with its likely appealable new first instance ruling, appears to be a fairer solution, in spite of all the inconvenience of a trial repetition.

On reflection, fair appellate proceedings on both facts and law, as part of a punishment and trial theory, are best harmonized with a flexible appeal system—which may entail the use of the first instance trial recorded evidence, an appeal hearing, or a retrial, depending on the cases and on the criminal procedure principles implicated—than with a rigid model.[45]

---

[44] See the dissenting opinion of Judge Karakaş, § 15, to Kashlev v. Estonia: '(. . .) it is difficult to understand how the possibility of lodging an appeal with the Supreme Court – *an appeal on points of law* – could be a safeguard for the applicant's defence rights (. . .).'

[45] An exemplification of a flexible solution can be found in Article 83 (2) of the Rome Statute of the International Criminal Court, although it does not define in which situations each of the alternatives should be applied:

> If the Appeals Chamber finds that the proceedings appealed from were unfair in a way that affected the reliability of the decision or sentence, or that the decision or sentence appealed from was materially affected by error of fact or law or procedural error, it may:
>
> (a) Reverse or amend the decision or sentence; or
> (b) Order a new trial before a different Trial Chamber.
>
> For these purposes, the Appeals Chamber may remand a factual issue to the original Trial Chamber for it to determine the issue and to report back accordingly, or may itself call evidence to determine the issue. (. . .).

As specified by Staker and Eckelmans (2016) p. 1969: '(. . .) if as a result of the appeal, the final verdict depends only on one or more narrow issues of fact, it may be appropriate for the Appeals Chamber (. . .) either to call evidence itself or to remand those issues of fact to the Trial Chamber. The Appeals Chamber is likely to use these powers rarely. (. . .) if the Appeals Chamber chose the unusual step to itself make findings of fact at first instance, the defence could be considered deprived of any possibility of appeal against those findings; this could be regarded as contrary to article 14, para. 5 ICCPR, to which those provisions are intended to give effect. (. . .). In any case, if wide-ranging new fact-finding was necessary, a new trial may be the more appropriate remedy.' Differently, under Article 49 § 2 of the Draft Statute for an International Criminal Court, the Appeals Chamber could not reverse or amend a decision in an appeal by the Prosecutor from an acquittal, only annul 'that decision as a prelude to a new trial', which "was thought to be desirable, having regard to the existence of only a single appeal from decisions at trial' (International Law Commission 1994, p. 61):

Through the critical and interdisciplinary approach unfolded in this volume, we sought a scholarly interpretation proposal of the ECtHR's fair appeal immediacy standard that could be useful to European domestic law interpreters and lawmakers. We hope, thereby, to have contributed to fill a gap in the less researched area of criminal appellate fairness studies, and to make criminal appeals more than just an afterword to criminal process textbooks.[46]

Cited Case-Law

ECtHR

hudoc.echr.coe.int

Botten v. Norway, no. 6206/90, 19 February 1996
Michael Edward Cooke v. Austria, no. 25878/94, 8 February 2000
Strzałkowski v. Poland, no. 31509/02, 9 June 2009
Moreira Ferreira v. Portugal, no. 19808/08, 5 July 2011
Kashlev v. Estonia, no. 22574/08, 26 April 2016
Chiper v. Romania, no. 22036/10, 27 June 2017
Lorefice v. Italy, no. 63446/13, 29 June 2017
Pereira Cruz and others v. Portugal, no. 56396/12, 26 June 2018
Bivolaru v. Romania (no. 2), no. 66580/12, 2 October 2018
Styrmir þór Bragason v. Iceland, no. 36292/14, 16 July 2019
Júlíus Þór Sigurþórsson v. Iceland, no. 38797/17, 16 July 2019
Paixão Moreira Sá Fernandes v. Portugal, no. 78108/14, 25 February 2020
Tondo v. Italy, no. 75037/14, 22 October 2020
Di Martino and Molinari v. Italy, no. 15931/15 and 16459/15, 25 March 2021
Maestri and others v. Italy, no. 20903/15, 8 July 2021

Italian Constitutional Court

www.cortecostituzionale.it

Sentenza no. 26/2007
Sentenza no. 34/2020

(. . .) the Appeals Chamber (. . .) may:

a) If the appeal is brought by the convicted person, reverse or amend the decision, or, if necessary, order a new trial;
b) If the appeal is brought by the Prosecutor against an acquittal, order a new trial.

[46] See Marshall (2011), pp. 1–2: 'Despite being both important and prevalent, however, very little scholarly attention has been given to the subject of criminal appeals. Texts on domestic criminal procedure often deal with appeals almost as an afterthought. Comparative studies are virtually non-existent.'

Portuguese Constitutional Court

www.tribunalconstitucional.pt

Acórdão no. 289/2020

Spanish Constitutional Court

hj.tribunalconstitucional.es

Sentencia no. 120/2009
Sentencia no. 142/2011

References

Bohlander M (2021) Principles of German criminal procedure, 2nd edn. Hart Publishing, Oxford
Brito AB (2013) Os Poderes de Cognição das Relações em Matéria de Facto em Processo Penal. Terra de Lei – Revista da Associação de Juristas de Pampilhosa da Serra 3:56–64
Capus N (2018) Written records of statements and fairness. In: Jackson JD, Summers SJ (eds) Obstacles to fairness in criminal proceedings – Individual rights and institutional forms. Hart Publishing, Oxford/Portland, pp 205–219
Ceresa-Gastaldo M (2017) La Riforma dell'Appello tra Malinteso Garantismo e Spinte Deflative – A proposito dell'imminente varo del d.d.l. C 4368 (e dei recenti interventi delle Sezioni Unite). Diritto Penale Contemporaneo 3:163–172
Council of Europe (1984) Explanatory Report to the Protocol No. 7 to the Convention for the Protection of Human Rights and Fundamental Freedoms. http://www.coe.int
Damaska M (1975) Structures of authority and comparative criminal procedure. Yale Law J 84: 480–544
Díaz-Roncero MJJ (2019) La Inconstitucionalidad de la Regulación del Recurso de Apelación contra Sentencias Absolutorias en Materia de Violencia de Género. Cuadernos de Política Criminal 127:89–113
Dubber MD (2004) The criminal trial and the legitimation of punishment. In: Duff A, Farmer L, Marshall S, Tadros V (eds) The trial on trial, vol. 1: Truth and due process. Hart Publishing, Oxford/Portland, pp 85–100
Human Rights Committee (2007) General Comment No. 32 – Article 14: Right to equality before courts and tribunals and to fair trial. http://www.ohchr.org
International Law Commission (1994) Draft Statute for an International Criminal Court with commentaries. http://legal.un.org/ilc
Langer M (2014) The long shadow of the adversarial and inquisitorial categories. In: Dubber MD, Hörnle T (eds) The Oxford handbook of criminal law. Oxford University Press, Oxford, pp 887–912
Levy N (2016) Cognitive science in the courtroom. Anatomia do Crime 3:169–182
Marshall PD (2011) A comparative analysis of the right to appeal. Duke J Comp Int Law 22: 1–45
Morão H (2020) Pela Renovação da Renovação da Prova. Anatomia do Crime 12:171–195
Roxin C, Schünemann B (2017) Strafverfahrensrecht – Ein Studienbuch, 29th edn. C. H. Beck, München

Schabas WA (2016) The International Criminal Court – A commentary on the Rome Statute, 2nd edn. Oxford University Press, Oxford
Spano R, Bårdsen A (2020) On the right to a fair hearing in criminal appeal proceedings. In: Spano R et al (eds) Fair trial: regional and international perspectives/Procès Équitable: Perspectives Regionales et Internationales – Liber Amicorum Linos-Alexandre Sicilianos. Anthemis, Limal, pp 583–594
Staker C, Eckelmans F (2016) Article 83. In: Triffterer O, Ambos K (eds) The Rome Statute of the International Criminal Court – A commentary, 3rd edn. C.H. Beck, München, Hart, Oxford, Nomos, Baden-Baden, pp 1965–1985
Thaman SC (2019) Appeal and cassation in continental European criminal justice systems: guarantees of factual accuracy, or vehicles for administrative control? In: Brown DK, Turner JI, Weisser B (eds) The Oxford handbook of criminal process. Oxford University Press, Oxford, pp 937–959

MIX
Papier aus verantwortungsvollen Quellen
Paper from responsible sources
FSC® C105338

If you have any concerns about our products,
you can contact us on
ProductSafety@springernature.com

In case Publisher is established outside the EU,
the EU authorized representative is:
Springer Nature Customer Service Center GmbH
Europaplatz 3, 69115 Heidelberg, Germany

Printed by Libri Plureos GmbH
in Hamburg, Germany